BACKSTAGE
PASS

BY

JOHN FORD COLEY

Escape from your everyday life . . . into the
life of platinum-award winning, Grammy
nominated entertainer who takes you on an
amusing journey of his treks into the bizarre
world behind fame.

To Vivian & Ken
Hope you enjoy some of
my mis adventures.
G-d Bless
John Coley

Backstage Pass

by

John Ford Coley

TABLE OF CONTENTS

Chapter 1 – Nights Are Forever Without You .... Page 9

Chapter 2 – Mistaken Identity .... Page 11

Chapter 3 – Family Support .... Page 15

Chapter 4 - I'm Not Only Bi-Coastal, I'm International .... Page 17

Chapter 5 – Who Were Those Masked Men? .... Page 27

Chapter 6 – It's All About "Feel". .... Page 37

Chapter 7 – Bread .... Page 43

Chapter 8 – The Women, They Really Love Me .... Page 51

Chapter 9 – It's Nice To Be Remembered .... Page 55

Chapter 10 – Favor .... Page 59

Chapter 11 – You Never Know Who Knows You .... Page 63

Chapter 12 – Sad To Belong .... Page 71

Chapter 13 – Are You Still Here? .... Page 75

Chapter 14 – I Love S-L-E-E-P. .... Page 83

Chapter 15 – How Did I Get Into This? .... Page 91

Chapter 16 – Southwest F.O.B .... Page 101

Chapter 17 – Living On Faith... Page 109

Chapter 18 – Talent Or Lack Thereof .... Page 113

Chapter 19 – Athletes .... Page 121

Chapter 20 – Actors .... Page 129

Chapter 21 – The Illusion Of Movies .... Page 139

Chapter 22 – Musicians .... Page 145

Chapter 23 – Keeping My Head and Watching What I Breathe .... Page 155

Chapter 24 – The Tower Of Babel .... Page 161

Chapter 25 – On The Road With Seals & Crofts .... Page 169

Chapter 26 – Interviews And Critics .... Page 179

Chapter 27 – How Do You Know When Your Time Is Up? .... Page 189

Chapter 28 – OK, It's Tuesday. Who Wants To Be Me? .... Page 195

Epilogue .... Page 203

FORWARD

Several years ago, I decided to go back to school and complete my college degree. I lacked a total of eighteen units or one semester, to have a degree in English Literature. At 22, I left in my senior year at North Texas State University, (now called the University of North Texas) to pursue a recording career in Los Angeles. I liked school but sometimes most important priorities must take precedence over simple important priorities and no one in their right mind passes up golden opportunities.

Many years later, I seriously began to investigate completing my degree, but at the time I lived in California, not Texas. I decided to check out one of the universities there. As I spoke with the counselor at the school, I was amazed at how she didn't attempt to fake the fact she wasn't really interested in where our conversation might possibly lead. As she shuffled through some papers on her desk she very blandly ask, "Well, tell me what you've been doing over the years since you've been out of school."

I began to list out some of the accomplishments and the things I have been involved in. I spoke of places where I had traveled, having been asked to speak at colleges on music, helping to start a school for the Hmong people in San Diego, the TV and radio shows, the films, the awards, the concerts all over the world, etc., etc.

After I was finished, the lady looked dazed and confused. Alternating between a squinty glare to one of eyes that were glazed over with a mouth that was half opened; all she did was stare at me. She never uttered a word. I felt as if she was trying to see someone behind me, only instead of looking around me, she seemed to possess x-ray vision and was capable of seeing them through the back of my head. At a certain point, her staring became quite uncomfortable and I began to feel like an ant under a magnifying glass and the glaring heat is getting hotter. I finally asked her if there was something wrong.

She incredulously asked me, "Have you really done all of what you've just told me?"

Now it's my turn to stare. I thought I had been quite sincere and clear. I didn't stammer or stutter or anything like that. It honestly never occurred to me that she wouldn't believe me. With a twisted smile I slowly nodded my head up and down, laughed and smartly said, "No. I'm a pathological liar. I'm just making this up as I go along."

Although I tried to be as serious as a Franciscan monk, my true nature had seeped out. Now, those that know me will tell you that I laugh as much as humanly possible. But, there's a good explanation for it. The reason I joke and laugh as much as I do is because I have such an intense, serious nature. Heck, I'm a former English

Lit student for crying out loud, and there's always ample opportunity to reach down into the core fabric of my inner self and explore any deep, dark, depressing existentialist theory . . . see, there I go. So I try to make others laugh. If they do, great. If they don't, who cares? I'm not doing it for them anyway. I'm doing it for me. It's better than therapy, and cheaper. I'm deeply aware of my true nature and quit trying to change it years ago.

So, I said to her, "Of course I've done those things. You want me to bring in the newspaper articles?"

What she said next completely caught me off guard. "If I were you, I wouldn't worry about a degree. You've already got more degrees than you can possibly imagine. As a matter of fact, without knowing it, you've already got a Master's. All you probably need is a thesis because of all your life experience. You should write these things down. I'm sure there are universities that will give you credit for life experience."

That sounded like a good idea. Actually wanting the degree from the university where I had spent so much time, I decided to call up a North Texas State counselor to inquire about it. He didn't seem to care much about life experience. It seems the only "experience" that mattered to him was to be found entirely within the university library. There hidden among only the mustiest, dustiest and most unread books was where any true "reality and worldly wisdom" would possibly be located. Other than that, there was no real, life altering knowledge.

This guy was funny. He made me laugh. I told him I loved the library too and that I used to go make-out with girls where some of those unread books were. It was so nice and dark and there was hardly ever anyone around but the ghosts. Did that count? He got quiet as this seemed to be out of his range of "experience" or anything he might possibly be able to relate to. He then proceeded to inform me that my eighteen units would now be increased to thirty-six units to complete my "formal" education and get the coveted degree. He had noticed that I didn't have college algebra and a couple of other additions that were now required since my obviously wasted time in school. (Transcripts don't lie). I asked him if he'd ever seen a film called "Peggy Sue Got Married?" He said "No." So, I patiently explained to him that just like the movie, I had been out of school for 20 plus years and I knew, for a fact, that I personally had absolutely no need of college algebra and hadn't used it in all my time out in the "world of the barbarians."

I never did get that coveted degree. But, I did take the advice to write some of those living and breathing experiences down. Anyone who says the following events are not true was either not there when they occurred or has never spent more than two minutes in my imagination. Being a linear thinker, the past and present tense are the same to me and are always happening "now," just like "Spaceballs." Also let's refer to this as my "Unauthorized Autobiography." I did not give myself permission to write it.

And by the way, if any of you college deans or presidents are reading this book and would like to honor me with a college degree from my life experiences, read on, because here's my thesis.

SPECIAL THANKS

Quite honestly, there are so many different people that have come in and out of my life over the years that my 'Thank You' list would fill up an entire volume.

To start off, I truly would like to thank God. You gave me life, gifts, a warped sense of humor and unbelievable opportunities. You've never failed me even when I thought You did and without my faith in You, life would be very meaningless and empty. To Jesus for finding me at the end of a rope and pulling me back up. My wife Dana, not only for helping me in getting this book out and all the hard work she put in it, but mostly for always being there, through good and bad, and incredibly bad. Thank you for not giving up on me when others would have and for believing in me. I love you. To all of my children, Ahnjayla, Shane, Dakota and Ciara for keeping me young at heart. To my mom and dad, Walter and Eula for constantly encouraging me and training me up the way that they did and Grandma Pace for all that wonderful banana bread.

I'd especially like to thank my old friend and partner of many years, "England" Dan Seals. I spent so many great years with him. We made some terrific music, laughed often and saw a lot of the world together. Many of my adventures were shared in part with him and without each other we might both have done something else with our lives. It was fun and I've got a truckload of unforgettable memories from it. You're a good man Dan and I love you.

To Rich Richeson, Ed Cole, George Pace, Danee Samonte, my friends in the Philippines, Ambrosia, Joe Puerta, Burleigh Drummond, Christopher North, Shem Schroeck, David Pack, Doug Jackson, Dave Lewis, Terry Sylvester, Jimmy Griffin, Herb Alpert, Doug Morris, Dick Vanderbilt, Mishel Kocheran, Susan Joseph, Kyle Lehning, Jim Seals, Dash Crofts, David Gates, Louie Shelton, Chris Thomas at Martin Guitars, Tony Gottlieb, Ovid (Larry) Stevens, Wanda Gardner, Doc (Mike) Woolbright, Buddy Lay, Randy Bates, Zeke (Tony) Durell, Marc Rocco, Danny Eisenburg, Jennie Frankel, Dick Clark, Pam Lewis, Rich Rees, Wendy Kay, Tom Wurth, every single person I've ever had the privilege to play and tour with and everyone I went to school with from Urban Park to W.W. Samuell. I've never forgotten nor will I ever forget where I came from.

Chapter 1

NIGHTS ARE FOREVER WITH YOU

For the female of the species
is more deadly than the male.

Rudyard Kipling

Nights are forever without you.

Sung by England Dan & John Ford Coley

On several occasions I've been asked, "What's it like to have recorded or written songs that made people all gushy or are remembered for years by people who fell in love to them, danced to them or every time they look at one of their kids they remember that song of yours, etc?"

Well here's a story that should answer that one:

Not too long after my former partner, England Dan Seals, and I had split up our partnership, I was traveling and playing in the little town of Chico, California. I used to get it confused with Chino. I would forget which one of them had a prison and which one had a State University. This was the one with the University. It was a good crowd and as far as I could tell, everyone seemed to enjoy themselves.

After the show was over, I was signing records and autographs for people. When her turn came, this very sharply dressed lady stepped up and asked me to sign one of my records for her. I did. (You know, come to think of it, she was a little too nicely dressed for me, kind of corporate, but then again, I'm no slave to fashion). Then she stared me intently in the eye and gently took my hand and began to squeeze it tighter and tighter. In a very sweet and soft voice, she began to tell me, "I really love romantic songs. My fiancée and I fell in love to your song, 'Nights Are Forever Without You.' He proposed to me to your song; we danced to your song; we loved to your song. As a matter of fact we did just about *everything* to your song.

Not being remotely interested in what her "everything" might possibly include, I politely said, "Thank you. I'm glad you enjoyed it."

At which point, her face literally morphed into a wild-eyed, crazy Charles Manson stare. For a split second I thought I was eye to eye with and possibly staring down the devil. I've been in quite a number of very interesting and unusual situations in my life, so I wasn't unnerved by her antics. Besides, since I'm pretty sure I might have dated the devil's daughter once just how scary could she be?

Her hand turned into a vice-grip and she began to squeeze my hand tighter than any bull-rider holding on for dear life, all the time looking me dead square in the eye. Then, in a deep, gravelly voice and especially one that I didn't recognize as coming out of her before, she said with a low, ominous spine tingling chill in that voice, "And then that blankety, blank so and so left me and I've hated YOUR song ever since." She never raised her tone and I would doubt that her blood pressure ever got over 120 on the top end. Some nights you just don't see 'em coming.

Being taken slightly off guard, trying to get my hand released from her grip while still surrounded by other people waiting for an autograph, all I could think of to say was, "Well . . . uh . . . cool." I think that comment about covered it.

I wonder whatever happened to that autograph and how her former fiancée might feel about the song? Maybe he still likes it.

But on the up side, it's so nice to be remembered in such a kind and warm-hearted manner. The very thought that something I sang years ago could have such an effect still today thrills my heart. So, in the event that any of those songs happen to bring a fond remembrance or small tear to your eye or even if the "blankedy blank so and so" has left you years ago and you begin to experience feelings of anger, regret, violence, emotional anxiety and start frothing at the mouth and really want to call them up, talk mean to them and even exact a little revenge, "well . . . uh . . . cool." And remember . . . Nights Are Forever Without You.

Chapter 2

MISTAKEN IDENTITY

When I was born the Doctor took one look at my face . . .

turned me over and said, Look . . . twins!

Rodney Dangerfield

Now I crept up from behind her

She looked so fine to me

But when I stepped around her man

My eyes could plainly see

She was ugly from the front

She was ugly from the front

She was ugly from the front

And I said ugly-ugly-ugly-ugly-ugly

Lyle Lovett, "She's Hot To Go"

In the latter part of 1976 things really began to pick up for me. I was enjoying the rise out of the dismal darkness of resigning myself to the fact that even after all the years of preparation, hard work, sweat and unintentionally starving myself to get that emaciated rock star look, that I might possibly forever be a "never-been" in the music industry.

However, as fate turned its other cheek, we soon found ourselves appearing on national television shows everywhere. There were some big ones at the time like "The Midnight Special", "American Bandstand" (me, being interviewed by Dick Clark) or "Don Kirscher's Rock Concert". We were interviewed by countless radio stations, opening shows for a myriad number of very successful recording artists and I had my picture posted in almost every record store in America and half the known world. It had only taken me 10 years to become "an over-night success." Life was good.

After "I'd Really Love To See You Tonight" became a huge success, I took a trip back to my home in Dallas to see my mom and dad. We decided to go out and eat and invited my grandma Pace to come with us. We were in one of the nicer restaurants (one that actually had table cloths) when my mother began to nudge me saying, "Johnny, I think that our little waitress knows who you are. She keeps staring over here like she recognizes you."

I nonchalantly said, "That kind of thing seems to happen a lot these days. I've sort of gotten used to it."

Grandma's impressed. She now knows all that banana bread she made me as a kid was worth it. Momma and daddy are beaming and knowingly exchanging glances back and forth across the table at each other.

Now all this time I'm thinking, "They must be so proud of me. I've become "a somebody," someone they can brag about in church. Their little Johnny became known the entire world over." Yeah, they're probably saying to themselves, "We made the right decision giving him piano lessons and buying the Wurlitzer so he could play in the band. Should've gotten his teeth fixed though. It all paid off just the same. It was worth it. Yep, our boy Johnny, he's something alright." We all seemed to sit just a little taller in our chairs pretending we didn't notice the waitress's constant ogling.

After a while, the waitress mustered up the courage to come over and say something to me. In a most polite and delightful Texas accent she asked, "Excuse me sir . . . but are you Sonny Bono?"

Man, there ain't no place you can run to or hide after that one. I was really ticked. I told her that I was definitely not him. All kinds of evil thoughts shot through my mind. "Sonny Bono! Sonny Bono! God, is this some kind of sadistic joke? I've told You before that if You really loved me You'd have made me look more like Robert Redford or Tom Selleck. Haven't I already suffered enough being mistaken for both Ringo and Jimmy Buffet? But Sonny Bono! Why him? Everyone knows he looks . . . well . . . goofy. God, above everyone else, I thought You really loved me. You're behind this, aren't you Satan. I bet you arranged this, didn't you! She's one of yours isn't she? Come to embarrass me in front of my family." Inwardly I was like a rabid dog, but a forced smile covered me, complete with teeth that never had braces.

Grandma's got that squint in her eye reading that poor girl up and down like she's about to "pinch a pint-size plug" out of her. My grandma was always very sweet to me, but as a rowdy kid I'd seen that expression on her face too many times before. That look still made me sweat. If I read her expression right it said, "Looks like I'm gonna have to go cut me a switch off a tree and some little girl's gonna have a red rear end before I get to finish my dessert." Grandma probably didn't even know who Sonny Bono was. Wouldn't matter to her either. Grandma's a Texan. I know she's on my side, probably ready to put that little girl in a headlock and start plucking her like a chicken.

My mother calmly explained to her who I was. The waitress was quite embarrassed. Her response was a sugary sweet, "You're kidding me. Of course I know who you are. I knew I'd seen you before. I loooove your music." Too late. Damage done. But regardless, now I have to leave her a big tip because she knows who I am and I can't appear to be cheap or revengeful. Then she had the gall to ask for an autograph. It was a long, depressing flight back to Los Angeles from Dallas.

Now, like a stalker hiding in the fog this "mistaken identity" seemed to happen more and more. Once, my daughter Ahnjayla and I were in a supermarket when she grabbed my arm, pointed and said, "Look daddy. You're on the cover of that magazine." I turned around to look. Wow, when did I do anything for that magazine? We walked over for a closer look, only to discover that . . . what!!! That's not me . . . THAT'S SONNY BONO!! I don't look like a thing like him . . . but it's amazing how he certainly bears a striking resemblance to me. And a darn handsome fella too, isn't he?

To make matters even more bizarre, I know for a fact on several occasions that Sonny Bono was mistaken for me. Wonder what he thought about being told he looked like me? Guess I'll never know now. To make it even more bizarre is the fact that I had dinner with Cher once in Oklahoma City. She never said a thing about the resemblance. Maybe she just thought that I was Sonny too, and since she was accustomed to having him around all the time and ignoring him, nothing seemed out of place to her. She just kept looking at me and stabbing her fork into the table.

There must be some explanation in there somewhere. Maybe I'll ask God about my Sonny Bono good looks when I'm dead . . . but He'll probably tell me His first pick was that I'd be mistaken for Rodney Dangerfield.

Chapter 3

FAMILY SUPPORT

A fan club is a group of people who tell a musician he's not alone in the way he feels about himself.

Jack Carson

As I grew up my family was a constant means of support to me. We were a middle class family and not raised with any real excess, but I certainly had what I needed. I was trained with the notion that I could accomplish just about anything I set my mind to, except maybe getting that cowlick on the back of my head to lay down. My mom and dad (and sometimes my cousins, aunts and uncles) used to come to places that I played at and cheer me on when I first began in the band in Dallas.

Later, after we had "made it" and our songs were always on the radio and our career was fairly well established, about the only times they got to come and see me play was when I came close to Dallas.

My momma was the very embodiment of enthusiasm. Not much that I recall got her down for long. Most of the time I only remember her laughing. And that was mostly at herself. She had that great ability. She wasn't one to let much of anything get the best of her. She used to hold her hands in front of her as though she was praying and clap them with a quick motion, nodding and smiling. My parents held high hopes for me and what my life's calling would be. Momma was certain that I was going to become a medical missionary when I grew up, go out and save people physically and spiritually, and then conquer the world in my spare time. Daddy was equally certain that I would become a Christian attorney. Of course, I never knew that Daddy had that kind of sense of humor. I didn't even think that he knew what an oxymoron was. I made this remark at the Ryman Theater in Nashville once. Funny thing, but the lights cut out on me. I immediately laughed, threw my hands in the air and repented by saying "I'm sorry, I'm sorry, forgive me. The lights miraculously turned back on.

At any rate, they'd come to the arena shows where Dan and I would perform. As thousands of people enjoyed our music, I could almost see momma's beaming face, quick clapping her hands and then nudging the person next to her and saying to them, "That's my boy, Johnny. He's going to be a doctor, you know." Of course, they'd look at her, move a little closer to the other side of the seat like she was some kind of oddball, but she didn't care. She was too busy thinking about how wonderful it was going to be to have a doctor in the family.

Chapter 4

I'M NOT ONLY BI-COASTAL,
I'M INTERNATIONAL

"I've been everywhere man, I've been everywhere"

Sung by Johnny Cash

In December of 1971, Dan and I were invited to tour England for a month with Elton John. This had to be one of the biggest thrills in my life. We had filled in for 'Dan Hicks and the Hotlicks' when they canceled out Milwaukee and Minneapolis with Elton. They had gotten a career move offer to perform on the "Tonight Show" with Johnny Carson and Elton needed an opening act.

These were the days before Elton began dressing so flamboyantly on stage. At this time he only had strange glasses and funny pants, but he was a really serious and gifted performer. Elton was coming off of his big hit "Tiny Dancer" and "Tumbleweed Connection" album and about to release the "Madman Across The Water" record. He asked us to play with him down in San Diego after the dates in Milwaukee and Minneapolis. When he came back from Japan we got the call to go to England with him. Our record company, A&M Records, was ecstatic. We thought we'd be really big there, especially with our name. Elton was quite a gentleman and treated us exceptionally well.

We traveled all around England, Wales and close to Scotland. We performed in cities like Manchester (next door to Liverpool, where the Beatles came from), Leister, Nottingham, Bristol, Newcastle-on-Tyne and many others. I was even able to go to Stratford-on-Avon and see the Royal Shakespeare Company perform "A Midsummer's Night's Dream" on one of our days off. I hung out in some of the pubs in Stratford and just soaked up the atmosphere.

The trains were the coolest things I'd ever been on. The only problem we had was that they ran on a 24 hour clock and they always left the station on time, I repeat, always on time. They used butter for mayonnaise on their sandwiches in the dining cars and I learned to replace words like "Cookies" with "Biscuits", "Confectionery" instead of "Candy", "Beakers" for "Drinking glass" and "Sorry' in the place of "Excuse me." I also learned that they frowned on me drinking ice tea. (I had to ask for hot tea, a "beaker" and ice, and then make it myself).

I'd never been on a train before or on the Underground (subways). I pretty much looked like a coal miner every time I got off the Underground from all the petrol they used for fuel. Soot on my face, in my nose, my hair, soot on the buildings, but hey, I was in England. I was happy. I couldn't figure which stop to get off the trains and once got "forever condemned on the Circle Line." I just kept going around in circles.

The English audience was not like the American audience. After a song they particularly liked, they would clap their hands over their heads. I got emotional a couple of times because they clapped their hands over their heads often when we played and we seemed to be really accepted, especially since Elton would introduce us every night. I really was thankful to Elton for bringing us over.

Nigel Olsson, Elton's drummer, Dee Murray, his bass player and John Reid, Elton's manager were really great to us. (Nigel recorded "It's Only A Matter Of Time", a song I'd written, for his solo album). Elton is really quite a character and one of the hardest working people I'd ever met. He'd be up at 7:00 in the morning working on songs. Heck, no self respecting musician that I knew was even up at 7:00 a.m., much less playing music.

One night we played in Croydon, near London. At the end of the evening, Elton was in the middle of his encore when Marc Bolan from T-Rex walks on stage. He was famous for his song "Bang A Gong." He was quite the peacock and had on a satin crème color suit. I'd never seen anything like that before. I was impressed. The stage lights are shining on his trademark, long frizzy jet black hair. The crowd went nuts. They were jumping and screaming, clapping hands way above their heads. Bolan plugs his guitar in, Elton yells to him, "F" (meaning the key of "F"). Bolan can't hear him very well and rips into one of the loudest guitar solos in the history of rock and roll. However, he misunderstood Elton. He thought Elton said the key of "E", a half step off. He must have been drunk or something because he just continued to play and play and never changed to the right key. Either he thought he was playing jazz or else he was way ahead of his time for rock and roll. It sounded a little like a weed whacker at 6 in the morning. He was sliding on his knees; he was doing the Chuck Berry chicken walk. Even Pete Townsend couldn't jump in the air like Bolen was doing. All in all, he was having the showmanship time of his life at Elton's expense. He acted like it was his show. Elton and Bolen were cussing at each other like drunken sailors after the show. You know, cussing sounds really funny with an English accent.

Now, I'm a history freak and had studied quite a lot of English history. Some of my ancestors had been there before they packed up and moved to Jamestown in the early 1600's. To be able to see firsthand all of the places I had only read about was truly exciting and inspiring for me. This was my very first trip out of the United States and I planned to enjoy every single minute of it.

The British money actually had colors (or rather "colours") and sterling silver in it and there were signs posted on trashcans written in the international sign language telling dogs not to take care of their business in the street. I thought, "Dang. Even the English dogs can read. They must be so proud."

However, I do admit that I was, to say the least, disappointed when first in England. I discovered such eating establishments as "The Texas Pancake House" and "The Tennessee Pancake Kitchen." Heck, I'd been eating that way all my life. I wanted something English. Something that spoke to me of international, like the man I was becoming. Something that wasn't meat and potatoes. All I knew was that we didn't have any English restaurants in Texas or Los Angeles and dadgumit I wanted some real honest to goodness English food, and I didn't mean fish and chips either. I had people to impress back home. The one eating establishment that hadn't made an appearance in England as of yet was a McDonalds. I occasionally will visit a McDonalds but I most certainly could have used one by the end of the tour.

One evening, Dan and Chic (Larry) Day, our road manager and I went out to some party in London. This party was truly nothing more than a bunch of oddly dressed people standing around talking about absolutely nothing, but it actually sounded interesting because of the English accent. I'd try to tell them jokes to fit in and for some reason I'd laugh at all of their jokes, which I thought were pretty funny, but no one would laugh at any of mine. They would just look at me pitifully.

After a while with the three of us standing alone and counting the tiles on the ceiling, this nasal, whiny, arrogant, condescending twerp came up and began to talk to us. He made grandiose gestures with his hand and nothing ever spilled out of his glass (which actually is a skill). I was amazed at his ability to expound at great length on the most uninteresting of topics, stopping every now and then to push his Buddy Holly style glasses back off the tip of his nose. I mean, after all I'm college educated, well except for 18 units, now 36. I've sat through countless uninteresting subjects with boring professors similar to him so I know how to fake polite, sincere interest quite well.

He finally got around to asking our names and commenting on what English butchering accents we possessed. Now, I would have said "accents we had" but he said "possessed" like our accents were demonic or something. I told him my name and why we were in the land of some of my ancestors. He was unimpressed.

When Chic told him his name the man jerked his head back and began to laugh hysterically. He even laughed with a nasal accent. He kept saying, "Chik, Chik, Chik. What kind of name is Chik?!" Then he would throw his head back again and laugh like it was the funniest thing he had ever heard in his life (which in Chic's eyes appeared to be growing shorter by the minute).

Chic was a tall, lanky black man with a big Afro, a warm heart and a quick smile. It took a lot for him to get worked up, but he was starting to head that direction pretty quick. Chic had come from the streets of Philadelphia and had grown up in gang areas. His brother had been a gang leader, so needless to say, Chic knew his way around the block, especially with sharp objects that might possibly find their way into his hands. He used to tell us stories about some of the idiotic gang stuff he'd witnessed and all I know was that I wouldn't have wanted to be around any of it. Period. Those people needed horses to take care of or something else to fill up their day.

So, about this time I see Chic getting a look in his eyes like he might invite this guy outside to continue the conversation, Dan pops in and asks the guy what his name is.

In his flippant, sissy, nasal accent he proudly declared, "Ah yes. Of course. My name is Ronald . . . Ronald McDonald."

In a split second, all three of us were on the floor in uproarious, hysterical, obnoxious laughter. Why, I would go so far as to say we were actually cackling. Now, "Ronald" didn't seem to think there's anything humorous, much less funny about his name. He would have sadly seen the humor had he been standing where we were.

Because McDonald's had not been positioned on every corner in Great Britain as of yet, he had no idea what was so "bloody" amusing. We couldn't stop laughing. He's becoming more and more ticked and some of the other people in the room begin staring at us wondering what could possibly be so funny. He's screaming at us and starts to throw an honest to goodness conniption fit by stomping his foot, slapping the sides of his pants legs with his hands with every syllable that he spoke, demanding to know what was so blankety blank funny, pushing his runaway glasses back on his nose that kept inching and sliding down with each stomp of his foot. At this point, he again demanded that we "stop this incessant and childish giggling this instant." The three of us just couldn't stop laughing. I actually had water coming from my eyes, I laughed so hard and long.

For a brief second we'd catch our breath, slightly gain our composure, take one look at him and start "giggling" like real cowboys at a dude ranch all over again. I laughed so hard my sides hurt the next day. He finally got so exasperated that he threw his hands up in the air and actually kind of slithered out of the room, looking back at us over his shoulder, mumbling and cursing us the whole way. We never got to tell him what was so funny because we just simply couldn't contain laughter.

The next day, December 17, we caught a train and played in Sheffield. We told Elton and the other band members the story. They were howling because they had been to America and knew of "Ronald McDonald." I think that's the only time I told a joke on English soil and got someone to laugh.

We never got to explain to the "English Ronald McDonald" what had been so funny. However, I suspect that when the first McDonald's chain made its way across the great Atlantic Ocean to Merry Ol' England and the big red-headed clown proudly announced himself, ours wasn't the last "giggling" he suffered from such a numbing blow to his proud ancestral family name. I can't help but laugh when I envision him still slapping the sides of his legs in his therapist's office somewhere trying to recover.

****

Now, to the other side of the world.

I've had the pleasure of traveling to the Orient on several occasions. I truly love Asia.

The first time Dan and I traveled to Japan was with Three Dog Night in December of 1972. We had a big hit song called "Simone" and the concert promoters asked us over. I absolutely loved Japan. They called us "Engren Dan and John Ford Coreysan." When we first arrived at the airport in Tokyo, we saw our driver waving at us and thought he had brought his teenage daughter along. Then, when they were certain that it was us, we discovered there was a troop of people there to greet us. "Welcome" signs began appearing from everywhere. Wow! The Japanese really know how to treat their artists. Back in the States, this kind of thing didn't happen anymore. We were lucky just to get our name on a placard when the drivers would pick us up from the airport. But here, in the Land of the Rising Sun, they treated us like we were stars. Smart people, the Japanese.

However, no one has ever gotten hold of the fact that after a twelve or thirteen hour plane ride, no one looks like a "star" or even a human being. I've got pictures to prove it. Therefore, the last thing you want is a bunch of cameras popping all over the place. You normally arrive about the time you're going to bed at home. Your hair is greasy, your teeth need to be brushed and your breath smells like you've got a bear hibernating in your mouth. A single Certs or Tic-Tac doesn't even make a dent in the breath thing. I felt like I needed a couple of Certs for my socks too. I always wondered why so many immigration inspectors wear those nose and mouth coverings like they're painting a room. Self preservation I would guess. You've slept in your clothes and they look like you've slept in them, plus you need a shave and some serious deodorant. Then, you shoot out of the gate and greet the public, giving autographs, and smiling for the camera bad breath and all. Ahhh, the glamour of it.

Although I was really excited, at the same time I was a little nervous at first about going over. Some of my friends, who had obviously never been there, were telling me "Watch out Johnny. Remember, we whipped them back in the big WWII. They're shifty and treacherous. Be careful."

What I found in the Japanese people was the most gracious, courteous, clean, technologically advanced culture I'd ever come across. I liked the way the little girls covered their mouths when they laughed. And the bowing thing. I got a great joy out of that. They would bow. I would bow back. Then they'd bow again. I'd just keep bowing. As long as someone keeps bowing, this can go on for days. In shaking hands, whoever lets go first, loses. Really simple. Bowing's more fun, plus I lost some inches in my waist from the exercise.

I ate a whole bunch of stuff that I couldn't pronounce and had no clue as to what it was, except I liked it. Most everyone spoke English, which helped me. I learned a couple of Japanese phrases before I left home. I like to know little things to say when I travel internationally. Like "Where's the bathroom," "I'm hungry," "What do you mean my accent is terrible," "How much is this in American money?" or "Your shoe's untied," so you can flip them in the nose. Helpful conversation tidbits like that. I would advise anyone traveling internationally to learn a couple of phrases of the country you're traveling to, but if you like Dr. Pepper don't expect to find any. The world's not as sophisticated as it thinks yet.

We almost always had an interpreter assigned to us. I remember one day we took our interpreter when Dan and I went to eat. All of the restaurants have the food displayed in plastic in a case outside. The plastic food looked a lot like airplane food tastes. But, this way you can just order by pointing. We'd been there for about a week and we really wanted something we recognized. We both spied spaghetti with a small American flag on it and some chocolate pudding for dessert. I instantly knew what I wanted. Some good old spaghetti. Something American . . . or Italian . . . well, at least something familiar. As the order came to us, everyone in the restaurant began to laugh. What's so funny? This is good stuff and besides, as much as I've enjoyed it, I'm tired of rice and soy, more rice and soy and when you get tired of rice and soy you can always have soy and rice. And that tofu stuff. Although I haven't read it yet there's got to be some sort of Biblical prohibition against that stuff somewhere. Yuck!

Now the Japanese are, like I said before, very polite and won't go out of their way to make you feel uncomfortable or embarrassed. But I guess this was just too funny, even for them. So, we asked our interpreter why everyone was laughing. It seems that Dan and I had ordered the children's plate. American flag and all. At this point, both Dan and I were in hysterics. I think we laughed louder than everyone in the restaurant put together. This was funny to me. I guess it would be the equivalent of a small child ordering lobster thermador. All I knew was that the taste was somewhat familiar, although I personally think that somehow they might have slipped some soy in it. Don't get me wrong. I really like soy, and I like lemon pie too. However, I wouldn't want to have it three meals a day for an extended period of time. We made a lot of fun of ourselves by eating the spaghetti one strand at a time, holding it in the air like kids. All without the use of chopsticks. "Amazing", they must have thought. Some of the older people there probably wondered how we had survived for so long as a culture if people like Dan and I were its representatives.

I also learned some things not to do. On the last day of our second visit to Japan, we were eating in a restaurant in Osaka with our interpreter and a couple of the band members. After I was finished with my meal, I stabbed my chopsticks in the remaining rice of my bowl. Nearly every eye in the place turned to focus on me. Our interpreter politely took my chopsticks out of the bowl and placed them next to it. I asked her why? While I could still feel the eyes of the Japanese patrons eating around me, she patiently explained. It appears that when someone dies, the friends and family place a bowl of rice with the chopsticks sticking up in it for when they come back after forty days. So, it wasn't a good thing to do. They always lay their chopsticks next to the bowl and never, under any circumstances, stick them in the bowl. It's like a premonition for death. I guess they wanted to see if I was going to choke on some sushi or something and die on the spot. But of course I didn't. Not unless I've been living all these years like "Jacob's Ladder."

The only other problem I experienced there was having to take my shoes off so much. You walk in the house; you take your shoes off. You eat in a traditional Japanese restaurant; you take your shoes off. They take their shoes off at every given opportunity. It gets tiring because I wear cowboy boots almost all of the time. Do you have any idea how hard those things are to take off and put on? Drove me crazy. Also, you'd better have a good sock collection when you travel there. Holes in socks are frowned upon.

I remember the very first night we played the "Budakon" in Tokyo. This was a great honor because all the American groups that were anything in Japan played here. The house was standing room only and the evening was full of promise. They had provided for me one of the finest Yamaha baby grand pianos I'd ever played on and there was a huge banner behind us that read "Three Dog Night" and our names were beneath theirs.

We played our hearts out. They recognized our hit song "Simone." Since it was the number one song there, we did our best not to make sound like number two. However I think that they were expecting a full band. Dan and I only played two acoustic guitars and I sometimes played piano. We relied heavily on harmonies and very few were even attempting that folk style anymore.

After each song they would applaud in a rather polite, subdued manner and were very quiet and respectful for us. Out of nowhere, after one of our songs, someone yelled something out in the audience. Everything got very still. The atmosphere was so thick you could stab a chopstick through it. I could see the frozen look and wide eyes on some of the faces in the front rows. Whatever he had yelled had been "very, very un-Japanese." So, I reached into my bag of Japanese one-liners. Something I had learned from a Japanese girl before we came over.

I said, "Anata no akkusento wa ii desu, Nihingo wa kadi masen, but domo arigato anyway."

The whole place got quieter, then erupted in uproarious laughter and all of a sudden we were in. They were clapping and laughing. With one simple phrase, in Japanese, which I probably said with a Southern accent, we won the audience over.

From that point forward, they were ours and we even got a standing ovation after our encore.

After I had said the phrase, I happened to look over to the side of the stage and saw Mariko, our assigned interpreter. She was in laughing convulsions with one hand over her mouth and the other hand on her stomach. Our manager kept trying to get Mariko to tell her what I'd said, but she was laughing too hard.

While the audience was still laughing, Dan leaned his head over to me and asked what I had said. I told him I wasn't for sure, but it seemed to have taken care of any heckling problem.

Now, I didn't particularly think this was especially funny and I wasn't even really intending to be funny. It was a simple explanation.

Mariko asked me where I learned that phrase. She said I should use part of the phrase often. It would cover a multitude of sins. It did.

In case you're wondering, all I said was, "Although your accent is very good, I don't speak Japanese, but thank you anyway."

I also had quite a lot of fun with the word "Hai." That's the Japanese word for "yes." Every time I was introduced to anyone, I always said, "hi." For some reason, everyone seemed amused when I would first greet them. I guess they thought I was trying to speak Japanese. Again.

I really like being on tour out of the country because, as a touring artist, they take you everywhere and explain everything about their customs and country. You get to eat all the exotic foods in the finest restaurants and the good part is that you never have to pay for anything. But when you come home and hit customs you have to declare all this free stuff they've given you. It's hard to declare a price on a fake Rolex or two-foot long chopsticks that pour soy sauce.

But, when you're there you're pretty much treated like royalty. Except for one thing. Don't ever under any circumstances ride the subway in Tokyo at rush hour. What am I talking about? It's always rush hour there. Unlike New York, no one pinches you or hits you up for spare change. It's just hard to bow in there. I had to ride the subway on a couple of occasions. I gave up both guilt and riding the subway in Tokyo for Lent. I gave up riding the subway in New York for personal safety.

Also, there weren't any dents on the cars that the Japanese drive. That really shocked me because in the States we drive in "yards." You know, spread out. The Japanese drive close together, in "millimeters." However, if they are in an accident and their car gets dented up, they can't drive it on the street until it's been repaired. It's an aesthetic beauty thing. We should try that here.

We rode the Bullet Train to other cities. That thing is actually faster than airplanes. Or it seems that way. I mean, those trains can get out of here in a hurry.

Almost all of my photos taken from the train were blurred. It's as though I have two photos of Mt. Fuji on the same negative. Could have been my camera though.

****

International travel can be quite an eye opener. If you always stay at home in the U.S. you never have to worry about doing something wrong because you know the customs.

My very first time in Israel was in 1974. It was a couple of months after the Japanese Red Army had blown up Lod Airport in Tel Aviv. I was very aware of how sensitive the situation in the country was. As I came down the stairs from the plane I noticed three Sabras (native born Israelis) huddled not too far away. I had a big black bag on my shoulder that had all of my camera equipment in it. I guess it looked somewhat suspicious. I noticed that they were watching me like a hawk and never took their eyes off of me. As I neared the bottom of the stairs, they walked directly toward me. When I hit the last step they demanded, "What do you have in the bag?" I very quickly put my hands in the air and stammered, "Cameras and books and stuff. Here. Take a look. You can even have one if you want." They could probably see that they had scared me. The girl in the group smiled very big at my remark and said, "Let me guess, American, right?" I sheepishly grinned and said, "The accent gave me away didn't it." The two men looked in my bag and just waved me on. But the girl said, "I hope you enjoy your trip." She had a beautiful smile. After what they've lived through and still live with on a daily basis, I completely understand checkpoints. I've traveled all over the world and that was the first time I was ever nervous.

Sometimes my upbringing clashes with other cultures. I was back in Israel several years later, traveling on a bus from Haifa to Acca. I absolutely love Israel. The history alone is worth the trip and I've studied a lot of it, from Biblical through Partition. As you can imagine, the old and new are quite striking. I got to travel through a Crusader escape tunnel that led to the outside of the city and visit Acca Prison where the escape from the film, "Exodus" actually happened. Very freaky.

The only time I wouldn't suggest going to Israel is during Pesach (Passover), unless you're Jewish. This trip was the time period I was there. There's no bread or those great desserts anywhere. I would sneak into the Christian Arab areas just to get pita bread. Love that hummus.

As I was riding along enjoying the scenery, the bus would periodically stop and armed soldiers would get on, look at people and sometimes ask for identification papers. The bus was entirely packed except for the seat next to me. Two lady soldiers got on and walked toward the back where I was sitting. As they looked for seats, I got up an offered them my seats. One of the girls slid into the vacant seat. I offered the other one the seat I had been sitting in. She proceeded to really go off on me. "Why are you giving me your seat? What's the matter with you"? Can't you see that I'm a soldier? You sit there."

I was shocked by her response and didn't want to tick off someone in uniform. So, I tried to calmly explain to her, "Miss, I'm very sorry if I've offended you. That's not what I was trying to do. I can't sit and have you stand. Please, take my seat."

"You take the seat! Why do you offer me your seat? Can't you see that I am a soldier," she snapped back.

Again, I apologized and said, "Miss, like I said I didn't mean to offend you, but where I come from, men always give up their seats to ladies, soldier or not. If my daddy were to see me sitting in a chair and a lady standing, he'd probably pull my hair out, and then tell me he didn't raise me like that. So, I'm very sorry but I can't sit down. Please take my seat."

She said, "No, you take it."

I apologized again and said, "Miss, I'm sorry but I can't. Please take the seat." She would not sit down. Her friend seemed amused by this dialogue and just kept looking at her from her nice seat by the window. She would not sit down.

We both stood in the aisle, holding onto the pole. We rode with that seat empty for about a mile or so. She finally looked at me and said, "You're quite serious aren't you." I told her I was. With eyebrows raised, her eyes looked at me hard trying to discern a motive. She didn't say anymore but finally swung into that highly questionable seat. No more words passed between us.

When my stop came up in Acca, I headed for the bus door. As I made my way, I heard a lady's voice behind me say, "Toda raba. Thank you." I turned around and she nodded her head and smiled at me. I waved. They waved back.

****

When you travel out of the country, the chances of them speaking your language are pretty good, while the chances of you speaking their language are "slim to none."

On a recent trip to the Philippines, I was working with the band that would be backing me up for the concerts. Between songs, they would be speaking and laughing in their native language. There's a paranoia involved when conversations are being spoken around you and you don't understand any of it. "Are they laughing at me? Maybe they think I look like Tom Selleck." Of course not understanding a single word being said, I would laugh right along with them just as though I understood every word. After a couple of times of doing this they asked if I understood their language. I smiled back and told them, "No. But I trust you." They spoke English the rest of the time.

Chapter 5

WHO WERE THOSE MASKED MEN?

It is not the size of the dog in the fight,

it's the size of fight in the dog.

Mark Twain

Late 1974 and 1975 were some of the hardest years of my life. We had been reduced to touring only with "Seals and Crofts." I really loved touring with Jimmy and Dash, but I longed for the days when we toured with many different groups. Dan and I were at the same mis-management firm as they were and had pretty much been consumed into that environment, both socially and professionally. The only thing that made it even close to worthwhile was that we were paid a meager salary of $65.00 a week for food and they took care of our bills. Prior to that, Dan and I had made approximately $1,500-$2,000 per night touring (less expenses of course). Quite a dramatic drop.

Although I had visited Los Angeles several times, I didn't actually move from Dallas until after our first record was finished in May of 1971. With that record everything was looking up and I had been of the opinion that we would become an overnight success. We'd been plugging very hard since we recorded our first "England Dan and John Ford Coley" album for A&M Records in 1971. Our second one "Fables" in 1972 had been rather disappointing for us, even though it sold well internationally. We had a third unreleased album in the "can" at A&M, but we had been let out of our contract in late 1974. We had toured consistently prior to 1974.

I'd been performing and honing my craft since I was 15. We had traveled with just about the best of that time period, 'Chicago', 'Bread', 'Elton John', 'Carole King', 'The Youngbloods', 'Three Dog Night'. The list went on forever. Now, call me crazy, but 10 years is not an overnight success, unless you're exceptionally challenged in math.

Music was fun. I loved it, worked at it, wrote all the time and Dan and I practiced almost every day. We were dedicated to it.

However, in the music industry, you've got a small window of opportunity and that opportunity has to be seized upon quickly. At 15 you've got your life ahead of you, so you can afford to mess around and not be real serious. At 21, you still have time to play around. To still be unsuccessful at 25, there's the possibility that you might not "be playing with a full deck," to coin a phrase, and you might need to re-evaluate what in the world you're trying to accomplish. Age starts to work against you (unless you play jazz, where experience, practice and skill are truly appreciated. Unfortunately for me, I didn't play jazz).

Quite literally, 3 days after the birth of my first daughter, Ahnjayla, I got a call from one of the management company's assistants, Susan Joseph. She informed me that both Dan and I had been released from the management company and were off the payroll. She had also been released and wanted to become our manager. I was relieved and overjoyed all at once. Having what paltry bills I had and $65.00 a week was not worth the agony of attempting to fit in where I wasn't wanted nor believed in. You never want to be where you are not celebrated.

Susan and Dan got along with most of the officials in the company. I did not and as much as I tried, I simply didn't fit in because I had my own opinions and wasn't shy about expressing them. I just stayed out of their way and avoided them as much as possible. I got along with Seals and Crofts, but not management. Dash Crofts was a terrific guy. He was always funny and easy to get along with. He made me laugh.

Now, the real testing began. How do we survive?

For the second time in my career I went into a serious struggling mode. However, finances had now become ridiculously difficult and my sense of humor was hard to find anymore.

"Suffering" really doesn't quite describe it. I think that "suffering," with all the ugliness that the word possesses, was in all probability its most redeeming quality, if you could ever say being unemployed, un-bookable, without a recording deal, not able to properly take care your family, being turned down by every record company (on both coasts) and thinking that any chance of ever realizing the dreams of becoming a huge, bigger than life recording artist was never going to happen could ever have any "redeeming quality."

We had really tried every single avenue to get another record deal ever since we had been dropped by A&M Records in 1974. A&M was a good label and they did try, but sometimes no matter what is done by either side, it simply isn't in the cards. Can't explain it. A&M worked for Peter Frampton, just barely though. You see, Peter Frampton was just about to run out of a deal, but in his contract it called for a "live album." He recorded "Peter Frampton Live." The album became one of their biggest sellers and that forced A&M to renegotiate. I love renegotiations. A&M worked really well for The Carpenters. In my opinion, they were quite possibly one of the best vocal groups ever. I still miss Karen. So much heart in that girl's voice. A&M also worked for many, many others and made huge acts out of them. Just not for us.

We knocked around for awhile, attempting to pull in every favor that we had just to keep working and earning some kind of income. Anything to keep the dream alive. However, without any record product out in the field it was hard to find work. The promoters that had booked us in the past liked us all right; the acts that we had opened for before all liked us, but if you're unable to help draw in the audience and sell tickets then you're flat out of luck. Besides, record companies are always breaking new artists with new releases and those artists usually fill those spots in the touring world.

It's a hard business and more than anything that's the lesson I learned the most. The record business is precisely that: A business. You're up today and everybody loves you and wants to be your friend. You're hot and when you're hot everybody wants you. Tomorrow, you're on your way down the ladder and no one really cares because there's always new acts to push, money to be made, fresh flesh to be marketed and exploited. "Yes, we know you've gotten better and better with experience and you're actually playing better now than ever, but . . . well, nothing personal, but you're not hot anymore and it's business." Being a recording act has all the resemblance of the old cowboy adage "the fastest gun in the West." You're always looking over your shoulder because there is constantly someone trying to take your spot. Now, while this may be good for your neck muscles with all the exercise of turning your head around, you can become very suspicious; get brain freeze and a little cold in the heart.

It's difficult not to be discouraged by this industry at times. I remember that Dan and I had come to L.A. early in our career hoping for that elusive recording contract. We were just out of Texas and because we didn't know what we know now there wasn't anything that we couldn't do. You'll try anything when you don't know you're not supposed to. Experience can hamstring you sometimes because it can be the most beneficial gift and at the same time the biggest hindrance.

We would visit the various record companies, take our guitars and hopefully get to play live for the A&R people. Now, A&R people generally have to put up with a lot and can make or break a record for you. However, the lower down the A&R food chain you go, the more they are trained to say "NO" to everyone for everything, except for a free lunch. If they say "NO" to a hundred people, eighty-five to ninety percent of the time they're right. So very few would say "YES" and take the chance of failing while at the same time they saved their jobs for another six months.

When I first came to L.A., one of the very first record companies that Dan and I went to was A&M, which ended up being one of our future recording companies. Those were the days when you could walk in, bring your guitars and play and sing for the A&R people. We met with some guy and his comment was that he loved our sound, loved the group, loved the name, but hated our songs. But if we could come back with some hit songs then he'd talk possible recording contract with us. Dan and I were not defeatists and I for certain didn't like to get three out of four and lose.

So, we then went down the street to ABC Dunhill that same afternoon. We played the very same songs for the A&R rep there. He hated our sound, hated our group, hated our name, but he loved our songs. He even asked if we would give them to some of his artists he already had signed to the label. One hates us, one loves us. Go figure. This happened all over town. Most of these people we played for I figured didn't even know whether they were boys or girls yet, much less being capable of making decisions on what a group or song was or wasn't. One explained that "the recording industry was a dog eat dog world." I told him we ate beef in Texas, not dogs. We went home to Dallas for another year to write new songs and get some real barbecue.

So, where were we? Oh yeah, back to the story. In the midst of all of this losing and never really gaining any ground, I began to think "I really don't want to give up and quit, but I'm hungry, I need gas for the car (at least while I still have it), I've got bills to pay and I'm really sick and tired of the game. To add insult to injury, I hadn't even had the money to buy new strings for my guitar in over 6 months. (You can only boil strings down so many times before there's no sound left in them at all). Maybe I'll just go back to Texas and work for my Uncle George. Besides, they like me there and I haven't had an apricot-fried pie in a long time and I miss those. I don't fit here, anyway. Nobody loves me, everybody hates me, guess I'll eat some worms. Or in the words of Marlon Brando in a "Streetcar Named Desire," "Stellllllllllla!" Boy, I hate victims. Especially when I am one.

However, I developed a rather sick and interesting sense of humor about it all. Being a musician, you really learn to take life on the chin, struggle against the tide and laugh at a lot of it. Like the joke, "How do you make a million dollars playing music? Start off with two million." Or "the doctor whose son comes in and tells him he wants to be a musician when he grows up and the disappointed father tells him he can either grow up or be a musician, but he can't do both." Or, "What's the difference between a songwriter and a large pizza? . . . A large pizza can feed a family of four." Or, my personal favorite, "What's the difference between a musician and a dog? . . . A musician isn't afraid of a vacuum cleaner." Funny. Sick, but still funny. I like funny and to coin another phrase, "truth is stranger than . . ." well, you know how it goes. I like jokes.

About this time, good ol' Mother's Day rolls around. I don't have any money, much less the extra money to buy my mom a Mother's Day card. Heck, I'm looking for any change left in the coin return in the public phones. (Found quite a lot of it, too). However, I went to the drug store down the street to at least see what's available on my budget. As I was walking empty handed out of the store I happened to pass by a framed placard and it caught my eye. Thinking back, it's surprising that I saw it because my head was hung so far down that my chin was virtually on my chest. I was so depressed. But I couldn't help stopping to read it. I read it over and over and over again. Before I knew it, my morale actually began to pick up and the old fighting spirit flooded over me in a rising tide. My entire Southern upbringing, coupled with momma and daddy's untiring enthusiasm for my success, bolted out of me like a train that came right out of my sunken chest. In my head the words just kept ringing and ringing over and over, "You don't quit; you never quit; you were not trained to quit, ever period! So it's a bad idea to start now." I stood there until I memorized what was on the placard because as you know by now, I couldn't afford to buy it. It went like this:

Press On

Nothing in the world can take the place of persistence.

Talent will not; nothing is more common than unsuccessful men with talent.

Genius will not; unrewarded genius is almost a proverb.

Education alone will not; the world is full of educated derelicts.

Persistence and determination alone are omnipotent.

Anonymous

All I could think of was that God, Who had always looked out for me, had not brought me all this way only to desert me now. He was my Source for all of these things I had ahead and I obviously wasn't using my real gifts properly. The more I thought about how easily I had almost been defeated, the angrier I became. So, I redoubled my efforts, pressed in closer to God and things began to change. I had remembered being told many times, that about the time you decide to quit, you're really on the threshold of success. I still believe that. So, don't quit, no matter what.

At the beginning of 1976 our manager, Susan Joseph, found a song called "I'd Really Love To See You Tonight." At first neither Dan nor I really liked the song. We figured it was more of a female song, but our manager talked us into recording a demo on it. Louie Shelton, an extremely well known guitar session player agreed to help us out on the recording (for free). Louie had played guitar on just about everyone's records including "The Monkees," "Boz Scaggs," "Barbara Streisand," "Joe Cocker," "Lionel Richie," etc., etc., and the list goes on and on. Louie had been our first producer on the A&M albums and had been responsible for bringing us to the attention of Herb Alpert. Herb said he wasn't interested, but Louie gave him a tape anyway. Herb listened to the tape while he was shaving and as the story goes, called Louie while he still had shaving cream on his face and said to get us to L.A.

Louie was truly a great man. A real gentleman. I can't ever recall him losing his temper or having any nasty things to say about anyone. For someone in the music industry, he was about the most patient individual I'd ever met. He also had a sneaky, impish side to him as well. Once, while Dan and I were practicing for an upcoming recording session, Louie was playing guitar with us. I said to let me know when he was ready. Louie looks off into space and says, "On the count of four."

I'm waiting for the count off. You know . . . one, two. All of a sudden he says, "Four." I'm falling over the piano trying to get to the right note. I even banged my knee. Louie and Dan are laughing like there's never been anything funnier. I wanted to know what happened to one, two and three. I looked at Louie and said, "I'm going to have to keep an eye on you, aren't I?" That got him laughing. I don't trust anyone's count off but my own to this day. I'm always ready.

Louie performs his own CD's now, and if you happen to like exceptionally good guitar playing, then he's one to check out.

Louie later became the producer for Seals and Crofts after they saw how well he had done on producing Dan and I on A&M. For our demo, Louie put together a team of players we had worked with before and people who owed him favors. David Paich played piano while Jeff Pocaro played drums on the session. These were two of the hottest session players at the time in Los Angeles. They later both went on to play in the rock group 'Toto'. You never know how groups get their names, but on this one I'd be willing to bet "The Wizard of Oz" had something to do with it. I'm quick like that. It's a good thing I liked that film because since I've had children I must have seen it 500 times. Or, perhaps the name came because they had met one of my former managers, the wicked witch of the West. Oh John, that's mean. (Note to self. Take this part out. Don't forget now). My personal pick from that film was "If I Only Had A Brain." Long name for a music group though. But I digress.

When we were in the studio that evening about to record the song, I learned one of the greatest lessons on schooling I had ever had. School education and real life experience are light years apart and very seldom do they meet in the middle. You learn how to do it one way in college and you get a degree for your time and effort. When you get into the "real world," although you get to keep the degree for a wall decoration, you simply toss out most of what you learned and relearn to do it the real-life way. Worked for me.

Parker McGee, the writer of the song, was at the session and handing out lead sheets to all the musicians. He had meticulously written out every single note, precisely like he had learned in his music classes. It was beautiful paper, complete and ready to go to sheet music stands in your favorite local record store. When he handed the paper to Louie, Louie took a long look at it and in his polite matter said, "I can't read this. Give me some paper and play the song down for me." All the pros needed were the chords to the song. Almost all of them, in unison, threw the lead sheets on the floor and took up pencil and paper. Not that they weren't grateful for the effort, but these boys were pros and knew how to use their God given imaginations.

Our manager, Susan, took this demo of "I'd Really Love To See You Tonight" around to every record company in Los Angeles, looking for any sign of life and that we would get a possible recording contract. All she met with was rejection and resistance. Every single record company turned the song down. It looked as though there was no future for us in recording. However, I kept to my beliefs and with every rejection I could only say, "You will not defeat me. We *will* have a contract and we *will* be successful." Fortunately, Dan and I really encouraged each other and we worked hard to keep each other's spirits up. When I was discouraged, Dan was upbeat. When Dan was down, I was upbeat. It was good chemistry.

Now, no one in their right mind likes rejection. But, in all fairness I do have to thank everyone that ever turned us down on our songs or denied us recording contracts. With every rejection letter, it personally only strengthened my resolve to succeed. So, I owe a lot to those people because they only caused me to try harder and keep doing it and as a result I got better at my craft. And since then I've been on top of the recording industry and I've been on the bottom. The top is better.

The three of us were completely steeled in determination. One way or the other we were going to succeed. I used to say, "If at first you don't succeed, you're simply not vicious enough to play the game." That quote even made it into the book "Tales From The Casting Couch."

The only thing that we didn't have was a gimmick. Now, you need a gimmick. That's important. We had a great record (but maybe I was just a shade bit prejudiced . . . but then again, maybe not). We had a unique name; terrific songs, (Now look at that . . . I am prejudiced after all), polite manners (in Hollywood you can't get more unique than that), but there was nothing that would really set us apart from the pack. Now, some of the bands at that time were setting their hair on fire or using make-up or were demon possessed, eating live rats on stage, or licking their eyebrows with their tongue, falling drunk off the concert stage, weird hair, smashing amps and guitars, you know, your average garden variety rock star. You literally had to be more insane than the last group on stage just in order to get a 'ho hum" out of the audience. We didn't do that. We played music. I couldn't bring myself to even think about being involved in those sorts of antics. We were musicians, not a side-show carnival act. Besides, I thought being normal was a gimmick all in itself. Fortunately, the other kind of behavior had become so "normal" in the music industry that our type of behavior had become quite unique. I didn't even have to work at it. So, as far as I was concerned, we had a gimmick. Problem solved. Next.

As a last ditch effort, our manager went in to see Bob Greenburg at Atlantic Records in Hollywood. Bob had been quite successful in signing many of Atlantic's big acts and you would certainly expect him to be able to pick a great song out of a batch of songs. Unfortunately, I guess no one can do it every time.

After our manager had played him the song, he just sat there in his chair rocking back and forth. Unexpectedly, a head popped in the door and asked if he was interrupting. Bob invited him in and his friend followed. Bob introduced them to Susan as Dick Vanderbilt and Doug Morris, the heads of Big Tree Records, a subsidiary of Atlantic Records in New York. Now, these guys were a couple of promotion wizards. They were like the 'Lone Ranger,' except there were two of them. (I'd be hard pressed to say which one was the Lone Ranger and which one was Tonto until I learned that Tonto meant "wild one"). They would visit various radio stations to plug their artists and get air play on their records. They always left a "Silver Bullet" with the program director or DJ's. Who were those masked men? It was quite a clever little trick, but like I said earlier, "You need a gimmick to stick out." Fortunately enough, they were very good at what they did as well as having a recognizable gimmick. Maybe, they watched a lot of cowboy movies like I did when they were younger.

They chatted for a few minutes with Susan and Bob and then, Doug asked Bob what he thought of the song Susan had just played for him.

Bob, (I was told later), looked a little sheepish and said, "Susan, I'm sorry but I'm going to have to pass on the song."

Susan was dejected again, especially since Bob always took a meeting with her and continued to invite her to bring in any demos she had on us. He genuinely liked our group, but he needed a strong single and he obviously didn't think this one was it either. Radio was changing back to a single format from an album format.

That's when Doug and Dick said, "Are you sure you're going to pass on that song?"

Bob apologized once more to Susan and told her Atlantic was going to have to pass.

Almost immediately Doug and Dick turned to Susan and said, "We want the group. That song's a hit."

Susan was completely staggered. How had they known of the song or the group for that matter? It turns out that when Susan was playing the song for Bob, Doug and Dick were conducting business in the office next door. They had actually heard the song coming through the wall. Through the wall for crying out loud!!! You never know what God has planned for you. Through the wall. I could not get over it. Through the wall. Just how fortunate can you be? God has such good timing.

Bob gave them his blessings (which was good because he ended up working the song later, which was really good for us. Bob was a good guy).

We went on to sign a single deal contract for Big Tree Records with an option on an album. We then re-cut the song in Nashville with Kyle Lehning and some terrific Nashville players. When they released the single of "I'd Really Love To See You Tonight" that thing came out of the shoots bucking. Within two weeks Doug and Dick called us and said get to work on the album quick. The next thing you know we're back in Nashville, recording on our first Big Tree album. We had it completely finished in 30 days.

We had hoped that Louie Shelton would be the producer on the album for us, but he was busy with other projects and wasn't available. Kyle Lehning, known better as an engineer at that time, had produced the original demo on "I'd Really Love To See You Tonight" in Nashville with its writer Parker McGee. Parker had hoped to have a recording deal himself on the song, but it didn't happen. He eventually got his deal with Big Tree though. Susan was of the opinion that Kyle would be a great producer but he had no track record. Dan was adamantly opposed to him at first, but softened a little later. Dan listened to his older brother far too much and had been convinced that a big name producer who already had a reputation was the only way to go. I didn't care at that juncture. I simply wanted to press ahead and what Kyle had done so far sounded pretty doggone good to me, so let's give him a shot. We did and it proved to be one of our wiser decisions.

Years later, after producing Dan and I, Kyle went on to become the head of Asylum Records in Nashville. He also produced such astounding acts as Randy Travis and Brian White. One of Kyle's greatest gifts was that he knew a great song. If you could get a song past Kyle, you'd really accomplished something. He helped pick a lot of them for us. Through his leadership at Asylum he brought more than a few great acts into the country market as well.

There was a lot riding on the outcome of our project and Kyle put everything he had into it. Our first Big Tree album, "Nights Are Forever" was the first RIAA certified Gold Album for Big Tree. With the joining up of Doug, Dick, Susan, Kyle, Dan and myself, life began to smell infinitely sweeter.

Chapter 6

IT'S ALL ABOUT "FEEL"

Of all the things I've lost,

I miss my mind the most.

Mark Twain

In 1981, I went back to my old mentor, Herb Alpert, at A&M Records. Dan and I had called it quits in early 1980 and I had formed another group with two sisters, Leslie & Kelly and myself. I really loved the sound of this group.

I had always liked and had a great respect and admiration for Herb. I truly thought of him as the last and only real "musician" in the position in any record company of making decisions about music. Almost everyone else had marketing degrees, but couldn't tell you a "C" chord from a broken shoelace. But on the plus side, they did hang out at all the currently hip restaurants and knew all the greatest vacation spots. As a musician, we didn't. We were too busy creating music.

Herb had this wonderful secretary that was just as friendly and sweet as the day was long. She used to sit and chat with me when I'd go to visit Herb. This girl could talk up a blue streak. She was going 90 miles an hour, laughing and telling jokes with this sweet edge to her voice. She was funny and I truly enjoyed being in her company. When the phone would ring, she'd say, "Wait a minute, I've got to answer this." Then, out of the clear blue sky, she transformed right before my eyes and her alter ego took over. She became a completely different female. Her voice and demeanor entirely changed. She became this soft, sultry voiced sex kitten, flipping her hair with her free hand and batting her eyelids. In her most sexually engaging, deep throated sensual tone she'd say, "Herb Alpert's office. This is Cheryl speaking." If it was someone she knew, in the blink of an eye, she'd transform back into Cheryl again, talking in the same manner she had been speaking with me previously. "Oh, hi Cindy not much-what are you doing? I'm just sitting here talking to John Ford Coley and I was telling him about the time when tayada, tayada, tayada." No breaks or time for breath. She was worth the price of admission. I used to go see Herb, get there early just to talk with her and hoped that the phone would ring. She was a sweet character and is probably going to kill me if she ever sees this in print.

Herb signed our group onto his label because he had a particular song called "Long Distance Telephone" that he believed in. He had waited for a group such as ours to sing it. We learned the song. He loved the way we did it and planned to produce it himself. I was really excited about Herb producing the song because I knew he was really a master at "feel." What I mean by "feel" is that sometimes the performance on a song will be technically perfect but it has no feeling, no heart, it's just technical and played well. Other times, it won't be technically correct, but it feels so good. When the two are joined, then you've got something to really be proud of. For example, I've heard well-known singers that are perfect, have beautiful voices, could do anything with it, hit every note, sing where only dogs could hear, or make it jump up and over the Empire State Building and break glass. However, it was so sterile and sounded like a donkey braying to me as they were singing the song and probably thinking about needlepoint or something even less exciting. However, on the flip side, there are some singers out there that technically couldn't find a note with a sawed-off shotgun standing in front of it, but man, do they have heart. Give me that kind of singer or player every time.

Years before, I had learned much from Herb Alpert when I was a recording artist at A&M Records. We'd been signed to A&M in the early 70's and Herb had always been good to Dan and me. The fact that he had taken such an interest in this new act was huge for me. I mean after all, this was Herb Alpert from the Tijuana Brass and not only did I like his music, he was a genuine hero of mine.

The only distracting thing about Herb, for me at least, was the fact that I could never get a "read" on him. Herb had this amicable face with deep, dark penetrating eyes. They were always friendly, but they had a tendency to bore right through to your soul. He never gave away anything when you spoke with him. His facial expression didn't change. He'd just stare at you. It made me uneasy, with a slight tinge of irritation. I thought I knew him one minute and then didn't know him at all the next. "Poker face" is what we called it. It always left me wondering if I'd gotten through or not. I seldom knew. I always gave him the benefit of the doubt. Maybe he was just admiring the chiseled shape of my Irish nose. Yeah. I can see how that could happen.

I made mention of this to my manager once and the comment I got back was rather startling. They said, "Then talking to him must be like looking in a mirror for you. You're the same way." Whoa, what an eye opening revelation. I'd never thought about it, but I was almost exactly like that, except I'd put two fingers on my lips. I wondered what church he had been raised in because where I came from you never gave any indication that anything got you out of sorts. That was one of the things I'd learned in church.

No matter what is said, no matter how much you disagree or think about what's said, never, never change your facial expression. Keep them guessing. Always give the impression that you're in deep, penetrating thought. "You're going to burn in Hell son", no expression, but what I'm thinking is, "I wonder what momma's making for lunch?" "Young man, if you don't straighten up and fly right, you'll never amount to anything." No expression, but I'm thinking, "That new girl in the back pew is hot."

"I don't want to be in Heaven without you," blank expression but what I'm thinking is, "*You're* going to be there? I wonder if they really give out accordions in Hell?" Stoic. I learned it from my daddy. He had a gift for it. I'd been taught by the best. Church was a tremendous training ground for many things. I feel sorry for kids that don't get to go to church. They're really missing more than they know.

Herb was a master at "stoic" as well. I wonder if he could ever read me. That would be interesting to know. Two people who couldn't get a read each on other, each wondering why I was never a hit for his label.

On the very first recording session with Herb he only wanted Jeremy Lubbock to play a Fender Rhodes piano and my group to sing the song. We fiddled around for a while and finally put down a take (performance). For the moment Herb was really only interested in recording the piano and not in our vocals per se. We were just fodder for the piano player so to speak. We sang our hearts out on that take and Jeremy played with a skilled, deft touch. It was perfect.

After we had finished the song, Herb sat in the control booth for a couple of minutes rocking back and forth and to and fro across the recording console. He had his eyes closed and just kept to his rocking motion. We nodded at one another and I thought we'd nailed that puppy to the wall. This was a cinch. He had to know he'd made the right decision to bring me back. After all, Herb was the "feel meister." Jeremy was smiling back over at us. He had given his very best and he had, in one take mind you, pegged it.

Herb finally got up and walked into the studio. He stood over Jeremy at the piano and said, "Jeremy, what I'm getting is this." Herb closed his eyes and began to make a slow rocking motion back and forth over and over like he was in a rocking chair or praying at the Wailing Wall. As he was in the middle of that motion, without stopping he said, "Now, I don't want this . . . what I want is . . . this." Then, he smoothly began to sway from side to side.

Without a split seconds hesitation, Jeremy said, "I think I know exactly what you mean."

Herb's pleased that he had been able to communicate his cryptic feelings so effectively.

Herb headed back to the control booth and Jeremy looked at me, shrugged his shoulder and rolled his eyes up like, "What in the corn bread dickens is that man talking about?"

I don't remember being stoic when that occurred. I was caught in the middle of myself trying not to foolishly laugh, look stupidly bewildered or ask him to come back in the studio and please explain in simple "Texan" what he had just done and furthermore what in the tarnation he meant by it. I'm your basic guy. I'm simple. Just when you think you know somebody.

Rocking back and forth or swaying side to side. What in the world kind of direction is that? I'm having short bouts of disconnected thoughts. Going to the beach or having your hand run over by a golf cart. Riding a bull or not using the new guest bathroom hand towels. As unrelated as they are, this I understand. Hey, I'm a divergent thinker, but give me something where I don't injure myself.

At this point, I'm trying not to shake my head in amusement, but now, how do I sing this song again without laughing while Herb's loving every minute of it?

Jeremy played the song again, swaying this time, of course. Herb's swaying side to side in the control booth. He's smiling. We're all swaying. I'd never swayed before. I wasn't sure I could even do that. I think I two-stepped once, but it was by accident. Even in church when the music's being played, I rock back and forth, not side to side.

When Jeremy was done, Herb got excited and said, "That's a take. Let's go home." Jeremy's got this shell-shocked smile on his face, teeth half showing, and a glazed look in his eyes obviously wondering, "Whoa, what'd I do? That was tremendous. I hope I don't have to do it again."

Jeremy ended up producing the rest of the album for us, except for "American Boy," which Herb produced. I had already spoken with Larry Carlton about producing the album, but Herb had other plans for us. He knew Larry and said he'd talk to him for me. I wasn't happy about it, but Herb wanted to do it this way. Maybe I should have fought a little harder.

Larry Carlton was and still is a tremendous guitar player. He had been with the Crusaders and had gone on to record his own solo projects as well as being a highly sought after session player. He recorded for everyone from Joni Mitchell to Michael McDonald to Linda Ronstadt to Michael Jackson and Quincy Jones with too many more to name here. He also wrote many theme songs for TV. One of his biggest was the Grammy winning theme from "Hill Street Blues."

He was reputed to have broken a guitar string on stage one night during a performance. Right then and there he got mad and ripped off two more strings and proceeded into an out of this world instrumental solo. Don't know how true it is, but hey, it got around and that's how legends are born. And if it comes down to the truth or the legend, you always print the legend.

A couple of years later, as he and an aide were about to enter Room 335, his private studio in Burbank, he surprised some robbers and was shot in the throat, shattering one side of his vocal cords. It was a long recovery, but he survived and continues to perform and record today.

Meanwhile, back to Herb land. Herb failed to call Larry. He didn't feel he had enough "stripes" to produce us on his own. So, without consulting us he chose Jeremy. Jeremy Lubbock was a string arranger and went on to work with David

Foster, whom he became friends with after I had asked David to play piano on our record.

I called Larry later when I found out he hadn't been informed about Jeremy and before I said anything to him he defensively asked me how the recording was going. He had already heard he'd been replaced via the Hollywood grapevine and I had a good relationship ruined. Sometimes things are completely out of your control. I really felt bad because I really like Larry and know he would have done a great job. So, as a result of not producing our album, I never got to ask him . . . does he rock back and forth or does he sway side to side. Guess I'll never know.

Chapter 7

<u>BREAD</u>

"Night after night who treats you right baby it's the Guitar Man

Who's on the radio, you go listen to the Guitar Man

Then he comes to town and you see his face

And you think you might like to take his place

Somethin' keeps him driftin' miles and miles away

Searchin' for the songs to play"

"Guitar Man" Sung by Bread

Here are a couple of stories about one of the bands I'd traveled with. Dan and I toured with the guys in the group "Bread" for quite some time. We both really enjoyed being on the road with them. They were a terrific bunch of guys and I learned a lot about life and the road from them.

We had first played with them at Brigham Young University in Ogden, Utah in 1971. We ended up picking up a couple of more dates with them in '72. One day, our manager, got a call from our booking agent, Dan Weiner, at ICM. Dan also booked Bread at that time. He wanted to know what in the world Dan and I had said to the members of Bread and David Gates in particular. Our manager said she didn't know. Had we offended him or something? She assured him it certainly wasn't the kind of thing that Dan would do, but if anything was said or done wrong, it was probably John. (Which was a fair assessment). He told her that he had gotten a call from David that morning and had been informed that he was not to book Bread at any venue on the tour unless Dan and I were booked on it as well. Needless to say, we were all stunned. David hardly ever said anything to us. David had written many of Bread's hits and pretty much kept to himself. Usually he read the "Wall Street Journal" on our plane trips while everyone else read "Rolling Stone," "Soldier of Fortune," or something else equally related to our industry.

One of the most attractive thing to promoters about Dan and my act was that we were easy and we didn't eat very much. They knew the food for the headliner was pretty safe. We only played two acoustic guitars, and sometimes a piano; therefore, there was no breakdown and set-up between the opening act and the headliners. Nothing really had to be moved and therefore the time in-between sets was much shorter. We ended up opening for many acts during that time period for the very same reason. I used to think it was of our stunning personalities and precision harmonies, but it was really because we weren't much trouble.

The first time we played with Elton John in Milwaukee, we did our sound check for stage and were done in five minutes. We weren't picky and as long as we were able to hear ourselves, we were fine. So, we'd just check the level of our guitars and vocals in the monitors while the out front sound engineer would get the levels for the house. When Dan and I were finished we just said, "Ok. I think that gets it. Sounds good." The sound people and Elton said in disbelief, "That's it. That's all you want? We love you guys. You can tour with us any time" which translated out in roadie vernacular as, "Hallelujah. They're done and the food's still hot."

This was not lost on the guys in Bread. Having us meant they could take a longer than usual sound check, play and rehearse more, get the sound just the way they wanted it and would know that we weren't going to mess up their stage set-up or sound. Just as long as we had our five minutes we were hot and ready to go.

There were a couple of small events that happened touring with Bread. The first evening we played with them was at Brigham Young University in Utah. The school had met with us before the show and told us that in no way, shape or form were we to bring up anything political or religious from the stage. We had a song called "National Official" which was a turn of events on the JFC assassination. Dan began to explain the song. It got very quiet. Realizing what he had done, he laughed and quickly said, "Oops. I guess I wasn't supposed to talk about that was I?" The audience started applauding and laughing so we went ahead and did the song. I don't think the audience agreed much with school policy and they did ask us back many times, so I don't think they were too mad. However, Jimmy Griffin had watched our portion of the show and when we came off stage, he introduced himself and poking fun at us said, "You're trouble makers aren't you?" We said, "We don't mean to be, but for some reason we just can't seem to help it." Jimmy and I got to be good friends.

One event that particularly comes to mind was on one dark cloudy morning when we had to catch an earlier-than-anyone-in-their-right-mind-would-ever-want-to, plane ride. I forget exactly what town it was, but I do remember the weather being quite cold and dreary, so I'll take a wild guess and say somewhere in Ohio. We had plenty of time on our hands that day and not much to do. We usually had sound check around 4:00 or 4:30 in the afternoon. Many times there wasn't a whole lot to do before the shows. The boredom can be stifling at times, giving rise to the joke, "I spent a week in that town one night."

Most of the time, life on the road is pretty exciting. There's always new places to play and see. Some really interesting people to meet. New foods to try. It's mostly always different, even if it's only the difference between Boise, Idaho and Fargo, North Dakota.

Jimmy Griffin, the lead guitar player and co-founder of Bread, went walking downtown after we landed that morning. Jimmy was fun because he liked to play chess and most of the time I carried a board on road trips with me. I liked chess, but finding qualified people to play with on the road was a major challenge. Jimmy told me the first time we played that he'd never been beaten in chess and to prepare myself to get a royal "thumping." Six moves later he was wondering how the "thumping" had become a pharaoh's curse and landed on him. He's been seeking revenge with every "thumping" I've given him in chess ever since. The score is about 6000 to zero, give or take 5999 or so. I'm doing mental math here and I'm not really good at math. Ask my accountants or the IRS, but I do know that there's either 2, 3, 4, 5, 6 or 8 beats to a measure, unless it's Turkish music.

On his way through town, he stopped by a pawnshop and stuck up a conversation with the owner. Before you know it, he had talked the guy into trading him four tickets for him and three friends to come and see the show that evening for a used Colt 45 automatic pistol. This was before the "Brady Bill." That gun was in great working order, too. Jimmy came back to the hotel and showed me what he'd gotten. Now that's a good trade. The tickets didn't cost Jimmy anything. After all, he got them for free. The promoters always gave us "comps" in the event we had friends or family we wanted to get in.

I should have gone with Jimmy that day. I had tickets to trade, too. The man might have had an extra Nikon camera lens lying around somewhere that I could have used. Jimmy put the tickets at "will call" under the man's name so he could pick them up before the show.

That evening, Willie Leopold, Bread's road manager, came in and told everyone about the big fracas that had happened in front of the auditorium. The police had caught someone scalping tickets to the show. The man had resisted arrest and they had tackled him to the ground. It was quite a fun and exciting evening, especially for the police.

Lo and behold, the man that Jimmy had given the tickets to was the scalper. So, the pawnbroker had not only traded away a valuable gun, he didn't get any money for the tickets, and as an added bonus, he got to spend the night in jail. That's a hard day's work. Jimmy felt bad about it and wondered if he should give the man the gun back. We said, "What are you going to do Jimmy? Go to the jail and give the guy back his gun? The police might frown upon that." Jimmy kept the gun. I would have too. It ended up not being much use to him though. I mean, what's the use of having a gun like that if you can't shoot some terrorist with it. Just kidding, ma'.

****

Another time we had a show in Lubbock, Texas. We had played at Texas Tech, the University there. We had to leave out very early the next morning because

Bread had to be in Oklahoma City for a show and Dan and I were supposed to catch up with Seals and Crofts in New York City to play the Philharmonic.

On this tour, Bread had hired a photographer to travel around with them and shoot photos for "The Best of Bread" album. He and I got along really well because I was an amateur photographer and we had lots to talk about. That's one of the difficult things about being with the same people all the time. After the first few days, all the jokes are gone, and before you know it, you've run out of things to talk with anyone about. So, he was fresh meat for me.

We had arrived at the airport at about 6:00 a.m. on a very chilly and foggy morning. I felt like I was in a werewolf movie because I had never seen that much of or as dense a fog before. It literally had taken us about fifteen minutes to get to the airport from the hotel, which was virtually just across the street. Nothing was coming into or leaving the Lubbock airport. In a word, we were stranded. The photographer must have shot up 6 rolls of film in that airport out of pure boredom.

"Video Pong" and the trivia games were the rage at that time. We played them in whatever airport we landed in. They were great diversions. As you can imagine traveling all the time, we'd gotten pretty good at those games. But this day, we searched the entire airport over and couldn't find one to play.

So, here we were, stranded, fogged in, can't find any video games and we've already read every magazine in the rack because we've been on the road for two weeks and have had to sit waiting for flights in dozens of other airports across the country. I remember I used to jokingly think, "Oh . . . let's see if the magazines in this airport are different than the ones in the airport we left out of yesterday. Oh. Look at that. They're the same." We hoped that we'd be booked to fly different airlines so that we would have new crossword puzzles. If you flew on the same airline all the time, you'd already done the crossword in that airline's in-flight magazine. Being an English literature student in college, I was very seldom without some book of value to read.

Now, Willie Leopold, Bread's road manager was not one to sit around and do nothing if a problem arose. He was one of the most resourceful people I've ever met. He could make a dead ahead decision quicker than most banks in California could go bankrupt. Willie later went on to manage Melissa Ethridge. She shot off like a rocket with tassels.

The fog began to clear a little, but all commercial flights were still canceled. Willie immediately recognized the severity of the situation, got on the phone and hired a private plane that could fly out of the fog in a matter of minutes.

When the pilot arrived with the private plane, he stressed to everyone over and over and over again, "If you've got to go to the bathroom, go now. It's about two and a half hours to Oklahoma City and this plane doesn't have a toilet." Now the airport might not have had video games but they more than made up for it with soft drink machines. I think Dan was already on his 6th or 7th Dr. Pepper of the morning.

We piled into this little plane. Willie had to sit in the co-pilot's seat. I prayed there were no problems or the pilot wasn't going to get sick because I know Willie didn't know how to fly (not a plane anyway). There weren't any seats in this thing. They were more like small cushions from some hippy love-in or something. We didn't have seatbelts so we're bouncing all over the place because of the turbulence and it was really hard to read, sleep or anything else except get a little queasy.

We couldn't have been in the air more than ten minutes when, you guessed it; Dan had to go to the bathroom. The pilot was grumbling and yelling back over his shoulder, telling him, "I told you to go at the airport. We don't have a toilet."

Now, Dan's a big guy and should have a bladder about the size of the state of Montana, but that many Dr. Peppers can make a 90 pound weakling out of just about anyone. Dan's whimpering as he told him, "But I tried to mister and I didn't have to go then."

Dan's teeth were beginning to float in his mouth and it was hard to tell if the water in his eyes were tears from the pain or else he was backed up to the brim. He was curled up in the fetal position, moaning and holding himself. The rest of us were trying to ignore him, thinking, "Better him than me." You can become quite mercenary in those kinds of situations. I tried to pretend I didn't know him.

"Mister, I've really got to go. I mean it." Dan whined. "Do you have anything? Can we open a window or something, anything?"

I heard words to the effect of, "be a man" coming from the pilot. I think I might even have overheard the phrase "sissy longhairs" muttered under his breath. We've got more than two hours to go before we were to land in Oklahoma City. Finally, the pilot told Dan there was a small can he could use. Dan jumped for that can faster than a groupie after a backstage pass.

Now the rest of us began to feel his pain because Dan filled the can to the brim. I actually remember that "small can" being about the size of a large Maxwell House coffee can, but Dan was a big guy. If anyone else had to go, the only container is full. The rest of us began moaning and by now our eyes burnt from the acid. Dan's eyes were flittering half closed and he looked like some junkie who was relieved to get his fix. Just think. We've only got to deal with the smell for another two more hours. "Happy, Happy, Joy, Joy." At least Dan was smiling.

We were all disgusted and wanted to wring Dan's neck. So far as I know, no one has invented a roll down window on a plane that you can use at 10,000 feet. We needed one. The guys in Bread had to be rethinking this glamorous lifestyle they were living. If this was glamour, I must have misread the brochure because this wasn't what I signed on for. Parties, Grammy ceremonies, girls all wanting to touch you, pull your hair and have you sign stuff, while the guys all want to be you because they think all you get is girls. Yeah, a rock and roll lifestyle that goes on for 24 hours a day. All day, every day. (Incidentally, even after all these years, I'm still waiting for the glamour part to materialize). This was why we were in this business. Glamour. Instead, we got a two and a half hour plane flight in a cramped, twin engine prop, with no bathroom, that got tossed back and forth with every bit of turbulence, and a flyer with ten minute kidneys. Fun, fun, fun.

When the plane finally landed in Oklahoma City and the door was opened, we shot off of it like a bullet. Most of the time, we'd complain about having to travel by commercial airliners, but after that episode, I've never complained again. They had restrooms.

Somehow we ended up on the "Best of Bread" album jacket from the photos the photographer shot at the airport. If you have one, Dan is the person on the left hand side looking through a camera lens, with the Dr. Pepper can between his feet. I'm the one at the ticket counter with my back to the camera (with the Dr. Pepper can in front of me. Just because you can't see it doesn't mean it's not there).

****

Another story about Jimmy Griffin. I've worked with Jimmy on several occasions since he was in Bread. Jimmy and Terry Sylvester (who replaced Graham Nash of the Hollies after Nash went to Crosby, Stills and Nash) and I played together in a trio sometimes. Of all the music I've played this is one of the combinations I think I've enjoyed the best. It's a lot of fun playing all those hits and watching people throw their backs out trying to dance to them now. Slow dancing has its purpose, even to the most upbeat song. And besides the road is so different now. At one time girls used to throw hotel keys and other more intimate items at us. These days they still come to the concerts but now they bake us cookies and cakes and stuff and bring their children to hear us. So much has changed.

Jimmy, a Memphis boy, had to be the most humble, quiet and soft-spoken person for a rock musician that I've ever known. We both lived in the Nashville area and sometimes I would go to his house to practice when we had gigs together.

One day, I happened to see a rather odd shaped gold looking thing on his mantel that looked something like a man praying. I went to take a closer look and to my surprise I recognized it as an Oscar. I'd only seen people get these on TV and use Sally Fields quote of "You like me. You really like me." I personally thought that was kind of cool. Real emotion.

As I had never been up close and personal with an Oscar before, I took a double look and ask Jimmy where he got it. In his affable manner, he told me he had gotten it for a song he co-wrote for the Carpenters and that song had won the Oscar at the Academy Awards.

I told him that he must not be very proud of it and if it were mine, I certainly wouldn't put it on the mantel. How many times had I been to his house and never seen the thing. I told him that I bet very few other people had ever seen it either if they'd come to his house.

He got a little defensive and asked, "Yeah. Then where would you put it?"

I immediately said, "In the bathroom."

He pulled his head back and looked at me like I was nuts.

"Why in the bathroom, may I ask?" he retorted.

Although I was younger, I put my hand on his shoulder and assumed the older and wiser brother figure and patiently began to explain to him some of the things I had learned in a rock music course I took in life called "Ego 101." I spoke loudly and slowly because it's an axiomatic fact that everyone knows how most musicians are hard of hearing and not generally the brightest crayola in the box. Simple fact of life. Except for Jimmy and me of course.

"Now, Jimmy," I gravely said, "I've been to your house, say, maybe half a dozen times and this is the first time that I'm seeing this Oscar. This is a major achievement, a milestone in your career. Do you realize just how many musicians ever win one of these things? Not many. If it were mine, I'm put it in the bathroom, throw a lot of parties and always have plenty of salty things to eat and therefore everyone would want something to drink. The more they drink, the more they would constantly need to go to the bathroom. Then they see the Oscar; marvel at it and at you too of course and you would be a big-time hero. Grammys are common place. But I mean, how many people do you know that have won an Oscar? However, no one will ever see it on the stupid fireplace mantel. Make sense?"

He looked at me with one of those "Get thee behind me Satan," kind of looks.

Then he said, "That would make it an idol, wouldn't it? You wouldn't be trying to make me an idol worshipper would you?"

Bummer. I'm trapped and Jimmy knows it too. I had felt that way once before; the time that I cut down a tree that started falling the wrong way. It isn't wise at that point to take the time to think. You simply react, drop the chainsaw and run . . . or die. Your choice really.

So, not wanting to admit that I had suffered any momentary lapse in spiritual judgment and had reverted to my former pagan side, I quickly and adroitly said, "Good point. Come to think of it, it really does look good on the mantel. Got anything to drink?"

I knew that I shouldn't have taken that stupid "Ego 101" course. It was apparent that Jimmy had taken the "Wisdom and Logic 101" course. I would have taken that course too, except that the books cost too much, which isn't wise or logical to begin with. Maybe I should have paid and opted for that course anyway.

Chapter 8

THE WOMEN, THEY REALLY LOVE ME

It's gonna be a long night. If you need me, I'll be in with the girls.

Igor from "Young Frankenstein"

After Dan and I ended our partnership, I formed a singing group with two sisters, Leslie & Kelly. A couple of longhaired beauties. I loved the way this group sounded and we had high hopes. We were on A&M Records for a short while in 1981. Unfortunately a very, very short while.

During this time, A&M released our first single called "Come Back To Me", a song that I had co-written with Kerry Chater, one of my many favorite writers. We shot a video for this song and it was the first real video that I had done. Dan and I had only shot a video once for "Simone" in Japan. We did a quick one on "I'd Really Love To See You Tonight" for the foreign markets as well, but that was only one of the two of us playing on a stage with the camera passing over us at different angles. They must have played the song three times and what we got was what we got. Not the standard of today.

Although the song "Come Back To Me" was not a success in the U.S., it was a huge success in Brazil. In Brazil, they had soap operas that were immensely popular and every character on the show would have a theme song that introduced them each time they made an entrance on the show. They liked our song so much that they created a new character for the show who would be introduced to the song.

We were invited to perform on the Merv Griffin show to showcase our song for the American audience. Now, I had been on "Merv Griffin" on several occasions before with Dan and really liked Merv. You had to watch him though because he was a very intelligent man, but he had an impish side and could be a tricky rascal. On our first "Merv Griffin" show after we finished our song, Merv came and stood between us to talk a bit. He asked me all kinds of questions and I'm responding in kind. Then, he asked me another question. When I began to speak, he suddenly turned his back to me and faced Dan. Dan was looking off into the audience and not really paying attention. I continued to talk and eventually Merv had to turn around and face me again. I'd learned tricks like that over the years.

After the Merv Griffin Show the girls and I had played, I was backstage eating and talking with everyone. Jim Stafford was there. He was famous for his songs

"Spiders and Snakes" and "My Girl Bill." I had also seen him perform at the Universal Amphitheater one evening. He's an extremely talented guitar player. I was knocked out with his rendition of Mason William's "Classical Gas." This is a terrific piece of work and not the kind of song for some untrained beginner. Jim really shined through on it that evening.

As we talked, he asked me a very funny question. Of course, "funny" is a relative term. Most things are funny to me, and what follows is one of those funny-provided-you-don't-have-to-live-with-it-on-a-daily-basis kinds of funny. He said, "What's it like to play with girls now instead of guys?"

Okay. Okay. Now here's every guy's fantasy. In fact, it's Fantasy Island. Tattoo runs to the plane. I get off and there, on the beach, are thousands of the most beautiful women on the planet. All scantily clad, with those over-sized pouty lips, waiting breathlessly, hanging on my every word. Their long hair sways in the afternoon sun, amidst the palm trees of perfection. They all want me I can tell. Oh, yeah. They tell me, "Oh John, you're wonderful. You're so smart, you're so funny, so cool and soooo brutally handsome." (Shut up, it's my fantasy). Well, in my version two very gorgeous women surround me as we get a record deal on A&M Records. Just think. As the only man in the group I'm the only hero these two will ever need. Suddenly, the needle on the record painfully screeches to a halt.

Back to reality. So I said to Jim, "You really wanna know?"

He said, "Well, I asked, didn't I?"

Jim's a Southerner. We speak the same language.

Since a picture is still worth a thousand words, I told him to follow me and I'd show him. The show had been short of dressing rooms for that particular taping of Merv and I had to share a room with my two lovely companions. I stood at their/my/our dressing room door. I nodded to Jim and knocked soundly on the door. What we heard next were these two angelic voices that sweetly said, "Who is it?"

I said, "It's me, John."

In a heartbeat, the angels turned into snarling dragons. Venom spewed through the two inches of wooden divide and rolled down to the doorknob. Terse and tense their words blurted out, "NOT NOW JOHN, WE'RE DRESSING!!!!"

I looked at Jim and dryly said, "The women. They really love me. Is there anything else you want to know?"

As his head shot back he dropped his mouth open and gasped, "Whoa! What'd you do to them?"

I swallowed hard and said, "Honestly . . . I can't remember."

What I do remember was Jim sympathetically patting me on the shoulder, looking me in the eye while searching for something meaningful and compassionate to say. I think he might have suffered from that "Fantasy Island" vision as well. They were beautiful girls. Although he tried his best not to, all of a sudden he burst out laughing. His infectious laughter got me to laughing. We both just stood there laughing so hard we had tears running down our cheeks. He really does have a nice laugh.

Chapter 9

IT'S NICE TO BE REMEMBERED

It is sometimes expedient to forget who we are.

Publilius Syrus (c. 42 B.C).

Periodically I still get surprised. When you're in the public eye, you never know what publication you're going to show up in or what dim light you're going to be presented in.

A couple of years ago, I was scanning through the Internet. I still periodically check under my name to see if copies of CD's are being pirated or just to check out places I'm playing, or in some cases, to correct errors like "being born in Austin, Texas, instead of Dallas, Texas." I think some publicist thought that because Austin and Dallas each had 6 letters they were interchangeable and that Dallas was the capitol of Texas.

However, on this particular occasion, I happen to travel down the listings pretty far. I don't think I'd ever been dragged down that far into the net before.

Most of the time there's an article talking about the worst or best songs they've ever heard. My songs usually make it in there somewhere. Some of the articles are written by people that must hate everything and everyone that ever spoke to them, looked at them or smiled at them because some of them can get pretty nasty. I guess that they think by what they say somehow they're going to help me change my opinion of myself. I don't pay much attention to those, but if you like a good laugh sometimes they are fun to read.

One of my favorite articles was in some newspaper from Las Vegas. The sports writer was spewing about Oscar De La Hoya and his upcoming boxing match. He referred to the time that De La Hoya had fought Derrell Coley and registered a seventh-round knockout in New York's Madison Square Garden. The writer obviously didn't much care for De La Hoya, Derrell Coley, or me either for that matter. In his opinion, he thought that "For what it was worth to restoring his image, it might have well been singer, John Ford Coley." This was cool. A new career. I'm open. I mean, it could happen; I could be a boxer, although I'd need to learn how to dance better. I can duck and move and avoid taking a shot. After all, I've been ducking and avoiding being hit by music critics for most all of my career. Besides, if I could get in the ring and fight De La Hoya, I'd slam my face into his fist so fast and hard; it'd hurt his hand.

Teach him a lesson. And I've seen him fight. He's never seen me fight. Maybe the experience could jump career boundaries.

The readers of that article who had no idea who I was or what I had been involved in, probably thought I was a younger brother or something of Derrell Coley. Maybe a welterweight, only from a completely different culture and mother and father.

When I played in Las Vegas not too long ago, I thought I'd invite this writer to the show. I wanted to thank him for spelling my name correctly in his article. However, I guess that he'd gone somewhere else to boost someone else's career. At any rate, I couldn't find him. Who knows? Maybe he's writing articles at another paper. Maybe in Pocatello, Idaho. They do seem to move around a lot.

At any rate, I happened to come upon a site that sparked my curiosity. It was entitled "England Dan and John Ford Coley Fan Club Members Hold Annual Reunion in Boston Area." I was intrigued. Wow! I still had fan club members running around out there somewhere? I had lost contact with our fan club president, Jan Schaffer, years before and I know that Chris Wolf, who had taken over the club before Dan and I split the group, had passed away several years ago in St. Louis, Missouri. Chris was a terrific, caring girl. She was sweet and worked really hard.

Running a fan club, I found out, isn't easy. You have to deal with managers and record companies and such. I have trouble getting information from them myself and don't like to work with them, so it must have been quite an eye opening revelation for fan club officers. However, these girls used to run some pretty interesting contests, so I was genuinely interested to see what this reunion was all about.

My computer was slow and it would take me forever to download anything. I'm anxiously wanting and waiting to see this. What do these people look like after all these years? Come to think of it, what kind of people were actually in our fan club? Who in the world would still be attending a fan club reunion for us? Would I happen to remember any of them?

When I finally got to the photo of the reunion, I stared at it for a split second before I was literally on the floor rolling and slobbering all over myself. I couldn't stop laughing. I'm howling. They had to hear me on the next 10 acres over. It had to be about the funniest and most clever things I'd ever seen. I called everyone in the house to come and check out the people at "my" fan club reunion photo.

The site was called McGuffin's Untrue News. I hadn't seen the "Untrue" part at the site, just the reunion notice. In the photo there were four people and they all looked to be octogenarians. I don't think there was anyone under 75 in the photo. There couldn't have been a full set of teeth between them. Each in their own wheelchair or lounge chair, complete with that "I haven't had this much fun since I staked my kid brother down to an ant bed" painted on smiles. I suppose it had been taken at a senior citizens home and on top of it, they looked like someone had dumped them there like a stray dog on a country road and they couldn't ever leave because they'd never get lime Jello that good again.

Now, I've played so many pranks over the years that I really appreciate a good joke when I see one. Even at my own expense. I love to laugh, especially at myself. I learned that from my momma. Heck, like it or not, life is funny.

I couldn't stop laughing and thought this was so clever that I did something I very rarely do. I responded. I got the e-mail address of the site and wrote to them. People get kind of nervous when they do something like that and the artist finds out about it. He probably thought I was going to hurt him or something. I told him how funny I thought it was and how much I laughed about it. I wanted a copy of it for my collection. So, he gave me a free subscription to his "untrue news" stories. Hey, the job comes with some perks you know.

I periodically ask people that come over to the house if they'd like to see some members at a recent ED&JFC fan club reunion. Unless they've been around me before and know how I am, they look at the photo embarrassed and don't quite know what to say to me. It's still fun to watch their faces. Sometimes I'll make up names for the people in the photo. "Yeah, that's Samantha. She looks hot since she's been on that watermelon, beet and pickle juice diet, don't you think? And here's Annie. That face-lift has done her wonders. Took fifty years off her. Don't hardly recognize her, especially after the doctors botched the first one."

However, I still couldn't help but think if any of our former "real" fan club members happened to see that photo and did recognize any of the people there. Now, that would be funny.

Chapter 10

<u>FAVOR</u>

The two hardest things to handle in life are failure and success.

Unknown

We used to tour with the group, Chicago, when they were still "Chicago Transit Authority" or "CTA." At this time, Terry Kath was still playing guitar in the group before his untimely death. Terry died from an accidental self-inflicted gunshot wound. Terry was always nice, but quiet.

We had been on tour with them for a couple of weeks from Utah to Washington State and back. They were a great group to travel with, especially James and Lee. To be the big recording artists they had become, they were nothing but nice to us and always willing to help.

At this time in our career, I used to play some of the bluegrass banjo songs, like "Arkansas Traveler" and the like. I really liked banjo. Still do. Unfortunately, I saw too many Bruce Lee movies and I took up karate. I ended up hurting my thumb and was never able to finger pick with a thumb pick again. That accident killed my professional banjo playing days. It also affected by piano and guitar playing and I had to adjust and learn to pick with a flat pick. I really thought my music career was finished. Karate and musicians don't mix. If you're a musician and reading this and want to learn karate, don't. Learn to use a gun and pay someone to clean it. It's safer.

We were in Seattle playing the Dome with CTA for two nights. On our second day there, Dan and I were out driving around just taking in the sights of the city. Seattle is such a beautiful place and if you happen to be there when it's not raining, it's a great drive. Seafood galore and you can stay in the infamous "EdgeWater Inn" and fish from your room while hearing Led Zeppelin stories all night long.

As we were driving, I made an illegal turn. Back then, the laws were different everywhere. In some states, you can turn right on red, in other's you can't. For example, in Carlsbad, California, a stop sign means "Stop, stop and then stop again. Wait 15 seconds, look over your shoulders, scan the buildings to see if there is a cop hiding in the bushes and then continue." You still might get a ticket. Where I came from, a stop sign was a place to check out the sighting on your '22 rifle. (For those of you not familiar with guns, this means target practice on a stop sign. It's probably outlawed now in most states, but if not outlawed, certainly frowned upon). Another example: In Los Angeles, a stop sign doesn't actually mean, "Stop." It's really nothing more than a polite, hopeful request. In some places you can get away with anything because the city's sole means of support doesn't come from ticket revenues. In others . . . well, I'm sure most you have experienced it already.

I look in the rearview mirror only to see the red flashing lights. A motorcycle policeman has me dead to rights. A long haired type driving a nice car with an out-of-state driver's license means one thing and one thing only; they take you to the precinct and you pay the fine right then and there. Otherwise, you'll never pay it. They know this.

He gets off his bike and does the policeman shuffle. You know, the slow one that says "I may have a wedgie but I'm still in control. One smart-alec word and your hippie haircut, along with your head, will get shaved." It really loses its effect though if the day is hot and he's peeling his pants off of his sweaty rear-end as he walks up to the car. Now, I'm Texas born and raised. I know my manners. "Yes Sir" and "No Sir" are as natural to me as taking my feet out of the stirrups on a rearing horse. I know the drill and no person in his right mind would ever do battle with a policeman. To this day I still can't help saying "Yes Sir" and "No Sir" to everyone. It's just polite.

When the policeman comes up to the window, he stares at me a little too long like he knows me or something. I smile and am on my most polite behavior. He asked for my license. He takes a long stare at my license. He glares back at me. He stares at my license again. He stares back at me. I'm getting nervous. He's big. He's looking at me like I remind him of someone he put in jail once that shouldn't be out so soon and he isn't happy about it. He's not saying anything. Just staring. This isn't good. Even Dan's getting nervous with small sweat beads on his forehead and he's only the passenger.

Finally, he looks at me real hard and in his best authoritarian voice says, "You look familiar to me. Were you the banjo player at the Chicago concert last night?"

Oh no. He saw me play banjo and hates bluegrass. Maybe he hated "Deliverance" or is under the false impression that all banjo players are hillbilly mongoloids that think all weekend warrior, city boys squeal like pigs.

At this point, I'm not feeling very self-assured, but in my most hopeful, yet confident voice, I said, "Why, yes sir, I am."

He cocks his head to the side. That signals to me that I just said the wrong thing. Maybe I should have apologized for it or something. Then with a big toothy grin he said, "I saw you guys last night with Chicago. Man, you're a good banjo player. I play banjo, too."

Dan's relieved. I'm really relieved. The policeman's overjoyed because this is as close as he's ever come to someone that he thinks is famous, or at least someone who knows someone famous or is famous by association. All I know is that I'm not going to get a $100.00 ticket.

We talked about some of the old music, which fortunately both Dan and I knew something about. He was having the time of his life, joking, talking to us like he'd known us all his life and asking tips about banjo. I was lying my best on how to play this and how to use different fingerings on that. Heck, I'd only been playing banjo for a couple of months myself. What do I know? But, he seemed to know exactly what I was talking about. I was making most of it up as I went along.

We offered him some tickets to come back to the show that night but he wasn't able to go.

After we'd had this nice, friendly talk for a while he gave me back my license. Then in his most stern policeman voice he says, "Now, you boys be careful and watch the traffic signs. Next time I'll ticket you." Authority!

He turned, walk back to his bike and drove off. Didn't even wave goodbye. What's this mean to you? I don't know. But, a word to the wise. If you're ever in Seattle, it might be a good idea to carry a banjo. Just in case . . .

Chapter 11

YOU NEVER KNOW WHO KNOWS YOU

"Aren't you somebody?!"

Numerous comments from different people

When your records are all over the radio and your face is plastered all over the TV, people frequently come up to you, ask for your autograph and generally keep you from eating a decent hot meal from all the constant interruptions. At the oddest times, you can never tell when someone is going to pop their little head up, squint their eyes and say, "Hey . . . aren't you . . ?" Keeping a low profile when you're hot isn't always an option no matter how much of a disguise you wear. I did that to Pam Tillis in the Nashville airport. She was at baggage claim, dressed in a hat that was pulled down low, sunglasses and everything but a black bandana over her face. I called her name; she turned and said "Yes?" It's a dead give-away when you answer to your name no matter how inconspicuously you might think you're dressed. I told her, "You do that incognito thing really well." She could only laugh. We talked for awhile. Such a sweet lady. Although I have had some twisted moments where I wanted to see someone famous, run up to them and say, "Hey, aren't you . . . wow, I'm really one of your biggest fans and . . . hey, you're putting on a little weight aren't you?" Just a mean streak I guess.

Sometimes you really have to keep your cool when you don't feel like it. I was in New Orleans once eating in a really good restaurant. If you want a real challenge, try finding a bad restaurant in New Orleans. Go ahead. I dare you.

At any rate, we were at the height of our career and were being scrutinized by the locals in the restaurant. Most times people may recognize you, but don't say anything. The waiter was, for some reason, trying to be very professional and before he took my order he began to explain the choice of wines to me. I told him I didn't want a glass of wine, but would prefer a glass of sweet tea. When he returned with our salads and drinks, he unintentionally spilled an entire glass of Chardonnay down my back and shoulders. It got quiet. Now everyone is staring at us. Look what happened to the longhaired rock star. Ha, ha, ha, this is so funny. Now, I'm wet, ticked and I'm about to eat my dinner with sticky Chardonnay still running down the back of my shirt working its way down still further south. What I wanted to do was stuff a crouton up this waiter's nose, but, well, unfortunately my self-control got the better of me.

I looked up at him and in a loud voice firmly said, "No. Like I told you . . . I didn't want the wine. I asked for a sweet tea."

Several people began applauding and started laughing in the restaurant. I guess I covered myself well. He was profusely apologizing to me, but it could have been a cover up. The record company rep bought my dinner. Fortunately for the waiter, I wasn't the one that had to leave the tip.

****

One time Dan and I were in New York City on a leg of a tour. We were walking near Times Square in the afternoon with our publicist, Nancy Griffin. I loved Nancy. She was a really sweet lady who traveled with us and set up radio and television interviews. She had a great sense of humor. She was so mild and meek and very easy to pull pranks on because she never expected them. For some reason, I think she thought that after the last 40 times eventually we'd get tired of this infantile, Boy Scout camp behavior and stop. It never happened.

Our road manager, Ron, used to pull pranks on her constantly, like getting into her room before she did and short sheeting her bed, or taking all her towels. Once, he even hid under her bed and when she sat down, he reached out and grabbed her foot. I think Nancy aged quite a bit traveling with us. But she was a good sport and I think she must have had brothers, so she knew what guys were like.

While we were walking around the city, Dan made the casual remark of "I'd like to find a good pawn shop. I haven't been to one in a long time."

Satan, having power of the air, what both Nancy and I heard Dan say was, "I'd like to find a good porn shop. I haven't been to one in a long time."

I immediately said, "You really want to go to a porn shop?"

Nancy's disgusted with him. She's thinking that all the pseudo spiritual stuff he'd been talking about has been a cool, calculated front.

Dan immediately comes to his own defense and says, "No, not porn shop. A PAWN shop." Both Nancy and I said in unison, "Aha. Misunderstood you." So I start ribbing him, "Are you sure? You look sort of guilty to me? You got this secret life we're accidentally stumbling upon?

Dan's covering tracks. "No . . . I don't." But he's still got this guilty twitch and looks like he's possibly hiding something.

As we walked I remarked, "I've never been in a porn shop. Wouldn't go. I'd probably be there during a holdup or hostage situation and then I'd get recognized and I'd be explaining that one away forever. I'm sure it would make me popular with some people though."

Nancy agreed. I could see her face contorting thinking of all the fires she'd be having to put out over that one. A publicist's nightmare, or dream, depending which end of the horse you rode. Of course, that was the late '70's and the standard has lowered dramatically since those days. Now it's more like a badge of honor.

We hadn't walked thirty seconds down the street when this boy and girl ran up to me, touched my shoulder and said, "Aren't you John Ford Coley? Can I have your autograph?"

They were so excited, jumping up and down, talking about how their friends would never believe it, could they have a photo too, this was great, wait 'til I tell my sister, could she have one too, do you have any photos on you that you could sign, etc., etc. In a demented sort of way, you become quite accustomed to this and your ego really looks forward to it. So you smile, say 'thank you, ask where they're from, say 'I like your name,' etc., etc. It's a dance. You have no rights. You're a public figure. Get used to it or find another profession.

This happens in the middle of New York City. Do you have any idea how big that town is? And what are the chances of being recognized in a town of sixty-eight billion people hustling back and forth looking right past you. After they left, I looked at Dan and Nancy and said, "And that's just one of the reasons I won't go into a porn shop, besides being hit by some freak lightning storm after all the prayers my mother put in for me."

The only time that autograph seekers become annoying is when you've snuck out of your house dressed in your sweats with the paint stains and holes in them, haven't shaved for two days and generally look like you've been out cleaning horse stalls for a living and could oil a Mack truck from all the oil in your hair. Inevitably someone sees you and says something and your only remark is, "You're not supposed to know who I am when I look like this!" Image is everything. You never know who's out there with a pen and album jacket, or worse, a camera just waiting for you.

****

More recently, I was at the airport ticket counter getting my ticket to go and play a date with the group, Ambrosia, in Detroit, Michigan. I had met these guys in the Philippines a couple of years back and we've been working together since. Hands down, these are some of the best musicians I've ever worked with and they've had many great hits too. Just good people. If they're ever in your town you've got to hear them live. They're worth the price of admission.

I'm standing there reviewing all the new Federal regulations trying to get my ticket. I love to fly, and it's a good thing too since I've flown more than three million plus miles or more in the length of my career. I lost count long ago. I also love to read and sleep. I get to do both on an airplane as opposed to being home where I seldom get to do either.

As I turned to head toward my gate, I saw Brad Paisley, the country artist, getting his ticket at the next agent over. He didn't have on his trademark hat, but I recognized him. We'd met briefly once before when I was with songwriter and publisher friend, Chris DuBois, and he had introduced Brad to me. Chris and Brad go back many years and they'd written some great songs on Brad's first CD. I was really impressed with him because he seemed truly genuine and humble. That's the best thing about country artists. Most of them are really great people and it isn't an act.

I called out to him, he recognized me and we started a conversation. Come to find out, we were on the same flight to Detroit but then he was to continue on to Montreal, Canada to see his actress girlfriend, later to be wife, who was shooting a movie there.

We did the Bin Laden Shuffle through the security check point pretty effortlessly and sat down at the gate to wait to board. We covered a lot of subjects, from his current CD to buying a car to how many people are calling him to invite him to fish in their private pond. That fishing song did him a lot of good. At one point, his dad called and Brad was asking his advice about something. Now that's nice. Close to his family.

One of the things we discussed was the short window of opportunity that an artist has when the stopwatch begins their career and the sound of an enormous gong spells the end of it. For some, this may be one single, or CD album and it's over, and then you never get the chance again, which gives you a lifetime to be bitter and resentful, but you've at least got some stories to tell. For others, it goes on and on. But you still only get that short window to make your mark. At a certain age, it's over, never to return. I'm fortunate. I still get to play all the time, all over the world. And I'm grateful for it.

While we were talking, this nice lady came up to Brad. She sheepishly asked him to verify if it was really him - like two pieces of picture ID and a major credit card. Not having his hat on must have thrown her. She asked for some autographs for her kids and they swarmed all over Brad and wanted to have their picture taken with him. They were happy. "It's really him. He's taller with his cowboy hat. Does he have any tattoos? Can we see them? Are you single? My mom's single. You could date. Can we get the photos developed on the plane?"

The lady momentarily shifts her attention to me, stares me up and down, but never said a word. I smiled at her. She's probably mistaken me for some hanger-on or even worse. She had no clue who I was and wasn't interested to boot. She knew who Brad was and he's the one she zeroed in on. I was watching this entire process, seeing Brad make small talk with the kids and just being friendly. I was happy for him. All the while I was thinking, "This is great. This is the window of opportunity we were talking about. I remember when this kind of thing happened to me all the time. Now it's his turn. Enjoy it. You'll like it."

Now with all the attention he's getting with the flash bulbs going off, many people waiting at the gate now recognized him. They didn't come over or say anything to him, but he was certainly getting the stares and the buzz was goings around the boarding gate. He was just being nonchalant about it all and good-natured about it all. He said his good-byes to the kids, sat back down and we continued our conversation like nothing had happened.

We waited until almost everyone was on the plane before we headed to the jet-bridge to board. The agent who was taking our tickets was agitated for some reason or another, hustling about and just didn't generally seem to be in that good, overly pleasant, we-know-you-have-many-airlines-to-choose-from, and we-want-to-thank-you-for-flying-ours, for-as-always-you-know-how-much-we-appreciate-your-business, kind of sincere, grateful mood. When I stepped up to have my ticket taken, I presented my passport. (A passport, I discovered, is definitely better than a state license. If you're in Minnesota and you present an out-of-state driving license, the chances of being "randomly" searched are far greater). The agent looked at me, handed me my boarding pass and I was summarily dismissed.

Now, Brad, in his pale yellow polo shirt with the CIA emblem, stepped up. The guy took one look at him and motioned him over to be re-searched (for the second time). The look on Brad's face was worth a thousand pictures, but who needs pictures? (Sorry Brad, couldn't resist) It told the story of all of us frequent flyers: "Not again, I've already been stripped searched, (twice), taken-off-my-shoes, (you're after the wrong people, guys) unfastened-my-pants-so-my-belt-could-be-checked, the file's-been-broken-off-my-fingernail-clippers, (stop harassing that 80-year-old woman), see, there's nothing-in-my-hat, there's nothing-in-my-pockets, there's nothing-up-my-sleeves. Heck, I can't even carry my pocketknife anymore. You ain't a cowboy without a pocket knife.

If I ever see that Osama Bin Knucklehead, I'm personally gonna hurt him for all of this inconvenience." When we do catch him, and we will, I'm of the opinion that we put him through 24/7 airport security. We keep him in the air constantly, flying him one place, and then flying him somewhere else, over and over. Make him get out and go through the entire security process again, and again, and again. Take off his shoes, his belt, his watch, empty the coins out of his pockets, take the towel off his head, cell phone, etc. Then have the buzzer go off and pat him down. Life sentence. I know it's lenient, but I'm in a good mood at the moment.

But, you force yourself to smile and submit to the search.

I used to get "randomly" picked three out of four times for that second search before they stopped doing them. It's those latex gloves on the too-eager-to-do-our-job-searchers that are so unnerving. Too clinical looking. When my carry-on got searched, they usually stopped and put everything back once they pulled out my Bible.

Now look at this . . . I'm taking out my frustration in a public forum. Have to change my name to John Diatribe Coley. But, flying used to be more fun.

Oh well. Back to the subject. This seemingly demonically possessed ticket agent didn't have any idea who Brad Paisley was, and furthermore wasn't interested. What's so funny is that Brad didn't in any way, shape or form, resemble a terrorist, foreign or domestic. He's such a clean cut, unassuming guy. The people behind him in line knew who he was, but they don't count in this scenario, nor when the going got tough did they offer any assistance on his behalf. So, he politely and patiently did the frequent flyer tango, stretched out his arms and submitted to the magnetic force field that was about to point out every filling in his mouth.

I joked with him afterwards, "Just because you got your bags cleared, doesn't mean you aren't a terrorist. Maybe I shouldn't be seen with the likes of you. You could tarnish my reputation. Guilt by association, you know."

He chuckled and the look said, "I've got friends and I'll get you for that one." But he didn't really care. He was just happy to be going to see his girlfriend he hadn't seen in six weeks. Ah, love soothes the inner beast.

So, I sat down in my seat and the sharply dressed lady with the newspaper next to me leans over and said, "Was that Brad Paisley you were talking to?"

I said, "Whoa. You mean I was talking with Brad Paisley, the singer, and didn't know it? Do I feel foolish. He does that fishing song doesn't he? How 'bout that. You like to fish?"

The conversation abruptly ends. She pretends to read her paper and I hear her mumble something about being a jerk. She must know something about fishing after all. Now, I can peacefully read for a while and then go to sleep. I like to fly.

****

Recently on a flight from Philadelphia, I got to actually give a tip to a TSA inspector. I was waiting in the security line behind a couple from the Middle East. I really do not like waiting in line. No one really does. The longer the wait, the more I figure I'm wasting of my life and although I try my best to fight it, it still makes me cranky. I've stood in some very long security lines. Fortunately, I was early for my flight. The couple, on the other hand, seemed to have no place to go and were in no hurry to get there. They kept slowly asking the inspector, "Do you want us to takkkee off our shooooes? You want me to takkkee off my belllltt? My watchhh?" This went on for quite an eternity while I patiently waited to shove my things through the x-ray machine, get something to eat and relax before my flight.

After they finally got through, I looked at the TSA inspector and said, "Do you mind if you give you a suggestion to speed things up a little?" He said, "Sure."

So I suggested to him, "It might sound mean, but why don't you put a neck wallet and red sticker on some of these people's foreheads that says 'First Time Flyer' so the rest of us will know who to avoid."

He tried his best not to laugh but did anyway and said, "Good suggestion. I'll pass it along." I don't think he did though.

****

I mentioned terrorists a moment ago. This happened recently.

When the singer, formerly known as Cat (Moon Shadow, Peace Train) Stevens, who changed his name to something else, was not allowed into the country in September of 2004, and was forced to fly back to wherever the heck he came from because of supposedly helping to fund Islamic terrorist organizations. As a result, he received a lot of press over it. Don't even ask me how, but through the miracle of twisted minds and I guess a love or hatred for 70's music, I became associated with the Cat in a very underhanded manner.

In a spoof article called "Bad Reporter" it seems there were several 70's acts that had converted to and adopted Islam and Moslem names. My former group had been renamed "Islam Dan and John Ford Coley." However, an asterisk had been placed by my name, which stated that "Coley has yet to be converted." Now that part is good to know, especially since I'm a card-carrying Conservative, flag-waving military supporter (American, Texan, Confederate, Irish and Israeli), barbecue rib and cat-fish eating, disco hating, died-in-the-wool capitalist, Southerner, God and Jesus loving (the real Ones of course) worshiping Christian who also loves to go to Synagogue. Now, don't quote me, but I think that might just put me at odds with the vast majority of terrorist organizations in the known world, both domestic and foreign and especially those that wear masks on their faces or hide behind children.

Now, for the bad part. The article also stated that "Dan had put a fatwa (hit) out on Coley." Thanks for the warning fellows, but I just can't believe Dan would ever do anything like that. I simply hate having to check everyone at the door for WMD's and wearing that Kevlar vest to play in makes me look fat. Man, I'm a real lover of "freedom of the press."

Now, for the real, bizarre, not to be believed story. It seems that Terry Sylvester was actually coming with Cat Stevens to Nashville. Terry knew him and he wanted Stevens to meet James Griffin and me. Now, had we actually met him, we might really be on a "No Fly" list. You know I love to fly and buses don't give frequent flyer miles.

If anyone is reading this that is in the FBI, CIA, DTF, INS, DEA, IRS, local law enforcement or a former Mouseketeer that is suspicious or has no sense of humor, let me fly. They were actually teasing. I promise.

Chapter 12

<u>SAD TO BELONG</u>

It's sad to belong to someone else

when the right one comes along.

Sung by England Dan and John Ford Coley

When the song "Sad To Belong" was brought to Dan and me by our management and Kyle Lehning, we all thought it was a pretty good song. We never thought about it any other way, other than it was something we liked. It was unusual and in the music industry, the unusual ones are paid more attention to than the common, ordinary run-of-the-mill standard. We just never knew the amount of controversy that would be generated by it. It's just a song for crying out loud.

When it appeared on the radio, it moved consistently up the charts. Before long though, groups were calling those radio stations condemning the song saying we were promoting infidelity in marriage relationships, attempting to pervert and destroy the moral fabric of America, annihilating the Godly principles that this country had been founded upon as well as the known world at large. I told them they had obviously mistaken me for some attorney in the ACLU, and that I was more than willing to leave the moral and ethical destruction of our nation in their more than capable hands. I mean after all you call a pro when you want it done right (or left, depending on how you look at it).

We'd get calls while we were being interviewed on the radio stations, both in praise of and berating us for singing this evil headed monster.

Now, I had been in church most of my life and either was just too sheltered from the way of a hopelessly lost and degraded society, or else, the people who were making such a fuss over it simply had too much time on their hands and were perhaps themselves afraid of feeling what they believed the song suggested. I have to admit that I was perplexed by all this attention. I guess it could have had a negative effect on some people, but then so does ice cream. But heck, it kind of got to be fun too. I don't believe I've ever shook my head so often in both amusement and disbelief as I did during that time.

Now, what made this song so funny for me was its basic idea. You're with the one that you obviously thought at some point was the "right one" until this new "right one" comes along. How do you know for certain that this new one is the "right one" when before you thought the "other one" was the" right one." What happens if neither of them are the "right one" and then the true "right one" comes along. Wow. That's a major league lack of commitment from a very insecure and whacked out person. What a vicious circle. See why I thought it was a funny song?

Strange things happened to us in the time period of that song though. We'd been asked to return to the "Johnny Carson Show" because of a performance we'd given when "I'd Really Love To See You Tonight" was a hit everywhere. It was quite a thrill to be asked to play the show, although neither time we played the show was Johnny Carson actually there. The first time the replacement host was Gabe Kaplin from "Welcome Back Kotter." He wouldn't talk to us on the show though or in the dressing room for that matter, but I had a good time anyway. I met Erin Moran from "Happy Days" on the show. She played "Joanie", the younger sister. It was her birthday and I got asked to go to the party. This is cool. She was a very sweet girl and we hit it off well. Finally I'm getting to live that glamorous lifestyle I've heard and read so much about since I was old enough to watch TV, or at least something that I thought passed for it.

On our next appearance on the show, we were to perform "Sad To Belong." David Brenner, the comedian, was the host this time, instead of Johnny Carson. Johnny Carson's golf game must have been at pro level for all the airtime he missed.

We're backstage getting the usual make-over, people fussing over hair, etc. Some strange guy kept making weird remarks about how I must have gotten my chin from Kirk Douglas. I personally thought it was bizarre that he was noticing my chin to begin with. I said so. He looked around sheepishly at everyone and then left. I mimicked a photo of Dan and me that I really hated. I mean really hated. It made me look like the biggest goof to ever come out of stupid land, but for some unknown reason the record company and our management both thought this was a really good shot to use as a publicity photo and to even grace the back of the "Dowdy Ferry Road" album jacket. I hated it when I saw it and I thought I had communicated that sentiment quite effectively. I probably hated it so much because as much as I tried to, I couldn't deny that it was me. And it didn't make me look like a young Brad Pitt either.

We rehearsed with the house band on the song before the taping and everything was great. However, when it came our time to perform on the show, we count off the song and before you know it, instead of playing "Sad To Belong", I feel like I'm playing the theme from "Exodus." Dragging, dragging, ever deeper into the mire. I'm melting, I'm melting. It felt like a death dirge and we're being escorted in our own special tumbrel to the guillotine. (I discovered later that it was only me being escorted). The song starts to sound more and more like a car engine that won't turn over. The bandleader was slowing the song down to such a depressing tempo that it was going to take us about five minutes to play a 2:52 song. The audience is looking at us like a cow at a new gate, nodding off and drool hanging in mid-drip from their lips. The host David Brenner is probably attempting to come up with a new comedy routine from this, but it's so slow he can't get his mind to function in half-speed. Ed McMahon is trying to focus on his watch. If you're wondering how I can sing and still see all of this, remember I sing harmony on this song. I had time on my hands. As a matter of fact, I could have called and had a pizza delivered at this tempo before my harmony came in. What am I supposed to do? Just stand there and look stupid like the photo I hate? So, I take action. I waved my arms in the air and stopped the song. Bad move.

All of a sudden, the entire set is in an absolute uproar. Crew running at me like there's free, fresh donuts in the studio. Screaming and talking ugly to me, "What are you doing!!!!? Don't you know this is a live taping!!!!!." Cussing a blue streak at me. I didn't even know some of those cursing phrases could be run together and connected like that. I gained an entire new "expletive" vocabulary that day. In a really rough situation it's even come in handy once or twice. I guess all knowledge can be useful. They're foaming at the mouth. Yelling, yelling and yelling some more. Heck, like I said before, they didn't scare me. I had a manager once I thought was the devil. I survived that, what could they possibly threaten me with?

I'm standing my ground and defending my position. "The song's way too slow, I can't sing it. Do it right!"

Not being one to rock the boat in public, Dan's patiently waiting and observing this circus. So, I'm taking the entire heat. And I can take it. But I can dish it out too.

They finally do a pick up and to make a long story even longer, we played the song. It's a good tempo. We're finished. Boy, were we finished. We were never asked back again. I've got a barrage of people screaming at me after the show from management to record people and crew. Between the screaming and not talking to me, I was getting an earful. It might have been rebellious, but I did the right thing. I'm not unaccustomed to standing my ground alone; however, it was still a long ride home.

David Brenner, like Gabe Kaplan before him, didn't talk to us on camera either. However, David did ask us to open up for him in Lake Tahoe at a casino. So, he must not have been too mad at us. We played the first night, and after that he asked to open up for us. I thought that was nice.

I think they might have forgotten that episode since Jay Leno took over the "Tonight Show." Of course, I haven't been asked back in about 20 years, but hey, I'm an optimistic guy. It could still happen.

From the result of all the flak, Dan and I stopped performing the song live in concert. It just wasn't worth the headache and I was tired of hearing about it. It might have spoken to some people in a positive manner, but they weren't as vocal about it as the opposition. The song did reach #21 or #22 on the record charts, depending on which chart you looked at, so I figure it affected someone. I discovered from reading the liner notes on the Rhino Record, "Very Best of England Dan and John Ford Coley" that Dan and I seemed to have opposing views on the song than what I remembered. And I've got an excellent memory, even Dan would have told you that. For some reason, events get noted, catalogued and filed away in my mind for future reference. However, in my mind, somehow in re-telling these events they all seem to play out in the present as though they are occurring at this very moment, no matter how long ago they happened.

There seemed to be quite a number of things in the liner notes that I didn't know and they tested my "excellent memory" as well. For sake of illustration, according to Dan, our song "Lady" was written about a young Japanese girl named Mariko who had been our interpreter while we were in Japan with Three Dog Night. Now, being one of the co-writers on this song I don't, for the life of me, ever recall anything being mentioned about Mariko in the writing session. I mean it's possible that I could have been really lost deep in thought or something, but darn, I really hate not being in the loop, especially when I'm sitting right there and am one of those involved. Funny how that happens.

But back to the story, the song "Sad To Belong" always seemed surrounded by its own controversy. When I played with Ambrosia and Jimi Jamison from "Survivor" in the Philippines a few years back, "Sad To Belong" was one of the songs that the promoters demanded I play. I explained how I didn't play it any longer because of the negative dispute about it. They said that if I came I had to play that song because it was a huge hit in the Philippines. Again, I explained how the song was about cheating. They re-explained they didn't care and what a big song it was and that I had to play it. I said to let me pray about it. I did.

So, I began to reflect on what else the song could possibly mean, besides the obvious, if I twisted it a little. Twist it, I did.

Now, here's what this song really represents. It speaks about ways to end divorce. It speaks about a method of making alimony a thing of the past. It talks about the complete elimination of family law/divorce attorneys who, for the sake of more money, divide spouses further and further so that they completely hate each other by the time it's over. It speaks about children never having to come from a split family and suffer that generational curse. It shows us how to keep love in our relationships forever. Simply put, the song says "Marry your second spouse first." Hey, I did it. And in theory it works. But then again, in theory, everything works doesn't it. Experience is critical. There. Any questions? Good. Subject closed.

It was the song most asked about in radio interviews there. I was even asked to play that song on all the local TV shows. At the concerts, I watch the people, night after night, young and older, singing the lyrics to this song as I perform it. What have the Filipinos come to realize that it's taken us Americans so long to come to an understanding of? I don't know, but all I can say is, "Thank God they're our allies."

Chapter 13

ARE YOU STILL HERE?

I won't eat anything that has intelligent life,

but I'd gladly eat a network executive or a politician.

Marty Feldman

I've had the good fortune to write a couple of songs for films. I really love writing for film because you've already got a subject and you've already got a mood. All you have to do is follow the bouncing ball. There aren't hours and hours of trying to come up with a story, a hook and struggle with a conclusion. It cuts the workload down considerably.

On one occasion I had this girl call me who had a song opportunity on Morgan Creek for a film starring Sandra Bullock and Denis Leary. I jumped at it. I'm a guy, but I love Sandra Bullock films. She said, "They're looking for a "knockoff" song something like 'Brown Eyed Girl' by Van Morrison." No problem. I love that song. I can do that. When do they need it? Tomorrow?" I dropped everything and set off to write it. We knocked it off pretty quick.

Then, we play the song for the music supervisor, Mark Berger. He likes it but he wants a couple of changes. We make them and even give him credit on the song for his input. That's just business. Now, the song's a shoo-in. The music supervisor will surely want his song in the film. Good thinking.

We did the demo on the song and presented it the next day. Mark put the song up against the film. He played it a couple of times. He liked the song I could tell. Then he said, "It doesn't work. Sorry." That's it?!! It doesn't work? Sorry? It was over that quick. Oh terrific. Just what I needed. Another useless experience. I'm blown away, especially since he'd had a part in the song. The lesson I learned from that, contrary to popular belief, there are some honest, objective people in L.A. I had a little black book of those kinds of people that I'd been keeping and his name was about the third entry after 20 years there. Virtually unheard of. Like finding a real live musician working at a record company or a record store.

So, about a year later, Mark called personally. He's got a baseball film, a sequel to the "Major League" series called "Major League, Back To The Minors" starring Scott Bakula, the guy from "Quatum Leap." Mark asked if I would be interested in seeing it to possibly put a song in it. Of course I go in. Second time's the charm. Just so long as I don't get to the "three on a match" thing, then I'm ok (the third guy usually got shot). Or in the words of the smartest man in the world, Steven Wright, "The early bird may get the worm, but the second mouse gets the cheese." I feel like the second mouse today. Besides, if it comes to the early one getting the worm, be my guest. You're welcome to it.

Mark plays me a song that he almost likes for this film but it doesn't quite make it. (Been there, done that, got the t-shirt to coin a phrase). So, we study the film, angle by angle, frame by frame. He explains precisely what he's looking for. He sends me off with the footage of the scene and I study it harder than I did in the office. Suddenly, it comes. The pitcher extends his body way over the toe kick and steps forward about a yard beyond where he should be. He still just barely gets the ball to the plate. The batter tags it way to left field. Bingo, the line drops out of thin air. "I've been coming up short just a little too long." Off I go.

Mark likes it. But, then it changes again. We don't want to make the guy a complete loser. He has to win. After all, he wins in the film. It ain't life, but you can make a loser do almost anything in the movies.

I go back to the drawing board. Eureka this time. "I've been looking up from a long way down." Mark really likes it. So, the song gets written and demoed. We had originally set a very fast tempo. I mean that thing got out of here in a hurry. There's smoke on the tape player when the song's finished. Just listening to it makes me I feel like I just had six cups of Turkish double espresso and I don't even drink the stuff. My hair's standing on end and I'm beginning to feel like I've somehow gotten into an old Adams Family TV episode.

Now, Mark wants to watch the film opening again. He feels that the song's too fast. He begins to time the seconds between the runner at first trying to make it to second base. His metronome is ticking. He watches the pop fly that goes to the shortstop. He calculates and re-calculates and then checks his math again. Man, this is hard work. Dang, I'm sweating just watching him. Finally, he says, "We need to cut the tempo in half."

I don't mind re-writing, but when the fourth re-write comes along, I'm ready for new adventures. All of this for 60 seconds of film time, mostly underscored so low that no one in the audience even hears the darn song anyway. But, hey, I'm a professional. I can do almost anything. Besides, I've been trying to break into film music. It's like writing a good country song. It isn't as easy as it seems.

We re-do it. I demo it. He loves it. It works with the film. He wants it. Now, he wants to know how much do I want for my part of the song? Here's where I get to play the businessman part of this business. So, I revert to what I've been taught in my music scoring class. Never say "I want 'x' number of dollars." Always ask, "Well, what's in the budget?" You might ask for $1,000 and they've budgeted for $10,000.00. They love you. They've just pocketed $9,000.

So, I play it cool and become the negotiation guru. I nonchalantly remark, "Oh, I don't know. What's in your budget?"

He immediately responds, "There is no budget. We're over budget. Film production took the last of it."

I sat there, pretending to think. I don't recall this scenario coming to light in the music scoring class. I'm thinking when I see this teacher again he and I might just have a rather serious disagreement. I'm thinking my monetary portion for the song at this point is down to gas money for coming in here and a bowl of chili with no crackers.

So, I paused. I decided to let him talk. To make the short of it, we finally agreed on the terms, shook hands and he said he'd try to push it through. I didn't quite understand what that meant, but I would shortly. I thought it was a shoo-in.

For clarity, let me give you another example of how it should work.

I'd written some songs for another film called "The Spy Within" with Teresa Russell and Scott Glenn. Steve Railsback was making his directorial debut on this film. Steve is a real lover of the craft of film making, not just in it for the awards shows. As you know, Steve was famous for his portrayal of Charles Manson in "Helter Skelter," "Life Force," and "The Stuntman," and so many other great films I don't have time to mention them all. Steve and I had been in a couple of films together and had become good friends.

I just happened to call him one day, see if he wanted to go shoot some pool, and he told me about this film he was directing. I, of course, asked if he needed any songs and he said, "Yeah." I asked when I could show him something and he suggested about 3:00 that afternoon. It was about 1:00 at the time I had called him and in good traffic, it would only take me about an hour to get to his house. I hung up and my first thought was "Oh, no. I don't have anything for him. What am I doing? What am I gonna show him?"

At any rate, I took him a couple of songs; he fell in love with one of them and knew exactly the scene it would be good for. Now, I'd like to call it a stroke of genius, but it was actually good timing. Right place, right time. He even had me write a couple more songs for the film that he felt needed music.

Steve's a fellow Texan. A pretty intense fellow Texan at that. Steve can get in your face in a heartbeat. So, being the director, he didn't ask for permission, he just told the production office and "powers that be" that these songs were to be in his film and pay me what I wanted. Period. His wave, his beach. Nobody messed with Steve. He'd just get that kind of narrowed, intense Manson look in his eye and it was better to just let him do it the way he saw it. He was usually right anyway.

Now, when Mark had said he'd let me know shortly, I didn't realize that he had to pass it through the director. When the director cleared the song, then the producer had to hear and approve it. Then his wife and her girlfriends. Next her hairdresser and then the person that cuts and puts blue nail polish on the dog's cuticles and then there's what the housekeeper and pool man think. Someone's got to get fired if it doesn't work. Besides, housekeepers and pool men are easy to find in L.A. Heads do roll. It gets complicated and of course I'm exaggerating, but by very little.

So, finally everyone that needs to, finally approves the song and it becomes the opening song in the film.

Now, on to the next step. We've got to find someone other than me to record it. Mark wanted me to sing it because he liked what I had done on the demo, but I didn't have a record deal and they needed a single to play on the radio. No record deal equals no single. However, that wasn't a problem for me. I just wanted the song in the film. We then set about looking for the right person to sing it. Films can get complicated. I suggested a couple of people that I wanted to sing it. Lee Roy Parnell was my first choice. Mark liked the idea. However, according to "Sound Scan," Lee Roy hadn't sold the number of records that Morgan Creek needed to consider him. They wanted to put the song on the artist's CD and have a big hit single to promote the film. So, I dropped the jaded cynicism I had for the industry at large and said to Mark, "I forgot. We're going for numbers, not quality."

We went through a couple of others I thought would be great at it, Collin Raye, Ty Herndon, etc., but for some reason or another they didn't do it.

Finally, Mark struck up a deal with Curb Records to do the soundtrack on the film. Good move. Great artists on the label, good distribution, sounded like a perfect match. Tim McGraw's on the Curb label. So, I thought maybe him or someone of that caliber would be cutting my song. Cool, but wrong. Way wrong. I've just never quite grown accustomed to being that wrong.

It seems Curb Records had an artist that has never had or done anything really before and it might be a good break for him. By this time, I just wanted to get the darn song cut and over with. So, what they did was pretty much just fill up the soundtrack with the label's roster, whether or not the songs fit, which surprised me. The artist that sang my song didn't really want to do it because he had already finished his CD, written every song on it and now was going to have the one song he didn't write become the single on his pride and joy. Now, this scenario I understood and could have sympathized with. I've been in that very same position and it actually felt good to be on the other side of the fence this time.

Mark had them come to L.A. to record the song. Mark's been putting songs in films quite a long time and had directed the production of people from Barbara Streisand to the London Symphony. So, needless to say, I trusted him, but I wanted to be at the session anyway.

I meet the artist, I meet the producer, it's all smiles and tipped hats. Later, Mike Curb walks in. Not only is he the President of Curb Records, he used to be the Lieutenant Governor of California at one time. I'm happy to meet him.

Now, most of the time my mouth and mind work in tandem, but it's that occasional time when my smart-aleck mouth gets ahead of my over-imaginative mind that I concern myself. At that juncture, for some reason there isn't a governor, lieutenant or otherwise, on my mouth. What comes out, comes out. I used to wear a shoe around my neck just to remind me to keep my mouth in check.

Mark introduced me to Mike Curb. After the initial round of 'how are you's, he stood there looking puzzled for a second or two and then said to me, "Are you still in music?"

Fortunately, my mind was working quicker that day, but it was still battling with my mouth, and the "comment" section of my mind was tossing back and forth like a ship in a storm at sea, "That's got to be about the most stupid question I've ever been asked in my life. That's like asking a man in the Navy if he's ever been abroad. (That sounds kind of wrong doesn't it)?

So, laughing at my own joke, I dryly responded, "Yeah. It's a lot like being in the mob. You never really get out. We have to take a blood oath or something to become a musician. You've always got your fingers in it somewhere."

Now, he begins looking for the door or someone else in a tie he might know to talk to. So he just responds, "Oh."

So to redeem myself, I told him, "Yeah, I was one of the writers on the song being recorded, so of course I'm still in music."

The spark of recognition jumps all over his face. "Ohhhh. I didn't know. So you really are still in music?" I'm a "creative"; he's a "suit." We did not connect.

It went down-hill from there. We got a great track recorded from the musicians and now it came time for the artist to step up to the plate and hit a home run on this song. Only problem was he hadn't really bothered to learn the song and was going to sing whatever melody that might happen to pop into his head.

I'm ticked. There are tons, I mean literally tons of people who would give their eye tooth and first born to have a shot at singing a song in a film, and we happened to grab one of the few artists that didn't care or really want it.

Now, Mark gets mad too. So, being the music supervisor, he says he'll handle it, why don't I just go on home and we'll have him learn the song and sing it tomorrow. So, he goes in, tells the producer and artist that he needs to learn the melody to the song and that the attitude on the song is all-wrong. Good. It's corrected and my blood pressure never got over 220 on the top end.

The next morning, I get to the studio, have a donut, am reading all the current music mags when in walks the artist, late of course. He sees me and makes a beeline straight for me. He stands in my face and angrily says, "I know this song melody inside and out, backwards and forwards, upside down and sideways and I'm going sing this song John Ford Coley style, but I'm gonna use my voice! Have you got a problem with that?"

So I thinking, "This is funny. Now we've got two attitudes to contend with instead of just the one. I'm not getting into this right now. I haven't even had a real breakfast yet and I'm still hungry."

So, with tongue in cheek, I smiled and said, "Uhm. Nice shirt. Goes well with that chip on your shoulder. Want a donut?"

He didn't.

Later that day, he sang the song and got the melody pretty close to right. After he was finished, he came into the studio and sat close by. He had this self satisfied, cocky, "I'm a star" look on him that just cried out, "Beat that one Coley. I just nailed that sucker to the floor."

When I was in my twenties and thirties I was willing to be much more physical about things like this. But these days, I really try my best to avoid nasty confrontations as much as I can, I just don't have the time, energy or the inclination for it anymore. Besides, I've broken my hand twice. I'm actually getting better at that "being calm" thing as time goes by. However, this one, it's just screaming at me, "Confront me, confront me." My evil twin took over and stepped into it.

The control room was fairly quiet while they adjusted the pro tool composites. So, not in my usual soft-spoken manner I said to him, "So, let me get this right. In order to get it right and you to do what we want you to do, we just have to tick you off and make you mad, is that it?"

His lip curled a little and he just dumbly smiled at me and smirked, "Yeah, I guess so."

I sat there momentarily dumbfounded. This was a monumental waste of time. Why even get into this. There are people out there who would stab you in the back or shoot you under the kitchen table to get a chance at being in this industry. And this kid got the shot, but didn't really want it. "I'm gonna go play some pool. See ya at the yard, champ."

The film got released and the song sounded pretty good. It was the opening song. The film still plays all the time on the cable stations. I personally enjoyed it, but then again, I'm really a sucker for a baseball film. I think I've seen just about all of them, especially "Bull Durham" and "The Natural" which I've seen about fifty times each.

However, the single and the video they made didn't do as well as the film and record companies had hoped it would. As a result, the record company took my song off of his CD before it was released. Unfortunately for the guy, when his CD was released, it coughed, sputtered, rolled over with its feet in the air and then died.

But, hey . . . I'm happy. I got another song in a film, another day at bat doing what I love and a heck of a story to boot.

Chapter 14

<u>I LOVE S-L-E-E-P</u>

Nice guys finish last, but we get to sleep in.

Evan Davis

At times, it seems like I've been a road warrior since before Moses became a prophet. I knew that I'd been gone too long once when I came home, did my laundry and had packed it back in my suitcase before I realized that I was actually home. So, I finally just had my bedroom remodeled after the Holiday Inn. I got one of those "Magic Fingers" massagers put into my bed, had the bedside lamp screwed into the table, screwed the pictures into the wall and had the TV bolted onto a swivel. And I, of course, had boxes of free shampoo, sewing kits and body lotions to make the hotel experience complete. Never was able to figure out how to get room service or a wake-up call though.

When you're touring on the road and have been out there for six weeks to two months, there is one thing that there doesn't ever seem to be enough of. You covet it. You would kill for it. You get overly surly and become not your normal nice "happy to meet you" self because of being deprived of it. I'm talking about five little letters. S-L-E-E-P. Just a decent little eight-hour nap.

You can eat anytime you want to on the road unless it's after a show and about the only thing open is a Denny's. I marvel at just how far modern science has progressed these days. It's truly amazing what they can do with plastic and call it food. However, if you love and eat a lot of fast food, then the life of a road musician might be a career you'd be well suited for, provided you can play and sing, or these days just dance and jump up and down. However, do be prepared. It's a lot harder work than you might think.

You can watch all the TV you want, provided you're not in some small region where's there two local channels in the hotel. In the late 70's, when I did heavy touring, for some hotels the concept of cable hadn't entered their realm of existence as of yet and all that was on those two channels were farm reports or local news. Don't get me wrong. I admire farmers and as far as I'm concerned, they're one of the two most important classes of people we have in this country. When you're really hungry, you can begin to thank and bless them in a hurry.

You can read on the road. There's no shortage of books, magazine racks and crossword puzzles. I like to read and do it often. I could burn through a 600 page James Michener, James Clavell, Leon Uris or Dostoevsky novel in short order.

Also, you can always find a movie theater somewhere. Every now and then, you can even find a good film worth watching in them. I lost count of how many times I've watched "Blazing Saddles" in the hotels. To this day, I still bust up laughing every time I see it.

But sleep. That's a commodity that there's far too little of. Usually after a show, my system would be so wired up that I couldn't go to sleep. I'm a night owl anyway. I like staying up late and working, then getting up late in the morning. So, at around 3:00 or so in the morning, I'm finally dozing off. It's the getting up early to catch a flight that really does me in. It still does today. I'm pretty good at sleeping on a plane though. But a 6:00 or 7:00 a.m. wakeup call is a great way to ruin a perfect morning for me. With little sleep, I almost always wake up on the redneck side of myself. I'm not a prolific or profound conversationalist at that time, especially if I haven't had my morning Dr. Pepper yet. I don't know if Dr Pepper actually woke me up or kept me up at night. It wrecked by stomach, but that's another story. It's not that I require a tremendous amount of sleep, but if I don't get my normal 12-14 hours, I'm just not my jovial self.

One particular airport experience comes to mind. Dan and I had played in St. Louis the night before. We weren't flying very far, only to Minneapolis, but we still had to get up early to catch the flight. That means we would get there fairly early, get to the hotel, be able to get some sleep before the show and I'd feel human again. The entire band needed the sleep. We were well past the slaphappy point. Now, we're just withdrawn and quiet. Maybe a little on the surly side of nasty and looking for a good argument.

We arrived at the airport about an hour before the plane was scheduled to depart. All the guys went directly to the gate, but our road manager, Ron Cohen, stayed behind at the TWA ticket counter and checked everyone and their luggage in. Ron was a very efficient road manager. Being a road manager/baby sitter is much more complicated than you'd ever expect.

I acted as a road manager once. Once. I hated it. He has to put up with trivial, sometimes infantile behavior from people and all us over-the-edge band guys and our idiosyncratic tendencies and the me, me, me, what about me, lifestyles. (I'll stop talking about myself in a minute). One guy's mad and not going to play because he didn't get a window seat on the plane. Another is screaming because his new luggage got a dent in it, or the cook put powdered sugar on his French toast, so now I have the right to trash my hotel room, or what moron forgot to take yellow M&M's out of the bag. My dressing room doesn't have any towels or sandwiches and what kind of wine is this, it isn't French that means someone is going to pay and it ain't gonna be pretty. Or a lead vocalist battling with LSD (lead singer's disease, for which there is no known successful recovery program), screaming he's the reason everyone is coming to see the band and he can replace them all and nobody will ever know. You name it; a road manager has probably had to deal with it. But, as long as you're not him, it's still fun to watch this stuff.

We had a guitar player, Bubba, who was generally always nervous about flying. Somewhere on the road, in a brow sweating panic he told our road manager, Ron, that he had a dream the night before and that the plane crashed and the only person who survived was him and that he wasn't flying. Ron surprised him by telling him that wasn't it a coincidence that he had had the very same dream, but in his dream he was the only one that survived. Bubba refused to fly. Ron asked him how he planned on getting home. Bubba flew and I guess we didn't crash. So much for Bubba as a prophet.

However, Ron can be quite an eccentric character himself. His one renowned comment was "People are stupid." I never questioned his judgment. He spoke with such confident position about it. I just figured he'd dealt in the public sector more than I had. We even had a T-shirt made for him that he proudly wore everywhere. "People Are Stupid." Front and back. Don't think he got in a fight once.

I remember one time we flew into Chicago and checked into the Holiday Inn on Lake Michigan. All of us were looking to take a nap. The hotel staff was treating us like we're pond scum or have a dreaded staph infection or something. Eyeing us. Suspicious. Following us to the elevator. We had stayed here dozens of times before. What's the problem? That's when we saw the mammoth hole in the roof where the stained glass ceiling used to be. Now, it's all over the floor and on top of the piano on the other side of the lobby. I asked, "What happened here?" The hotel manager got an angry, sour and ultra-serious expression on this face, as if he wasn't grave looking enough already and said, "Dickey Betts and his band got into a fight in one of the rooms and threw a table out the window. This is where it landed. Fortunately, no one in the lobby was hurt."

So, I said, "Really. Well, who won the fight? Dickey's pretty tough." His eyes darted to me and he didn't seem to think my comment was very funny. I thought it was funny, but then again I was on the slaphappy end of no sleep.

Now, our road manager Ron, was a little bitty fellow, not as big as a minute. He was really into maintaining and building his muscles. He would actually carry a big set of barbells in his luggage. All of us battle-hardened road-warriors used to hang around and watch the baggage men get our luggage. Baggage men loved us because we carried all of these bags and they knew the tip was going to be huge. All of a sudden some little baggage guy would grab Ron's luggage and give it a manly jerk only to be jerked back to the ground himself and nearly tear the tendons and ligaments in his arm. I picked Ron's luggage up once. Only once though. That thing weighed more than my horse, including saddle. What was really fun to watch was if the baggage guy just so happened to pick up Ron's bag first. It would jerk him to the ground and you could see him stare helplessly at the other 20 or so remaining bags, like they must all weigh this much. There's no tip that big! It was a long day on the dock for that boy. In the words of Mark Twain, "It's funny when it happens to someone else." But Ron tipped really well. Of course, he could afford to. It wasn't his money. Dan and I paid for everything, so Ron could afford to be generous. No sweat off of him.

He used to lift those weights day and night and have everyone check out his biceps. He got so cocky and bloated about it that he foolishly challenged Nick, one of our roadies, to an arm wrestling contest. You don't mess with roadies. They've had a lot less sleep than you've had and can be in a terminally bad mood. Ron set the contest for a week out. He was pumping iron in his hotel rooms like there was no tomorrow and Nick was just eating a lot of donuts and drinking beer. Ron kept haranguing and teasing Nick about how he was gonna put him down and how Nick had better start working out. Big Ron's coming.

About as dry as a day-old biscuit, Nick replied once, "Don't worry. I'll be ready for you. I'm already up to one push-up a day." Nick was about as wide as he as he was tall, and he wasn't very tall at all.

When the day of the "big match" comes, Ron's got all of the band members there at the sound check, making certain that we all have a ringside seat to watch him whip-up on the road crew champion.

Now, Dan and I had traveled on the road for years before we had any sizable songs on the radio and the adopted, died-in-the-wool, not-to-be-neglected rule of the road was, "Treat the roadies good. If you've had five hours sleep, they've had three. They're at the gig setting up the equipment before you get there and they'll be there another two or more hours after the show is done. Give them respect and a wide berth." I think we had told Ron about this rule at some point, but either he forgot it or wasn't paying attention at the meeting.

Ron's got a table set up backstage. He's pumped. He's ready. He's breathing deep and slow, doing stretches, twisting his head side to side like a boxer and just generally making a complete fool out of himself. He's talking big while Nick spreads mustard and extra ham on a sandwich. He wants to know where the pickles are. Ron takes off his shirt to reveal a yellow muscle shirt. His rippling muscles fully displayed.

Someone says, "Where are your muscles Ron?"

We laugh.

Ron is undaunted. He's ready. He makes a few customary "your momma's so big. . ." remarks to psyche out Nick. Nick's just chewing on his ham and cheese.

They sit down and square off. Ron's practicing slow breathing, Nick's wiping mustard off his chin. They clasp hands, get their best positions, someone says " 1,2,3, go" and before Ron even has the chance to strain, bam, down goes his hand on the table.

Nick still has the half-eaten sandwich in his left hand.

Ron's dejected. What happened? He wants a rematch. Ok, let's do it again. Two out of three. Focus.

This time the match goes differently. Ron strains, he's pushing with all his might. Nick's just holding his arm still. He takes another bite of his sandwich while holding Ron at bay. Bam! Down goes Rons' hand on the table. Ron's looking at his hand shell-shocked. Nick stands up and says, "When supper coming, I'm still hungry." I've never heard so much laughter in my life.

Ron never carried the weights again after that tour. For all the good it did, Ron should have been "packing iron" instead of "pumping" it. However, it wasn't fun watching the baggage guys anymore. We were always looking for amusement.

So, meanwhile back at the St. Louis Airport, while I'm casually admiring Charles Linburgh's, 'the Spirit of St. Louis', and wondering how in the world did he land that thing without a front window, Ron is in a furious battle with the ticket agent. It takes him over an hour to sort things out.

Now generally Ron was pretty easy to get along with, but he did have a surly side. Kind of like a Doberman when the brain becomes too big for its skull and it's pressing and pinching in some areas. You just can't help going crazy to release the pressure. Sometimes, it's not the most pleasant situation to be around but most of the time it is amusing if you're observing from the distance.

Once again, back to the St. Louis airport story. As a result of TWA's mix up, our plane was pulling out of the gate by the time Ron got to us. He'd been running, he was out of breath and looking for a fight. The agent at the gate was snotty, arrogant, discourteous and wouldn't open the gate or recall the plane. She defiantly told us "tough" we could catch the next flight. So Ron told her he hoped her airline went bankrupt and she'd be out of a job. Incidentally, he got his wish. We didn't generally act that way, but we're tired. As a matter of fact, I remember being beyond tired. Musicians don't relate to the word "authority." It isn't in our vocabulary. All of us were about ready to create a real disturbance in the airport. We're furious. Ron was reading the agent the riot act and laying into her like he could most definitely take this highbrow, heartless sea-hag in an arm wrestling match. She was about ready to call security on him. So, I stepped up and calmed Ron and had him sit down. I said, "Let it go. We'll catch the next one."

Now I had got a couple of hours to waste in another airport. I could have been sleeping, but not in these hard plastic chairs and in such a public place.

I once saw Kenny Loggins passed out in a seat in an Iowa airport, waiting for a flight. We had played with him one time in New Mexico when he was part of Loggins and Messina. He was sprawled in that uncomfortable chair with his arms and legs all over the place, his head was tilted back over the chair and his mouth was wide open. He looked something like a Venus Fly Trap in that green shirt. Just waiting for some unsuspecting insect to try to get the nectar off his tongue. His girlfriend was sympathetically holding his hand. Not the kind of image you really want the public to see, and I wondered if anyone had ever seen me in the same condition. Kenny looked beat and he never woke up before my flight left.

Dennis Locorriere and Ray Sawyer of Dr. Hook and the Medicine Show ran across us once in the O'Hare airport in Chicago. Dan and I had played in Champlain, Illinois the night before. I was stretched out on my back, just trying to get a few extra winks. I heard this dry, monotone voice above me saying, "Yeah Ray. He looks dead to me. Look at the drool on his mouth."

I open my blood-shot, blurry eyes, see Ray's eye patch not three inches from my face and Dennis cackling like there's no tomorrow. I'd worked with these guys before in Boston. They were a fun band to be around. They were the ones that gave one of our songs a new title, "Nights Are Chopped Liver Without You." That was funny. I still use that title all the time. So, I said, "You guys, go away." I rolled back over and slept until boarding time. I didn't see Dennis for another twenty years. I still haven't seen Ray.

However, back to the original story for the third time and final time. I'd flown in and out of St. Louis airport dozens of times so I at least knew what the restaurants were like. But just the thought of sitting on those seats at the gate for a couple of hours was a lot akin to trying to get comfortable in your bathroom wash basin. Not the warm, comfortable Siren call beckoning feeling that invites you to sit down like it's a Lazy Boy. Not that I'm not saying it's impossible, but I usually stand up and walk around as much as possible. I had to spend the night in the Dallas/Ft. Worth airport once and sleep in one of those seats. I don't recommend it, unless you have some hidden masochistic tendencies that as of yet you might not have recognized.

I sat in my seat for about a minute and then stood up. I walked over to the ticket agent. She was hostile. I was polite.

I'm born and raised Texas Southern. We teach and practice polite down here. Polite charm can work miracles. I began to gently talk to her, just to soothe over the situation. I told her that the reason everyone was so upset is because we do this kind of traveling all the time and we had our act together from years of practice, but TWA messed it up at the ticket counter. I explained how we were really tired and had planned to get to Minneapolis to sleep awhile before the show. The Southern charm was having an effect. She's softening. I continue.

About this time, Ron kind of slithers up behind me. She eyes him like she's stalking prey. Then she looks back to me and says "Well, I'll talk to you about this. You have control."

I immediately said, "Nope. He's the one you ticked off. Talk to him." I turned and left.

Ron looks at her like a foaming rabid dog because he still wants to fight. She's really not happy. As much as I hate to admit it, I did enjoy the exasperated look that fell all over her face. I'm snickering as I walked back to one of those uninviting hard chairs. I guess I have a little sadistic streak in me after all. Those chairs must have brought it out. I was constantly looking for diversion from the daily routine.

It came back on me though. Our plane to Minneapolis was delayed too. For an additional two hours. We just barely got there in time to get our sound check, rush to the hotel, shower and then play. Needless to say, I was flat exhausted. For the life of me I can't remember where we went the next day. But, I do recall that we didn't have to fly back through St. Louis. No words can describe to you just how hard those plastic seats with no arm rests were and I still needed sleep. I covet sleep, you know.

Chapter 15

<u>HOW DID I GET INTO THIS?</u>

I don't know anything about music.

In my line you don't have to.

Elvis Presley

When I was about six years old, I'd sit on the footrest on the barber chair pretending I was playing the piano while daddy had his hair cut. My parents caught on to this and I've been playing a real piano ever since. The foundations that I received were something I really cherish because I know that I came up the hard way. Learning to play, write and sing. In church, in different bands, honing the craft day in and day out, night after night. Believe me; I never ever thought that I would make a career of it. I was doing it because I really loved it. And I especially like writing songs. That's where all of your emotional baggage comes in handy. When someone comes up to me and tells me a sad story about what's happening in their life, I grab a pencil and paper and say, "Tell me more."

But, the business end of TV and radio has changed the reason why we play music or act in films anymore. As far as I'm concerned, the object of music is music, not a recording contract. I'd still be playing regardless, even if it had never lead to a recording deal.

I remember once, my son had a friend over at the house. He brought along his spanking brand new electric guitar with him. They were prancing around the room, mimicking all the same moves they'd watch from countless rock and roll bands on MTV. I happened to overhear them when they said, "We need to start a band. Duuude, we've got the looks, we got the moves, we're a sensation waiting to happen." I thought this was funny. Hype. We all need it. I said, "Hey kid, let me see your guitar."

It looked hot. Black with chrome galore. When I strummed the first chord on it, I choked back my laughter and handed it back to him. Yep, they had the moves and they had the looks all right, but no one had taught him how to tune his guitar. It's just a prop, because after all, "we got the looks, we got the moves." We don't need no stinking tuners. Fortunately, my son has learned to play guitar since then, but it's just for fun. And from that experience as I occasionally surf through the TV channels and pass by "American Idol," in my typical humorous, cynical fashion, I often think there should be a special version for people that can actually play a musical instrument. Bless their little hearts, seems everyone just wants to be out front and sing and dance. But I get more than a little bored watching people who try to look "sexy," singing 247 notes to a measure while searching for some kind, any kind, of memorable melodic melody to sing that everyone else can sing along with as well while still making all the obligatory over choreographed dance moves. Maybe I'm just jealous. You know you can't do all those dance moves after you reach age 25. . . 30 tops. You're bound to hurt something. Perhaps it's just my imagination that there seems to be no shortage of inexperienced "Divas" and singers who can't play an instrument. We should let them do it acapella. I personally like acapella.

So, here's how I got started. I actually got into a rock band by default. When I was 16 years old, the hottest "combo" at W.W. Samuell, where I went to high school in Dallas, was the Playboys 5. This group had a lead guitar player that left the band. Dan Seals, my future partner, at 17 years old, was a year ahead of me and the saxophone player/lead vocalist in this group. He wanted to find another guitar player to fill the empty guitar spot. Larry (Ovid) Stevens, the rhythm guitar player, wanted a piano player. The remaining band members, Mike Woolbright, on bass, and Buddy Lay, on drums, voted with Larry and I tried out for the group. Now, I'm a classically trained piano player. I know my way about Bach and Beethoven, but I'd never actually played rock and roll with a band. I only listened to a lot of Beach Boy's music on the radio. But I auditioned, got the job and my mom and dad went out on a limb, stepped into debt and bought me a Wurlitzer electric piano. It was one of the first electric pianos on the market. That's when I regretted not learning to play guitar earlier. That piano was as heavy as my '57 Chevy and everyone complained about having to help me carry it. That piano and that piano alone could account for me as a skinny musician having muscles.

Even with my own piano, Dan still didn't want me in the group. He only wanted another experienced guitar player. I remember once we were practicing. I was playing the melody note for note while Dan was singing it. He stopped the music, pulled at his hair, looked at me and said, "You just play the chords, I'll sing the melody."

"Oh, is that how it works 'cause I don't know." I said. I was pretty green at this.

Fortunately for me, I had one of the best piano teachers anyone could ever have. Mr. Ed Cole. He was a local piano teacher that had been in big bands and played at church functions, with drums and the whole shooting match. I was a paperboy and happened to throw his sister's paper. She had a daughter close to my age and he had seen me messing around on the piano once at their house. He liked the way I played and offered me a great deal. For little money per lesson, I would play the classical competitions as his student and he'd teach me chord inversions, rock and country themes, etc. It was a terrific trade-off. Even while I was in the band, I continued to perform the classical competitions for him. I contribute most of my musical education to him.

Still, I hated those competitions. It was always like a scene right out of "Amadeus," with the king playing the harpsichord and the evil, Antonio Salieri, constantly hovering over him tapping out a pedantic tempo and correcting him. It's just you and a wand waving judge in the room, counting out tempo. What fun. "It's-too-slow, it's-too-fast, tempo, tem-po, TEM-POOO, technique, remember technique, hands tapping out tempooooooooooo. Don't tap your foot, precision, too much pedal, too little pedal, you're making Bach turn over in his grave, you're butchering Beethoven, it's lucky for him he was deaf the way you're playing his sonata, AHHHHHHHHHHHH." I actually think I might have had Salieri as a judge once, slapping his leg with his ruler as I stumbled through a piece. Over and over, no heart, just technique. Almost as much fun as bobbin' for french-fries. I've had a phobia about rulers since I began to study piano. You get your hands slapped with a wooden ruler enough times and you're destined for years of therapy. (Those of you who are recovering from parochial school know what I'm talking about). I don't even use them to measure things unless it's a tape measure and does that little winding speed trip back up into the case. I think that's the time period when I became so violently frustrated and longed to be around drunken people in clubs. It didn't take much to make them happy.

But hey, I'm moving up. I'm in a rock "combo" with the customary name of Playboys 5. I'm only sixteen. I'm thinking, "Yeah, I know you're all watching me as I walk to my classes. Yeah, you're right . . .I'm cool, I'm hot. You're jealous and you should be. I know you all want me." It was a great time to be alive. We even dressed in jackets just like the Beatles except I had my initials sewn on it.

Most parents, including my own, didn't even know about Playboy, or if they did, it wasn't discussed in the church circles I'd run in all my life. They probably just thought we were copying Bob Wills and his Texas Playboys. I never let on.

By my junior year in high school, the band split up. But then we got an offer to come to Nashville and record some of our songs after a country singer passing through Dallas just happened to see us play at the hotel. He told his management and producer about us and showed them the demos we'd recorded. That was my first real trip to Nashville to record. I'd been there before traveling through with my parents, but I was more interested in getting to the town where Davy Crockett had been born. But that was nothing like going there to record. This was big time. My momma and daddy were so proud.

So, the producer and his wife changed our group name to the "Chimeras." Where they came up with that one requires hours of research in either a dictionary or a deep appreciation and love of Greek mythology. But, they managed to get us the best musicians Nashville had to offer.

They record us, they love us, think we're "cute" and we sound good for our age. I'm having the time of my life. I'm a man of the world now. I'm gonna be a star; whatever that is. They keep telling us so. They send us home, saying they'll contact us soon. Well, how soon? Sooooon, they promise. Then, they proceed to steal our songs. Dan lost the two songs he had written from that experience. Copyright, copyright, copyright. Welcome to the big time.

We decided to keep the band going after all, but we needed a name change. It's the mid 60's. We needed something current. Even though we had a good fan base, the name had to change. Finally, Theze Few was picked. I didn't come up with that one. I am too much of a traditional speller. Misspelled words drive me crazy. When I see things like, "luv," "u," "4," and "cus" . . . oh . . . skip it! We continued to play the same high school dances, skating rinks, Goodwill openings and private parties. I was making $5-10 a night. For four hours. Not good money you say. Well, you're right. But I was on a learning curve and besides I was having fun. I make a couple of dollars more a night than that now and the jobs are a little better than the first one I got paid for playing for a Goodwill opening. To tell the truth, I love to play more than anything and pretty much do it for free. But these days, I don't get paid to play; I get paid to travel.

Besides, the girls loved us. Musicians really had it good.

The girls flock to football players during football season, then when basketball season came up, they'd drop the football players like greasy BB's and fall in love with the basketball crew. Guys that ran track never had a shot and the lucky basketball boys had the run until baseball season. I played football and ran track in grade and Jr. High school. It was a long break waiting for football to begin. All during the summer break, the girls waited for football season. At least, until they grew out of it.

Now, being a musician, we didn't have seasons. We were open for business all year long and some took great advantage of it. So there was a great rivalry between athletes and musicians. Not all, but most jocks didn't care for us "sissy, long hair" musical types much. The athletes usually got all the attention at school.

But to show you how attitudes can change, I even made some athletic friends later on.

Back to high school, even though the athletes got all the fawning and fussing over, us musicians got a lot of attention too. We got our attention after school and it was definitely a lot more fun and we didn't have to walk like roosters. The down side was that most parents didn't want their daughters hanging around with us because, as you might probably suspect, most musicians are not the sort of individuals that you can take to the debutante ball. Too rebellious. But hey, what's a dance without musicians? That nice-from-a-distance syndrome. Although I know, for myself at least, that I personally come from a long line of "different drummers" and as much as I tried to fit in, I simply was not debutante ball material. Had too much of my own opinion. Thurston Howell from "Gilligan's Island" does not swim in my gene pool.

Parents are generally pretty suspicious of their children's dating partners to begin with, but dating a musician who was probably a "dope-fiend, classless, rebellious, boozer, person-of-low-character who will most likely steal-your-youth and leave-you-with-a-shattered, shameful past, which, we're almost certain, because we're wiser and older than you, you'll regret later on in your life" was definitely frowned upon. Now, I personally resented being classified as a probable "dope-fiend and boozer." Of course, the rest was up for discussion. Fortunately, not all parents are like that. The girls I dated had parents that were pretty cool and we got along. "Yes ma'am" and "Yes sir" tames even the most "eyes over their glasses" parents. Even if they did think I was just a "little bit left of center." Okay, okay. You be the judge.

So, in my senior year of high school, I was the only band member in "Theze Few" left to carry on the swagger in school. All the other band members had graduated the year before. At this point, they're going off to college and getting involved in all sorts of deviant behavior. Heck, I'm still just a naive high school kid.

But, during this time, we also became very serious about musicianship and playing. Theze Few had become very popular in the Dallas area and were beginning to branch out. Our manager, Rich Richeson, was the stepfather of our guitar player, Larry "Ovid" Stevens. These guys were branching out and I was still thinking "high school." I grew up quick. We began playing fraternity parties and strip clubs. Those were wild times. I'm just this church-going Baptist boy trying to assimilate all of this under-belly from a world I'd never known existed. It was truly a "Blue Velvet" time of my life, without the severed ear.

I remember one instance, when we were scheduled to play a strip club over in Ft. Worth on a Friday and Saturday evening. The money is better than most places we would play. The band would always rehearse on Thursday evenings and Sunday afternoons to prepare. We'd learn all the current songs off the radio and really tighten up our show.

Our manager, Rich, was from Chicago and he had been around. I learned so much from Rich. He was truly one of my mentors. Although I gave him grey hair from my smart-alec mouth and constant badgering, I really admired him and contribute much of what I learned and how I grew up to him. My dad and Uncle George were the other men in my life that were my big influences.

Rich walked into our Thursday night rehearsal. He then began to explain that the job for Friday and Saturday are both cancelled. We got mad. I was counting on the money. It was very good money too. So, I said, "Well, since they're canceling at the last minute then we should still get paid, right?"

Rich gets tough and says, "You want to be paid, huh, hotshot? Well, I just got the call and they found Jimmy (the club owner) in the back alley last night, dead, with a bullet in his head. You still wanna get paid?"

My stomach's in my throat. I feel sick. Dead? Shot in the head? This kind of thing only happens in the movies. And only in places like New York, L.A. or Chicago. I knew this man. He was friendly to us, plus he always paid. But what kind of people have I gotten myself mixed up with? This isn't exactly what I signed on for. Shoot, I'm barely seventeen and not even legal yet. I wasn't even supposed to be allowed to play those kinds of places until I was eighteen. I can't tell my mom and dad, they're not happy about me missing so much church to begin with. They don't need this kind worry. Heck, them worried? I'm the one that's worried.

This was sobering and frightening all at the same time. I could have been there when it happened. I'd already been hit by a '22 caliber ricochet on the firing range in R.O.T.C. Bullets burn. I didn't like it. I've still got the dent in my forehead to prove it. But more importantly than all of that, my girlfriend broke up with me over playing these kinds of clubs. Now, girlfriends come and go at will . . . but a bullet in the head can be permanent. I know . . . this must be a sign.

So, we moved away from those kinds of clubs except for every now and then. But since then, I've always had a soft spot for the girls that worked there. They were sweet people, just lost and trying to make a living. We even played a "Strippers Convention" once. Being that young I never thought I'd get bored doing that, but I actually did get bored. Sensory overload I guess.

Dan and I began to hit it off during this time. When we first met each other we didn't like each other much. Dan still wanted another guitar player in the group and I have always been of the opinion that I didn't want to have anything to do with someone who didn't want anything to do with me. Sometimes we'd travel to gigs with each other. We discovered that we both could write songs and we began our writing career together during that time.

Not only that, we'd sing the Everly Brothers songs and found we had a natural harmony going. Our voices fit as if they'd been tailor made to sing together. I'd always loved harmonies. It was as good as a lead vocal to me. It made it interesting especially if the harmonies were unusual. So, when I'd hear Dan Fogelberg or Joni Mitchell or hear those tight harmonies of the Eagles or the Carpenters, I'd get emotionally involved. There's something so spiritually motivating about harmonies that my soul just rises out of my body and lingers. My eyes still get watered over when I hear music that brings out a deep primal feeling that I only know is in the genes. I've got a lot of Irish in me and just can't help getting emotional about things like that. Heck, we cry at card games, then fight. Great way to live life.

I'd been trained in church with those kinds of harmonies. They're even written in the hymnals. Church used to be a terrific training ground for music, especially with a mom and dad that sang in the choir. I was always surrounded by it. But I was also raised watching and listening to people like Mitch Miller and Lawrence Welk. Gunsmoke and Paladin came on after Lawrence Welk. If I wanted to watch Marshall Dillon and see the monotonal Paladin, then I had to sit through Lawrence Welk. Dad watched Buck Owens and Porter Wagonner on Saturday afternoon TV. I spent time trying to learn how to comb my hair like Denny from The Beach Boys. I really loved the music and groups like that in high school. Even Flamenco. Love Flamenco music. So much fire. I used to go to El Cid in Los Angeles on Friday or Saturday nights and watch the Flamenco dancers. But it was the music that brought me there. To tell the truth, I really appreciate just about all kinds of music because fortunately for me, I wasn't raised solely on rock and roll. I'd hear Stephen Foster, then West Side Story, then Doo Wop, then classical, then Irish songs. I'm eclectic. I like the sound of that word, eclectic. Rolls off the tongue. If you listen closely, it sounds a lot like lunatic.

Not long ago, I was listening to a Josh Groban CD. Great music. My wife came in and asked what I was listening to. I clumsily said, "Opera." She looked at me skeptically and said, "I'm going to the store. Call me when you come back to your senses." I can't help it. I love it and get emotionally involved.

During my college years, Dallas was beginning to lose its Western cow town image and was well on its way to becoming your basic generic let's-model-our-town-after-every-other-cosmopolition-city-in-the-nation-so-the-good-people-won't-know-if-they're-in-Chicago-or-Boise. Dallas is no longer the Southern city I grew up in. When I moved to L.A. to pursue a recording career, there was still right about one million people there. There's over four million there now. I get lost just trying to find my old house. And, I don't remember any drive-by shootings in my old neighborhood when I was growing up. They happen now, though.

But back in the late '60's Dallas was one terrific place. We had so many clubs to play and being surrounded by the State University system, there was always a fraternity party to play. Plus, we were a good cover band and highly sought after. The phone rang constantly for us to play.

Our manager, Rich, was a good businessman and crafty too. I remember once a local DJ named Jimmy Rabbit from KLIF radio had taken a shine to the way we played and liked the demos we'd made. He hooked us up with Dale Hawkins, who'd written "Suzy Q." Hawkins came out to a rehearsal one evening, said he thought we were a "happening" band, and got some money from Rich to do some projects with us. He then proceeded to disappear. Never heard from him again. In case you're wondering, these lessons I was learning were getting expensive. Jimmy Rabbit would be there at local gigs with us representing the radio station. It was a big deal to have the famous DJ show up and give away disposable junk. Now, after Hawkins had done us in, Jimmy "Rabbit" transformed into Jimmy "slippery pig." Rich would call and call and then call again, leaving message after message for the Rabbit. Now, Rich had five young men pestering him day after day wanting to know when we're getting to record. We're ready. We're impatient. We won't stay young forever, you know.

Rich, more or less, took us on to help his own stepson, Larry, learn about the world. But, what actually happened was that he ended up taking on five boys and later six boys to raise. He raised us good, and I received an education no university in the country was capable of providing. All I lack is a diploma on my wall from "The University of Rich Richeson."

The band was rehearsing when Rich's wife, Wanda, asked him what he intended to do about this. Rich wasn't your typical fly-off-the-handle kind of man. Instead, he coldly calculated, looked for the weak spot and would zero in on it. But by now, even Rich was mad. So, because of the direct avoidance and insult, he called the radio station. He disguised his voice into a deep, good-ol-boy, cigar-smoking, arm-punching, lie-swapping, hillbilly Southern accent (remember, Rich was from Chicago). For some reason or another, this is what most people think of when they think of a Southern accent. It isn't. Its hillbilly and it's usually the way we make fun of ourselves. When other people try to "talk Southern," they're really speaking "hillbilly." Simply put, they just sound stupid. Very stupid. Doggone, another diatribe. But, you've got to do what you do best. I'm getting good at it.

Anyway, he told the radio secretary, "Howdy thar young lady. I'm Colonel Davis, Col. Buuuuford Davis, and I wanna 'tawlk' to that Rabbit fellow about coming out, maybe hosting a little party I'm throwing for my darlin' little girl and what he'd charge me for it. He around there darlin'? Tell that boy I wanna 'tawlk' to him?"

Now, there's a possible job offer on the table. Rabbit picked up the phone in a hurry, "Hello, this is Jimmy Rabbit. What can I do for you, Colonel Davis?"

After weeks of avoidance, Rich has him. He coldly says, "Hi Jimmy. Rich. Richeson."

Dead silence. Rich said he could hear all the silent cussing going on. In Texas, no self-respecting Texan "curses." They cuss, in case you're wondering about the grammar.

The Rabbit starts fumbling and offering excuses from "I've been thinking about calling you" to "Wait, the song's almost over and I have to cue up the next one. Let me call you right back." Rich may not get anything from the Rabbit, but he did catch him in his own greedy trap. Rich went through the Rabbit like a sumo wrestler stomping on the inner child of a discontented 40-year-old new age therapist. If it would have been us guys in the band, we'd been looking for the guy that killed the strip club owner to talk to the Rabbit. However, Rich was a guy who did things on the up and up. I don't ever remember hearing Rich yell at anyone that I can think of, but I do remember when he was angry, you'd really wish he would have yelled or something. His not yelling was intensely threatening.

None of the band knew the extent of Rich's "threats," but the Rabbit was on his way to the next DJ gig at another radio station not too long after that. Maybe Moscow, Idaho or somewhere. We didn't get to record and we didn't get our money back, but that little trick was absolutely, unforgettably priceless. I've gotten to use that technique before myself. It's a dyed-in-the-wool winner.

Theze Few went back to making our demos again. We even managed to get a little local airplay. The radio stations used to do that back then. You couldn't get a local radio station to do that now. It's all about advertisers and the music on your local radio station is programmed somewhere in some factory where they can tuna or something. So, the majority of music you hear is programmed for advertisers, not listeners.

We used to get people to call up the stations and request our songs. Many of the girls that we had in the fan club used to call, then change their voices and call again. You couldn't do that now. Not with "Caller ID" and stuff. The one thing I've learned over the years is that sometimes having experience can hamper you. If you don't know you can't or aren't supposed to do it, you probably will. We did. We got some great airplay because of it.

I remember that happening to one rock group at my high school. The long hair craze was sweeping the West Coast but at my particular high school, it was not a welcome addition to the curriculum. This band grew their hair all summer long. By today's standards it wasn't really long at all, but we're talking 1967 Texas here.

These boys came to school the first day of my senior year. They were all seniors too. I had played in a band with one of them and one of the other boys I had gone all through the school system with. The school officials told them to go and get their haircut or they wouldn't be admitted to school. So, as legend has it, they went home, wrote a song about "Don't Cut My Hair," proceeded to record it and the darn thing was playing on the radio that night. I personally think they'd been planning it for months. Nothing worked that fast in Dallas that I ever remember, except maybe getting in dutch with a teacher and being sent off to the principal's office. There wasn't much delay in the discipline department.

All of a sudden we've got TV news crews swarming all over the school, camera's everywhere. Reporters sticking their microphone's in student's and teacher's faces. Irate school officials telling them to leave. Radio stations, in their mobile vans, playing the song back to back. The girls swooning over these boys standing in open rebellion on the front steps of the school, football players pointing at them and pounding their fists into their hands. But the "heretic musicians" standing defiant, pleading their cause to the press, secretly hoping the entire time that the school wouldn't readmit them.

They got their wish. And along with the wish, they received volumes of publicity. In the long run, the publicity didn't help them much and they ended up at some other school and as soon as the craze was over, no one would hire them to play. Good gimmick, but it just didn't take off.

But for now, the entire school was in an uproar. It wasn't the typical way our school year started, but it was entertaining to watch from a distance. I really resented this little drama at the time. Looking back however, here's some boys that were using their heads. It's all about promotion. Good publicity, bad publicity, the results are the same. The only difference is in the spelling.

Now, why didn't my band think of that? It could have been us with all that publicity. We could have been a flash-in-the-pan too, having to be transferred to attend another school. But, on the up side, our record would be playing on the radio stations in town. Our photos would be in the newspapers all over the Dallas/Ft. Worth area with our parents standing by us, patting our heads and defending us against the forces of evil school administrators and socialist satanists and how we were really good kids and such and it was all their fault for trying to squelch our normal-for-teenage-kids behavior. I'll tell you why we didn't. Because our parents would have torn our hair out by the roots for publicly shaming them like that and a band of bald headed kids just wasn't the current rage at that particular time. Respect was an important part of my growing up.

But Theze Few went to work even harder on the "tried and true" tested methods and stayed away from anything that might be considered "suspect." So, we languished, continuing to play the same gigs over and over while I continued to lose girlfriends, because of never being able to have a Friday or Saturday night date. I was always working and playing music and it beat the heck out of throwing a paper route, like I had done for years or bagging groceries on weekends. I always had money back then.

Chapter 16

<u>SOUTHWEST F.O.B.</u>

$5.00? Just for playing music at the roller rink for 4 hours? Dang. I'm in.

(a very young) John Ford Coley

This section could also be titled "The World According to John." One of the most prominent images that any group can present to the public is their name. It identifies you. It can actually make or break you. Some names are too bland, some too pretentious or gaudy. Some are just simply stupid, but for some reason or another, they seem to work. Above all, the name has got to be unique. We used to spend hours laboring over just the right name, just to stick out from the run-of-the-mill number of groups out there. I'm still amazed at just how stupid some of the names I personally came up with were. And in the sense of good taste, I'm not going to tell you what they were either.

However, it doesn't start there. Even a great name can't help you in the long run if you're no good. It's like a boxer who crosses himself before the match. It's a nice gesture but it doesn't really help much if he can't fight. I'm a real believer in foundations. Without the proper foundation nothing of any real value can be built on top of it.

During my senior year in high school, was the time I personally began to get serious about music. During this time, we added a trumpet player, Randy Bates, and changed the group name from Theze Few to the Southwest F.O.B. or "Free-On-Board." Our manager, Rich, came up with that one. We were constantly being greeted with, "Is it Southwest F.O.B. or S.O.B.'s?" At first we thought it was a great gimmick. We were always being called the "S.O.B.'s." It got old in short order.

We had been playing a lot of soul music and R&B - Otis Redding, Wilson Pickett, Sam and Dave songs. That was terrific music. Great melodies too. From the influences of the band members that were already in college, we jumped ship and careened headlong into the blacklight and parachute period of our life. My clothes got cooler. I got rid of my white socks and boots and changed them out for moccasins. Paisley became the design of choice and I swapped out my dress pants and pressed jeans for bell-bottoms, beads and hair that was over my collar. Whoa. Just by changing the style of my clothes I became one of the "groovy people." Shoot, according to some of the people at my church I was just "headed to Hell in a handcart."

Momma and daddy were a little worried, but never said anything negative and only encouraged me.

The change of style began to have an effect on everything about me, especially my school life. I pretty much began to think that I was "10 feet tall and bulletproof." I also learned how to pretty much talk my way out of anything. Case in point: I would usually walk a girlfriend to class or just piddle around and end up late to class. I'd concoct these wild, outlandish stories about why I was late. My imagination would just take off like it had a mind of its own. I even got written up in our senior class book because once I came in late to my American history class from lunch. The teacher didn't want to hear my excuse and immediately sent me to the office for a tardy pass. In the school office I told the attendance teacher that the reason I was late was because I was getting my books from my locker, quite naturally minding my own business, on my way to class, when all of a sudden this girl on crutches tripped me with one of her crutches. Then, out of nowhere, she abused me with the most unlady-like foul language and mercilessly attacked me. But, I bravely fought her off. First it was her on top of me, then me on top of her, rolling over and over, fighting, scratching and clawing the whole time. "And then you know what happened?" I said.

She eyed me cautiously and answered, "No, I can't imagine. What happened?"

Without blinking, I dryly said, "She killed me."

She never cracked a smile, but said, "That's a good one. You deserve an excused pass for that story." She gave me an excused tardy pass and shortly I was back learning about my ancestors. I was late a lot back then. However, it was good training as a musician for being "fashionably late." I've almost gotten better about it as I've gotten older. Almost.

I'd also begun to let my hair grow a little longer and longer and longer. Once, I had to go into the assistant principal's office because the radio had been stolen out of my car in the school's parking lot. He kept looking at me real hard, sizing up the length of my hair, wondering just how much to let me get away with. Finally he flatly said, "You're Miss Mac's friend, aren't you?"

I boldly said, "Yes sir, I am."

Nobody, and I mean nobody, messed with Miss Mac. She was the very embodiment of tough. She was the girls' gym teacher and head of the Girls' Drill Team, the Starlets. She was known for making the girls cry and even the boys would shudder and never crossed her. I had heard she was ex-military, a nurse or something.

In my junior year, I was setting up my equipment in the gym for a dance of some sort or another. She walked in and for no particular reason, began screaming at me. I was hot and sweaty and not in a good mood to begin with. Before my good senses had time to kick in, I looked up and started yelling back. She stopped dead in her tracks, stared at me for a short minute, and then stormed out the door. That gym got quieter than a church on a Monday night. Everyone kept telling me that I was "dead meat," and that no one had ever talked to Miss Mac that way. You always assumed the cowering position. I guess I caught her so off guard that she didn't know what to think or do with someone yelling back, probably out of her range of experience. However, she and I got to be good friends because of it, and being Miss Mac's friend had its privileges. Nobody else messed with me either. I walked around like I had a bulletproof vest on. She pulled me out of a couple of scraps with school administrators and teachers that would be considered by most as "too wet to plow" situations. I liked her.

About this time, "Dr. Zhivago" came to the theaters and my whole life changed. The mustache was in vogue. I was just barely shaving that peach fuzz covering my face, if you could call it that. I think I was up to shaving one time a week. Maybe two. I used to take some strands of one of my girlfriend's long brown hair and hold it up against my lip, look in the mirror and think, "Yep. That's me all over." So, now I had a look that as soon as my whiskers decided to cooperate I could see off in the not too distant future. I've hardly ever been without one since. Besides, without a mustache, I'm told I look too much like Barney Rubble. (Say what you want about the acting talents of all these new young actors, Brad Pitt or George Clooney, etc. But in my book, no one can hold a candle to Barney Rubble). So, by the time I was in my second year at college, I was finally able to get a decent mustache.

When I got to college, just about everything changed. First of all, my piano teacher, Mr. Cole, said he wanted to get me a scholarship for music. I told him I wasn't interested in studying that kind of music, I wanted to go into law. Man . . . what could I have been thinking? Law? What a useless profession. Didn't they ever read in the Bible what it says about those people? Of course, I'm certain it doesn't apply to or include any of those blessed and highly favored souls that negotiate my record, TV and book contracts. Saints ya'are. Love ya, miss ya, mean it.

Then a devastating event occurred. Buddy Lay, my friend and drummer in the band, got drafted. Viet Nam had kicked in high gear and the draft board was after everyone. I was never particularly for or against the war, but with Buddy having to go and then Philip, my childhood friend and neighbor from across the street going, I began to rethink matters. Now, I had got good friends over there. They deserved my support. Enough said.

One night, Buddy said that they woke up his team of men, walked up and down the ranks and pointed, "You, you, you and you." Buddy was one of the "you's." They took the biggest men over to the Marine Corps from the Army. He did come home, but didn't rejoin the band, and he had some crazy stories to tell.

So, with Buddy being gone, the search for a drummer began and went on and on and on and finally, one day, Tony (Zeke) Durrell walks in, confident and cocky as any of the members of the band he was auditioning for. He was very good and got the job.

Now, as far as I was concerned, we should have changed the name of the band. The Southwest F.O.B. was Buddy, Larry (Ovid), Randy, Doc, Danny and me. Zeke was not in the original F.O.B. But we kept the name anyway.

One weekend the F.O.B. played with a traveling group at LouAnns, a local teen club in Dallas we had been playing for years. The band was a San Francisco based group called, "The West Coast Pop Art Experimental Band." They changed our musical lives. They played a song called "Smell of Incense." We fell in love with it and recorded our version of it.

There was a group of guys from WFAA, one of the local television stations in Dallas that had formed a company together. They had money and were looking for a music group to invest in. Rich showed them our "Smell of Incense" recording and when they heard it, they knew they'd found their group and they liked the Southwest F.O.B. as the group name and didn't want to change it.

This was terrific for us. Now, we could get on the local TV shows and get even more exposure, which translates out to "more work." We'd already played things like "Tiger A Go Go" with Ron McCoy, a disc jockey in Ft. Worth. He had been especially helpful and he was a good guitar player himself. But, this was back when we were still Theze Few.

Now, finally shows like "Something Else" with Ron Chapman in Dallas and "The Larry Kane Show" in Houston weren't out of our reach. We'd already played a "Battle of the Bands" with Ron and lost, but got to play with Vanilla Fudge out of it. Ron was a local guy that brought us such people as Joanie Prather, who went on to the highly rated television show "Eight Is Enough." She had been one of the "Go Go" dancers on the show. Maybe it wasn't "Go Go." It looked more like improv or swimming out of water to me. I just remember the day we were scheduled to appear on the show, Joanie wouldn't talk to me, or have anything to do with me actually. Imagine all the great things I could have said about her here if she had. Too late now. If you're reading this, it's in print.

Rich had an office in downtown Dallas and had become friends with an elderly lady named Marie and her husband, Larry, another tenant in the building. Marie was a seamstress who made costumes for strippers. (I know that has to sound funny). Rich talked her into making stage clothes for our band. She was a neat freak. She convinced Rich that a zipper in the front of pants was not as neat as a zipper on the side, like ladies pants at the time. Rich bought into it. Now, we felt stupid zipping up our pants from the side. How unmanly. Made us "Girlie Men" to coin a current phrase.

On our first appearance on the "Something Else" TV show, we're taping live before a studio audience (always scary), complete with commercials. For that segment, Larry (Ovid) was singing the song without his guitar and he was nervously stepping from one foot to the other. Just before we started to play, I grabbed his arm and in a panic said, "Ovid! For crying out loud man, your zipper's undone."

I've never seen anyone wheel around that fast. His fly is open on TV. He's scrambling and grabbing the front of his pants and still feebly attempting to be cool. But there is no zipper in the front; it's on the side.

I'm laughing and falling all over my Farfisa organ like there's no tomorrow.

The band wants to know what's so doggone funny.

Larry's fuming, but his mind was now off of his nervousness. He grabbed me by the arm, got up to my ear and said, "You're gonna pay for that," then turned back around and smiled like the professional he was.

The "on-air light" immediately comes on, cameras are rolling, Ron Chapman starts to talk with Ovid. He looks over at me and he wants to know why I'm laughing so hard. I couldn't tell him. Ovid never did get even with me for that little stunt. However, he's still young and has a good memory. I guess he figures he has time left.

Ron Chapman went on to own the radio station KVIL in Dallas. He also became the stand-in for "Now for the rest of the story, Paul Harvey. Ron played the dickens out of England Dan and John Ford Coley songs. Thanks Ron. We appreciate it. (See Joanie. I could be saying those nice things about you right now. Talk to me next time).

All of a sudden, we're all over the radio with "Smell of Incense." Radio is our friend. We're getting job offers everywhere. People knew me at college; everybody wanted to be my friend. I liked this.

Then, like the grim reaper, out pops the Musician's Union. We weren't in the union. I didn't want to be in the union. I don't like unions. They were wonderful when they began because they were needed. However, we didn't need one. We told them Texas was a "Right To Work State."

They said "So what!" and issued us an ultimatum. I really hate ultimatums. "Either join the Musician's Union or we'll have your record pulled off the radio."

They meant it and they could make it happen. So, we had to join the union, pay an initiation fee, and from then on pay local union dues every time we went to another town to play, all under the guise that we were "putting local musicians out of work." Plus, for a small nominal fee we received the added bonus (and privilege) of renewing our unwanted membership every year. What a deal. Should be called the "fee" union. However, they did give us a thousand-dollar burial plot. Personally, I would have preferred a car phone as my token gift. I could have used one of those.

To show you how serious union stuff could get, once when Dan and I really hit the road as a duo, there was a national truckers strike. A couple of local union boys took a shot at our truck driver's semi when he was transporting our musical gear to the next gig in Pennsylvania. But he just kept going.

When Dan and I moved to Los Angeles to record, we happened to run across a couple of musician union reps one night at A&M studios. We said that since we lived in L.A. now, we might as well change over to the local musicians union here. They got really excited and said, "Great, great. Now all you have to do to transfer is pay the $150.00 initiation fee and we'll transfer your membership here." I said, "We've already paid the initiation fee in Dallas and it was only $100.00. Why would we want to pay it all over again and for more?" "But, you're in L.A. now," he said. Dan jumped in and said, "Well, it's all the same AFL-CIO isn't it?

The guy kept defending the fact that this is L.A., the big time and not little podunk Dallas. So, we asked if we had to transfer over. They hemmed and hawed and kept giving weak explanations and we finally said, "We'll just stay in the Dallas local." We did. I've had to join other unions over the years. I emphasize the words "had to." Protesting doesn't help.

So, anyway, "Smell of Incense" remained on the radio. At this time, the men that had the faith in us got bought out. STAX Records was forming a new label called HIP to take on our kind of act. STAX is considered a black label, but they wanted to expand. Their forte was R&B and great music like Sam and Dave, Steve Cropper, Wilson Pickett and tremendous groups like that. Now, you might not know it by looking at either of us, but we were about as white as anything you could imagine. Heck, you couldn't even see us in the bright sunlight. We'd just fade. The only other group that was on the HIP label was a group called "The Nobody Else." They became known later as "Black Oak Arkansas."

We released an album called "Smell of Incense." If you hear it, it's so 60's style you'll start looking for all your old vests, beads and blacklights and things like that.

I remember when Rich came in with our album cover; he only had one thing to say. "They won't be selling this one in your Sunday school at church." He was right. Many record stores wouldn't sell it in their stores either because of the cover. It was very risqué, even for the open-minded '60s. It's considered plain and bland now by today's lower standards.

All during this time, Dan and I were getting restless. As a band, we had already opened up concerts for Three Dog Night, Led Zeppelin, Vanilla Fudge, Paul Revere and the Raiders, Blue Magoos, The Standells, Poco, Johnny Rivers, to name a few. I'm getting bored playing the same things and places over and over though. Besides, we changed members again and drugs were popping up more and more in the group. The new bass player was nuts, and at that time that was his most redeeming quality. Once Dan stopped him from beating up his girlfriend for getting stoned and not giving him any of it. Lovely. I just sat there, eating my dinner. I didn't like him or his girlfriend. I was beginning to lose any sensitivity or compassion being in this group and didn't much care if they killed one another or not. Bass players were easy to find. Both Dan and I wanted out because the time to leave was long overdue.

Shane Keister became our piano player and actually took my place, but I stayed on to play organ and sing. I was the only one still in college and college had begun to take a toll on me in my music. I was at school all the time and didn't have a piano to practice on. I was getting rusty. Shane used to come to school with me and help me cheat on my music tests. He had perfect pitch. I only had a desire to get out of that music class with a good grade. Together, we were a perfect match. He went on to play with Elvis and later on Dan and my records.

Dan and I began to open the shows for the Southwest F.O.B. with acoustic guitars singing some of the songs we'd written. That got my blood pumping. We eventually left the group, even though we gave up our $100.00 a week share of the loot and went directly to starvation row. But . . . was it worth it? Ya ding danged bet cha.

But this is where I learned a very hard, sad and difficult lesson; one that very few people in my age bracket knew because we were considered "self-employed." A simple little thing like saving for your taxes, which I hadn't done or known to do. If I could make the money, I sadly discovered the I.R.S was more than willing and even happy to take it away from me and then tell me how they had been remiss in their duty of not relieving me of it. I told them I needed my money that I worked for more than they did. They laughed and told me there were less fortunate than me that needed it too. That's when I learned what a "deduction" was. I got pretty skinny back then paying them off. And between me and you, I'm not a real fan of that "starving artist" thing. I had already done the "Top Ramen" tours, thank you very much. Food is my friend.

Chapter 17

LIVING ON FAITH

Success is the ability to go from one failure

to another with no loss of enthusiasm.

Winston Churchill

After leaving the Southwest F.O.B., Dan and I both began working "real" jobs. We did pretty much whatever we could to keep my school tuition and horse board paid and food on the table for Dan and his family. Dan had a wife and small boy to take care of.

We also took a giant leap of faith in our duo and began to play local folk clubs like the "Rubiyat," owned by Bob Johnson. Everybody played there including Townes Van Zant, Guy Clark, Michael Martin Murphy, Boomer Castleman, Mike Williams, B.W. Stevenson, Ray Wiley Hubbard and Alex Harvey. The list just went on and on. I really have to thank all those who owned the clubs that we played at. That was where we were able to learn our craft. In front of an audience is where you really find out what works and what doesn't. I really feel sorry for those that don't get to have that experience. It's hard to offer anything when you go from singing and playing in your bedroom, to the recording studio, directly to the big stage. You can't develop a personality that way.

The Rubiyat was located right next door to a transvestite club. I guess the lease was cheaper or something. I never paid much attention to it or even knew that place existed, or those kind of people for that matter, until I saw a man running, or actually kind of sashshaying, into the club one night in full makeup with an evening gown under his arm. It just kept getting weirder and weirder in Dallas. People make me laugh.

I remember once, Dan and I played the community college in Dallas where Dan was spending some time pretending to study and get a degree in music. While we were in the middle of our set, this beaded up kid with hair that hadn't been combed for weeks walked up and asked Dan if we played anything by the Buffalo Springfield. Now this was one of my all-time favorite groups, but Dan and I only played original songs, not covers anymore. So, Dan explained we only performed our own songs.

The kid shook his head and snottily said, "Oh. I was hoping you'd play something good."

That was funny. When I heard him, I cracked up laughing and thought, "Music lover."

However, Dan was genuinely insulted and quite ticked. After our set, we headed out to the Rubiyat to play an unscheduled set because Dan was so affected by the kid's comment. Now, since that time, I've adopted a rather firm, dyed in the wool theory about music and the related arts. Goes like this. "If you like it, you're right. If you hate it, you're right. It's all a value judgment anyway." That has helped me repeatedly. The other one is, "If you don't have the ability to send me to either heaven or hell, what am I trying to impress you for?" Oh, how I cling to life's little experience book.

Now, Dan and I got the opportunity to deal with the ol' "search for the perfect name" game again. For a while we worked under the name, "Colley and Wayland" and began traveling back and forth to L.A. playing the "Ice House," the "Golden Bear" and clubs like that. We were searching for a name that would really identify us. Also, what works in Texas might get you laughed off the stage in California. There were duo named groups everywhere. Seals and Crofts, Sam and Dave, Peter and Gordon, The Righteous Brothers or The Carpenters, etc. We were looking for something unusual.

Finally, Jimmy Seals of Seals and Crofts, Dan's older brother, chanced upon the name of England Dan and John Ford Coley. When the Beatles exploded and overtook the music scene and the entire known world at large, Dan used to walk around faking an English accent. In other words, he just plain talked funny. It sounded very authentic, provided you'd never been to England, but if you had, it sounded hillbilly when you're attempting to speak Southern.

So, Dan became England Dan and since I was working at the rodeo and had been a cowboy type all my life, Jimmy thought John Ford Coley sounded better. I'd always had people mispronounce my last name Colley. From grade school on, I've gotten, "Coolen, Cooley, Coley, Cauley, Calley, Colly, Cowley, Cotton, etc., etc." And that's just in the Federal Census records. Everything but Colley, (pronounced Collie, like the dog. My nickname was Lassie). I wonder if that ever happened to Sarah, my somewhere along the line distant relative. Sarah Ophelia Colley was her maiden name but she was better known as "Minnie Pearl."

One time, I got delayed by Israeli security in Tel Aviv because my plane ticket read "John Ford Coley," but my passport read "John Edward Colley." I'm fumbling for some identification with the other name on it, trying to explain to them, "Don't you know me? My records were number one in Jerusalem. Strip search? Terrorist? No, I'm a musician. They're closely related I admit, but spelled differently. What do you mean you didn't like my records? Critic, everyone's a critic. Nice beret. Where can I get one of those? What do you mean? Of course I ate at McDavids." I made it out fine, kept my clothes on and everything, but didn't get the beret. Just barely got my guitar case out of the country. And why is it that everyone that has on those latex gloves has the same glint in their eye? A word of advice: if you travel and have a pseudonym, make certain that your passport and plane ticket have the same name.

Anyway, the name caught on. That's how it happened. That's the official version anyway. The unofficial sounds remarkably the same, only different. Nice oxymoron.

However, we had our share of difficulty with that name as well. Once, while playing with Bread, we were reviewed as "English Don and John Portfolio." Now a trend had begun.

As our success progressed, we even thought of more names for ourselves. We considered that perhaps we should cultivate a more international flavor. Unfortunately, this was not a vision that was supported by our record company. We thought that maybe each new album could have a different theme or name, like "Polish Dan and John Ford Coleyoski", or "Italian Dan and John Ford Cappucino." There's always, "Norwegian Dan and John Fjord Coley; Japanese Dan and John Ford Coreysan and Hawaiian Dan and John Ford Okole (yeah I know what that means)." But my all time favorite was "Mexican Dan and Juan Queso Frijoles." That one just has a certain ring. As you can see, the possibilities are endless. It might well fall under the category of "idle pursuits," but, hey, you've got plenty of time to sort these things out on the road, when you're not sleeping that is.

So, in other words, what it took about three chapters to explain, simply put, I survived high school, college, countless bars, strip clubs and fraternity parties, girlfriends, the '60's, '70's and the '80's, Dan and I got a name, we made it, lived to tell about it and with God's blessing, continue on. Whew.

Chapter 18

TALENT OR LACK THEREOF

"Get it in one take!!!!?? For God's sake.

I'm not an actor, I'm a movie star.

Peter O'Toole in "My Favorite Year."

Over the years I've met and been involved with some truly intriguing and interesting characters in all forms of entertainment. Some are funny, but not like "ha ha" kind of funny, some are funnier and some, even at the mention of their names, I'm rolling on the ground laughing.

One time we were asked to play the Mike Douglas Show in Philadelphia. Dom DeLuise was scheduled as a guest. Dom is one funny guy. He does three things, all of which he does well. Laughs, acts and laughs some more. While he was being interviewed by Mike, a chimpanzee was brought on to the set and before you knew it, Dom was picking fleas or bugs or something off the chimp and still answering questions put to him by Mike.

He had the audience in absolute stitches the entire show. I felt good though because much to Dan's dismay, I opted to play a joke version of "Lara's Theme" from "Dr. Zhivago" on the piano because I thought Dom might enjoy it.   I had learned it from Shane Keister and it went like this. I'd play the first part correctly and then on purpose hit a wrong note at the end of the phrase, say "oops" and continue on and do the same thing on the second phrase, until I quit. Dom's on the side of the stage, just falling over and rolling on the ground.   He was laughing so loud and hard that the audience was looking over to him and caught up in his laughter. Dom has quite an infectious laugh.

Dan's furious with me and has that real piqued tone on his face. We're supposed to be "serious musicians."

Besides possessing one of the finest voices I had ever heard, Dan had to be one of the funniest people I had ever known. He was always goofing off and making really funny comments. He had a quick mind and could come up with the most outlandish comments. He kept me laughing often. However, the instant that he set foot on stage, a whole different personality emerged and it was as if some invisible steel trap clamped across his mouth. He became deadly serious and was afraid of looking foolish. I was just the opposite. Because I was always joking and goofing off on stage, I learned what to say and what didn't work. And Dan and I would have some pretty terrific arguments about it. But, hey, who you are is who you are. I'm a guy. I'm not changing, regardless of things I've been caught in and claimed I could "change" to stay out of trouble.

After Dan and I had split and he began his solo music career, he once told me that the hardest thing he ever had to do was to try to talk to and communicate with the audience. I'd always done it for him. He said it felt so unnatural to him. Everyone wants to look good. I told him to be just as big an idiot on stage as he was off stage. It seems to work for me. Besides some of the things I say on stage are from material I've heard him say off stage. They're funny, trust me and they'll love it. But it was hard for him.

Back to the story. At the taping of the Douglas show with Dom, there was another guest who was a representative from the White House. She was the official person that taught people how to eat when they attended a function at the White House. How would you like that for a job? On her resume it reads: "I teach people how to eat." Maybe it's different in D.C. Eating comes pretty natural to most everyone where I come from.

Mike Douglas and Paul Anka are sitting in the middle, doing their best to comply. The lady is seated at the head of the table and Dom is at the other end. She's as serious as a taxpayer at an IRS audit and Dom's at the other end rolling up his pants leg to his knee and making hand signs under the table to her and the audience. The audience is busting up laughing. The lady's trying to get a handle on everything and remain composed. Mike's trying to be the perfect host and failing miserably. Paul Anka has got his hand over his mouth trying to keep a straight face and having about as much success as Mike. The only one is control is Dom. The lady exactingly explains to everyone how they should butter their corn-on-the-cob. "Butter one section, eat it and then butter the next section. Never butter it all at once. This isn't proper etiquette."

Dom's all over that one. He jumps in and says, "Hey lady, wanna see how we eat it where I live?"

This lady has absolutely no place to turn for help and before her secret service guards can shoot him, Dom picks up a slice of bread, cuts a big slab of butter and sticks it in, grabs his piece of corn-on-the-cob and swirls it around in the slice of bread. "That's how we do it at my house. Hey lady, watch this." Dom grabs his same knife he cut the butter with and digs into his peas. "See, lady, the peas will stay on your knife with a little butter. Oh, no. Help me lady, I got peas stuck in my nose." Dom's snorting peas out his nose onto the table, into the audience and the audience is loving it. The cameramen are laughing and having trouble keeping the cameras steady, the lady's fuming, because her big moment has been upstaged, Mike's trying to regain control and not succeeding because he's laughing as much as everyone else. There is no one else on the show when Dom's around. He is the show.

****

While you have people like Dom, other people take this "star" thing far too serious and start to believe that they're something they're not: Privileged. As much as I think I'm not affected, I'm always surprised by their behavior. Sometimes, even by my own. But, I've always been of the same opinion as Bob Geldorf of the Boomtown Rats. Anyone who takes this business as anything other than a joke is an idiot. However, I prefer to speak of the people that I was surprised to meet and how terrific they were instead of those that were not "a pleasure to meet."

I might have expected an ugly kind of behavior out of Oliver Reed and Michael York because of the screen personas they had. I was reluctant to meet them, feeling they might beat me up or something. Instead, I was greeted with very polite and dignified men. Very personable, well educated and comfortable in their own skins. I like being surprised by celebrities.

Same with Ron Howard on the Mike Douglas Show. I'd watched him from "Andy Griffith" to "Happy Days." Just a really nice guy and besides, he had played with the Duke in "The Shootist." John Wayne was one of my heroes. As a kid, I always wanted to be a cowboy because although their life was hard, they never had to go to the bathroom. At least in the movies. By the way, I miss cowboy pictures. About the only actors making good cowboy movies anymore are Tom Selleck, Kevin Costner, Robert Duvall and Sam Elliot. Keep it up guys. I watch them.

Ron wasn't egoed out either. Besides, about everything I ever needed to know, I'd learned from either Andy Griffith or Roy Rogers. Ron, being on the show playing Opie all that time, must have learned it too. I used to work with a bunch of the old horse wranglers at the film studios. They'd trash everyone else, because they had worked with all the film greats, and because of it I have difficulty watching some of the old stars. I've heard too much about what some of their personal lives were like. But nobody and I mean nobody, would say a bad word about Roy Rogers. He was one of their heroes.

So, I never knew what to expect when I'd meet people.

****

Speaking of being on TV shows. Sometimes stories just come flying at you and drop dead square in the center of your lap. After all the heat, surprise and the passage of years, they become quite funny in hindsight. I might not be able to predict the future, but I can predict the past with 85% accuracy. I have this gift. Yeah baby.

I remember one very unusual story that involved Dan and I. It was near the end of our career together and we had been getting into some rather serious arguments.

On our very last appearance of the "Dinah" show the proverbial kettle had boiled over and its contents were being flung into the equally proverbial fan.

Before the show I had gotten so mad that I pulled Dan into one of the off-stage rooms. He and I were really going at it and that conversation was pretty much the end of us as a duo. The truly great thing about being in an argument with Dan was that neither of us was afraid of or intimidated by the other. So, the "debates" could get quite lively, but we knew that nobody was going to be throwing punches and we'd eventually work through it.

After we had pretty much chewed one another up and spit each other out, had called it quits and our blood pressures were returning to the normal range, we were about to head back to the sound stage where the filming was. Although I didn't really notice it at the time, there was a sofa turned with its back to us in the room. All of a sudden a man's head popped up from the front of the sofa. He was wearing huge glasses and a week's worth of grease in his hair. It was almost identical with the scene of "Gone With The Wind." All we needed was for "Miss Scarlett" to throw a vase at the mantel. He had been resting on the couch and stayed there without identifying his presence throughout our entire argument.

Then he boldly says, "I'm sorry to hear about you guys breaking up your partnership, but, I've got a tape that I'd like for you to listen to. It's got some great songs on it and in case you don't break up, I think you'll want to do some of my songs."

Talk about being in the wrong place at the right time. Dan and I stood there stunned. I just remember looking at him like he was a dead animal or something. I kept trying to picture him in a janitor uniform. Then, Dan and I looked at each other in complete disbelief and started busting up laughing. Finally, half-way composing myself, I briefly studied the guy and said, "So, let me get this right. You're a musician?"

He said, "Yeah, and I think you'll like my songs."

I'm not really over the last argument with Dan, still ready to go on to 'Round Two' and here's fresh meat. So I fired back at him, "Naw. You're not a musician."

He defended himself and assured me that "Yes I am, and I've got some great songs I think you'll like."

I reiterated myself and reassured him that, "No. You can't possibly be a musician. You know absolutely nothing about timing."

That remark confused him and put him into deep, puzzled thought. Dan and I, buddies again are now joined together in a common cause, exited the room laughing out loud. That was the last show we taped for "Dinah." I don't think anyone suspected there was any trouble between Dan and me on the show. We seemed happy. But really, we were inwardly chuckling about "Couch Man."

It's always fun to have the last word.

****

With all the hits, also came invitations to come to everyone's party, tennis and racquetball tournaments or TV shows. We ended up being invited to perform on "The Captain and Tennille," "Tony Orlando and Dawn," 'The David Soul Special," "The Gong Show," "Make Me Laugh," "The Lynn Anderson Special," along with the customary rock shows like "The Midnight Special," "American Bandstand," and "Don Kirschner's Rock Concert." The calls kept coming. Everyone wanted a piece of us. We ended up writing the theme song for "James At 16," a popular teen TV show and even landed a part to be on the show. I was having an absolute blast.

Dan and I had been invited to be part of the panel a couple of times on "The Hollywood Squares." This was a highly rated game show in the '70's. We had known the producer, Bob Quigley, for years, but had never been asked to be on the show. I remember talking to Bob's wife, Keith, once. That's right. Keith. I think maybe it was short for Dolores or something. Sweet lady though, and I remember how she had told me that things had not always been as good as they were now and that times had gotten quite rough for them. At one point, she confided to me, that they had actually been down to their last million dollars. What were they going to do? Yeah Keith. Tymes iz hawwd.

When it did happen, it was a real honor for us because mostly the people that were asked to be there had been on TV, film or were comedians and very few musicians were ever asked to participate. Musicians are usually much more unpredictable and don't come off well, chiefly because of all the inside jokes that no one else relates to. You very seldom see a musician sitting down and talking to the host on any TV show or ever saying things like, "I'll take 'Lithuanian Folklore' for $1000, Alex." We mostly think too far out of the box.

Paul Lynde was always on the "Hollywood Squares" and he was truly one round guy in a square box. Half the time, he'd just sit there in the middle square, not saying anything to anyone. When he was asked a question, he'd do or say something so completely outrageous, fall all over himself or else just stare out at the audience. Everyone would be laughing themselves silly, even if they never completely understood all the little inside innuendoes of what he said. I was one that laughed the hardest.

Before each show, the people in charge of us would give us fake answers for the questions. Never the real answer but something for us to say in the event that we didn't actually know the answer. Paul Lynde was never given any answers beforehand whatsoever. He was so quick and witty he'd make up the most unexpected one-liners. I spent a lot of time waiting for him to be chosen because of his nutso remarks. You absolutely never knew what was coming out of his mouth.

On one of the first shows we were on, they had given us the fake answer "Bering Strait," (not the multi-talented Russian Country/Alternative group which has a couple of future mega performers in Lydia Salnikova, the keyboard/vocalist, and Ilya Toshinsky, the guitarist, but Bering Strait the waterway between the U.S. and Russia). So, Dan and I would alternate between ourselves and each would take a question when we were chosen by the contestant. It's my turn next. The contestant looks and says "England Dan and John Ford Coley to win, Peter."

Peter flips through his celebrity list and gets the questions for Dan and me. He then asks the question, "What separates England from France?"

I'm a heartbeat away from answering, "The United Nations."

I mean, England and France hate each other, always have, and probably hated each other before the Garden of Eden. When I was in England, it went so far as to rearrange the pronunciation of names. If you said "Buffet" you were quickly told that the word was "Buff-it" and for "Filet," again we were chastised into pronouncing the word "Fill-it." So, "The United Nations" actually sounded quite logical.

In the blink of an eye, I'm a tortured soul. My mind's in a whirl and spinning. I'm asking myself the question of "do I try to be glib and funny?"

What if it falls flat like the joke Elvin Bishop tried to use on the show when asked some Biblical question and he stupidly remarked, 'Wasn't he the one that slayed everyone with the jawbone of an ass?" He smirked into the camera and thought he was so clever because he got to say "ass" on nationwide TV. Instead, there was dead silence. No one thought it was funny. Not the contestants, the audience nor the host, Peter Marshall. Now, he scrambled for something meaningful to say. He failed. He was never asked back again. His career in TV took a short and dreadfully anticipated downward spiral. I'm still reminded of what happened on the Johnny Carson show and I didn't want that to happen to us again.

The good side of me saying, "Don't get cute." The evil side is tempting me with "Go ahead. Wing it. I'm right behind you, pal." Dan's looking at me with that panicked, don't do it, eyes-as-big-as-the-State-of-Montana look. It always amazes me that all of these complex and complete thoughts can occur in a New York minute, but to say them out loud takes time.

I opted to stay on the safe side. So I responded, "The answer is the North Sea."

Hey, I've studied history and geography all my life. Piece of cake. Don't compete with Paul Lynde. He's better at funny than I am. Opt to look well read and highly intelligent instead. I sat there looking at the contestant with a self-satisfied, trust me kind of grin.

The contestant paused, studied me and narrowed his eyes, shook his head and said, "I disagree Peter."

I thought "OH NO! You blew it pal; you could have won the game, dumbo."

Peter Marshall jumps in and says, "You're correct. It's the English Channel. Congratulations, you've won the game."

The applause sign pops up for the audience and bells and whistles go off everywhere. The winner is elated because he just won some trip to Detroit to view the GM plant and watch them complete repairs on Pontiac Stadium or something. Dan was thanking me for not saying something stupid. The contestants were shaking hands with Marshall while celebrities were taking drinks of wine from under their table.

I was smiling like I gave the answer on purpose, but I was truthfully in shock. The English Channel? How in the world did that get past me? I knew that. It's the evil side's fault. He threw off my timing. Dan's nervousness jumped off and got on me. Yeah, I was trying to please him. Hey, I was in the correct hemisphere at least. Quick, put me on "Jeopardy" and ask me something from the "Dumb As A Box Of Rocks" category. Only this time I'll give whatever answer that first comes to mind.

From that day forward, I've opted to say the first, uncalculated thing that pops into my head when asked a question. It may or may not be funny, it may not be right or politically correct, but it is going to be unpredictable. I'm comfortable there.

Chapter 19

ATHLETES

1.7 million dollars for three years!!?

How am I going to live on 1.7 million dollars for three years???!!!

From the film "Jerry Maguire"

I've come into contact with a couple of pro ball players over the years. Being a musician, I never figured I'd ever have any pro athlete friends because I remember the guys who pulverized us in school. But when you're famous they become your friends and then only hurt you in charity events.

Linden King, a line backer for the San Diego Chargers and Los Angeles Raiders was really a talented musician. He was also one of the biggest linebackers in the NFL. That boy could play and sing. Good songwriter too. I wish he'd had continued with music after his football career ended. He would have made a terrific country artist. We even played a few gigs together. Linden always insisted on sitting down. I couldn't play sitting down, so I would stand up. Ironically, he was always a foot taller than me, even sitting down. The first time I met him, he came to his door wearing cowboy boots. All I could do was look up and up and up until my neck hurt. At that point I was prepared to like any song that he might want to show me.

He gave me his condominium in Honolulu, Hawaii when my wife Dana and I got married. We got to look out on Diamond Head every morning for a week. He even loaned us a car to get around the island. Funny thing was that just about every morning at around 7:30, with his girlfriend in tow, he'd pop his head in the door and shout, "Hey Coley, you up yet? Let's go eat." Just like a locker room. Dana and I had a most unusual honeymoon.

****

I also got to be friends with several other Chargers players during my time living near San Diego. I used to play racquetball with several of them, Hank Bauer and Bob Horn. Good people and great players. I played a racquetball charity benefit with those two once. It was a doubles match and Rolf Bernerska, the Chargers field goal kicker, and I were teammates. We were on the glass court and I was serving. A large audience had shown up and were there to support the charity. I turned to give the boys the score, which according to them was not correct. Both Hank and Bob jumped on me quicker than a cobra and gave me their version of the correct score. Anyway you looked at it though, Rolf and I were still ahead. I cracked a smile and casually retorted that I had been told football players couldn't count. They grimaced at that one and you could almost see the arteries throbbing in their necks. I looked for support from Rolf, but he's cowering against the side wall explaining to them that he'd just met me and we weren't friends. Now instead of a team sport, I was on my own. They told me they got to have "two gotcha's" for that remark.

During the next play, before I know what's happening, they pantsed me and my shorts are dangling down around my knees. My rear end's hanging out in the breeze and the entire audience is pointing and convulsing in a 'can't catch our breath' laughter. Mothers are shielding their young children's eyes. Bob and Hank are still holding my arms and I can't get my pants back up. I guess I'd have been laughing too if it hadn't been me.

Hank was rolling on the floor laughing himself into an absolute hysterical mess. Bob, really pleased with himself, said, "We've still got one more 'gotcha' you know." Blew my concentration big time waiting for that next "gotcha." Although Rolf and I lost the match, Rolf at least held on to his dignity.

I'm ok now though. I don't stutter anymore. I had friends in town that were psychologists and such. Therapy helped and they completely adjusted me to a seriously messed up world.

****

Another time I played racquetball against Doug Dieken, of the Cleveland Browns at a benefit in Cleveland. Doug's a big guy. I mean, a really Goliath-sized big guy. I'm just your average, garden variety, under six-foot, emaciated rock musician. Well, not so much anymore, but once.

Doug sized me up with scorn and his turned-up lip pretty much said it all. "I have to play this wimp? The things I do for charity."

Doug got a surprise with me though. I'd been taught by and often played with a professional racquetball player named Jerry Hilecher. Jerry was one of the two best-known racquetball pros back then. So, I had Doug running all over the court and he was a quick guy for being as big as my house.

At one juncture of the game, I hit a backhand slap shot that was designed to go behind me. Doug'll never get that. I hit it hard. Doug comes running across the court to get to the ball like he forgot this was for charity. Winning's all that matters. I feel like a "rookie" that was after his position on the field. A killer instinct is completely overtaking him, any shadow of reason has been left in the locker room and his only problem at the moment is, I'm in his way.

At first I'm flatfootedly stepping back and forth on my toes trying to figure which way to run. I begin to look like I'm performing a really bad imitation of a talented Michael Flatley in "Riverdance" waiting for the equally talented Jean Butler to lilt in and dance with me.

Then my last remaining faculty snaps to attention and I freeze, not moving left or right, trying to make myself an even smaller target, knowing I'm about to get creamed. Here's this 250 plus pound 6-foot, 27-inch freight train barreling down on me, my life's flashing before my eyes, I have visions of eating all of my future meals through a straw and blood splattered all over the room. My blood. It's a game for crying out loud, a charity benefit besides. Forget pride! It ain't supposed to be that serious.

Doug . . . fun dangit, it's supposed to be fun, remember? It's for charity!

Doug ran right over me, then whoosh! Lift off. I'm breathing the same pure air as the birds. Doug grabbed me by the arms just below my shoulders and completely picked me up and lifted me high off the ground. He stood there for about five seconds, just holding me up in the air, looking at me the way a hunter-views-the-prey-he-just-killed. My feet were dangling about a foot off the ground. I'm did my absolute best not to look intimidated way up there in the stratosphere. He just gave me a big toothy grin and put me down. Dang. I'm no longer in "Riverdance." Now I felt like a ballet dancer in the "Nutcracker."

Because I wasn't the sissy musician type he expected, but almost beat him in the game, we got to be friends after the match. He even gave me one of his own Cleveland Browns T-shirts. It was as big as he was. I mean, there was enough room for three other musicians inside that shirt besides me. I used it for a bedspread for years.

****

But personally, for a sport, nothing beats tennis or Rodeo in my book. Not Ro-day-o, like the overpriced drive in Beverly Hills. Just plain Rodeo. Pro Bull Riding (PBR). Now that's a man's sport. Cody Custer, Chris Shivers, Ty Murray, Don Gay, Tuf Hedeman and many others. Don Gay was a young bullrider back at the Mesquite Rodeo where I used to work for my Uncle George. Don went on to win just about every bullriding championship ever heard of. Plus, he was a pure Dizzy Dean of the PBR announcing team. It was as much fun to hear his colloquialisms as it was to watch the riders. He always reminds me of home.

Those are my kind of athletic heroes. A sport without the rooster strut. Can't get enough of it.

A couple of years ago, for no particular reason PBR disappeared off of the television network TNN. That was the only thing I watched on TNN. I ended up getting the real reason for the disappearance from a former employee. They told me that when TNN sold out its station to MTV, one of the new executives had a bunch of the boys come up to discuss PBR's future on the network. As a bona-fide, city slicker

New Yorker, she assured them just how much she loved Rodeo and the PBR especially. She said she was one of their biggest fans. However, the network needed to make a few changes. So, she offered some new guidelines and said, "Pro Bull Riding is boring. Is there any way the bull riders could ride for maybe a minute, instead of the customary eight-seconds? It would be more exciting that way." (Now as you know, even great riders have trouble sometimes staying on for four seconds, much less eight).

Then the coupe de grace. She said, "Also, the clowns. They have to go. They're simply not funny." (They're not supposed to be funny lady. They're bullfighters. They're there to protect the riders from getting trampled into the ground you silly tin horn, dude ranch, city slicker you). It's not like football or basketball. Every time they climb on the back of one of those 2000 pound beasts they take their life in their hands. Do you have any idea how dangerous a bull can be? I do. I've seen riders really hurt. I've worked with them at the rodeo, in the music, and film industry.

But hey, I do have an idea for you, lady. How about calf-roping instead? Over too fast you say? We can use three-legged horses and the ropers have to ride sidesaddle. You want excitement? Violence sells. How about ladies barrel racing with a lit timed stick of firecrackers tied to the horse's tail. Or better yet, how about land mines strategically placed around the arena? You can have some real "yard darts" that way. And if the bulls and cowboys don't get blown up during the ride, let's see how many can make it back to the fence without losing a leg. Talk about a ratings boost. I think we're on to something here. Yeah, I can see you'd be a fan all right. You might even want to try the rodeo clown thing yourself. What a story you'd have to tell to your friends. Getting in that barrel is a hoot and getting butted around by a 2000 pound animal in a constantly bad mood is a pure adrenaline rush. I'd do it myself, except for the fact that I've gained a little wisdom as I've grown older. Don't worry about dodging bull snot and the steamy bull ooze on the ground either. It all washes off. Just don't forget to wash your hands before you eat.

Hey. Now we're talking. Maybe I could get a job at your station. I've got ideas like those galore. No more silly spring break junk or the "do we really care if the scum live or die" reality shows. We could create truly clever, meaningful and uplifting programming where people would want to watch TV once again and walk away feeling good about spending so much time in front of the tube. Even with guys the remote control would be a thing of the past because no one would want to change the channel and . . . oh . . . yeah. You're probably right. We'd have to deprogram half the known world and it could cost so many non-creative, creatives their jobs. Never mind. Nice try, but it'd never work.

Incidentally. In the event that any of these proposed events do happen to show up at the rodeo . . . remember you heard them here first.

****

I apologize for that last section. For the life of me I don't know how it got in here. Now for something entirely different, but remarkably the same.

****

On our second trip to Japan in 1978, the members of the Cincinnati Reds were staying in the same hotel as us. They had won the Series and had been invited over to Japan to play a few games. The Japanese absolutely love baseball. They play pretty darn good ball too.

Johnny Bench, the Reds catcher, came through the lobby one day and I was introduced to him. He was huge. I was blown away by the size of all these guys. Even Pete Rose was huge. I'll bet their food bills were really gargantuan as well. That's about as close as I've ever gotten to that Goliath looking down his nose at David thing.

At any rate, when Johnny Bench and I shook hands, I was surprised that my hand completely disappeared inside of his. For him handling and throwing a baseball must be like me handling and throwing a walnut. I would guess the ball completely disappears in his hand. I often wondered what it would be like to be that big. But then again, I could kiss that emaciated rock star look goodbye. I personally kind of like that look. Although I can barely seem to fit in any of my old stage clothes anymore, I wonder if those guys can still fit into their old uniforms. Refrigerator Perry comes to mind. Wow.

****

Occasionally, some of these stories are painful for me. One of the biggest disappointments in my life came on the "Dinah Shore" show. It was a great line-up, including Billy Crystal, who was doing really well at the time on a TV show called "Soap" and Yankee's slugger, Mickey Mantle. Mickey was one of my all-time favorite baseball players. I'd followed him as a kid and was there, on TV of course, at all of the games. I had his trading cards, I knew his number, I tried to get his number on my little league baseball team, but everyone else wanted to be him too. I was there with him, in spirit when Roger Maris beat him out of the batting title. I pretended to be him when I played baseball at school. He was one of my boyhood heroes. He's a legend and you can't ever take that away. I was thinking that if the kids in my old school knew who I was standing next to, they would be filled with green envy.

Before the show, Billy, who knows more than any one should about baseball, was literally fawning and groveling all over him. He was giving Mickey play by play re-runs of when he saw him at Yankee Stadium various times and I'm just thrilled to be in the moment. Man, I couldn't get over it. I'm standing next to Mickey Mantle. I wanted a picture. Mickey's big and tall. My parents were going to be so proud. Billy was slobbering and asking him every baseball question under the sun. Billy was being such a huge, fawning fan. Mickey's answering him politely, but you could secretly tell he was enjoying it immensely.

I decided to ask Mickey a question. After all, I was also a big fan since my school days too. Mickey had been a huge inspiration to me. He slowly turned his head to me, narrowed his eyes and glared down at me so there was no mistake that he didn't want to talk to me and gruffly said, "Yeah."

"Whoa. What was that all about?" I thought.

He turned his head back to Billy. Billy's at the idol alter worshiping. Mickey was eating it up.

So, I decided to risk it again and ask him another question.

This time he turned his head slowly, looked at me hard for a second or two and finally in a "don't bother me again voice" said, "Yeah."

So I thought that maybe it was the long hair. Maybe he didn't like long hairs. We've certainly gotten a lot of bad press over the years. Let's give him the benefit of the doubt.

So, after listening to a little more quick witted banter by Billy, I was about to ask him a question when the make-up people asked him to get made up for the show. So I quickly said, "Mr. Mantle?"

Before I could finish he said, "What do you want?!"

And then Billy sided up to Mickey and chimed in with him, "Yeah, what do you want?!"

Now I'm ticked and my Irish flared up. I have a serious aversion to and don't like rude people.

So before I knew it, I shot out, "I just wanted to shake your hand so I could tell everyone back home that my childhood hero isn't the jerk the media has painted you up to be."

Well, honestly, I didn't really say that. But shoot, I sure thought it though. Maybe I would have if I had had more courage. So, I'm saying it now. Besides, Mickey was a big guy and he could probably call in the entire 1960 Yankees baseball team to help him if he needed it. Now I could take Billy. But, this was Mickey Mantle, one of my former heroes.

I did turn and walk away from Mickey. You never want to hang around anywhere you aren't celebrated. He left me alone. Didn't talk to him on the show or ever again. More than anything else I hate having my childhood heroes destroyed. Perhaps he was just having a bad day. Perhaps his eggs had been overcooked and the toast had been burned. Maybe he had lost a lot of money the night before in a poker game with Billy Martin or someone had taken his parking space. Perhaps he had been reading some of the media I was referring to. I don't know and by now I really didn't care.

I told everyone back home that I'd been on a show with and personally got to meet Mickey Mantle. They oohed and ahhed. They told me how lucky I was to meet all of these people and how he must have really been nice.

I just said, "Yeah."

I learned that from Mickey.

****

Now for the brighter side.

Dan and I had been invited once to attend the Football Hall of Fame induction ceremony in Canton, Ohio. It was when Johnny Unitas and Dick Butkus were to be inducted and the Dallas Cowboys were going to be playing in the exhibition game.

There was a big dinner and Peter Breck from the TV series, "The Big Valley," was a guest speaker. Peter was an extremely friendly man, not the tough talking cowpoke on his TV show, and he had brought his small son along and they were both like a couple of kids to be around all the excitement. We all seemed to get overly enthusiastic with people outside of our own element. The hall was filled with former pro greats and other guests.

The one person I was surprised by the most was Howard Cosell. He was the "man you love to hate" from "Monday Night Football." Along with him was Frank Gifford. The nice one from "Monday Night Football." Only trouble was, they seemed to have their roles reversed. When I was introduced to Gifford, from the manner in which he acted, I just figured he must have been hanging around Mickey Mantle or vice versa. The big screen is only an illusion folks. Sometimes you can just look at someone and see a future "Enquirer" headline.

On the other hand, Howard Cosell, big cigar in hand, was one of the most polite and interesting men I'd ever met. He asked all sorts of thought provoking questions about our careers and seemed genuinely interested in knowing about what I did. He laughed big and despite the stories about him, he was a real pleasure to be around. However, you did get the feeling that he was not a man to be trifled with. There was a sharpness to him. One look in those sad eyes and you knew there was something awfully deep in there.

The one person that I had hoped to meet was Roger Staubach. This would be one of the biggest thrills of my life. I had followed him when he played football at the U.S. Naval Academy. He was a man to be admired. In Dallas, the Cowboys had even waited for him to finish his stint in the Navy before he could join the team. The Cowboys were the team I followed, even when I moved to L.A. I've been a fan ever since they began. They were struggling in those days, being a new team and all. When

I was playing football at John B. Hood Jr. High School, we were given tickets to go and watch them play. That was in the days with Eddie LeBaron and Don Perkins. Tom Landry was the best coach in the world and it was back when the organization had a real team owner that cared about his players and coaches and not just the money and power and also the power and the money along with the money and power, coupled with the power. . .well you get it. Not like now.

Unfortunately, before we had a chance to meet him I was informed that he had already retired for the evening in preparation for the game the next day. We had to leave early the next day to play in some other city and I was greatly disappointed. But, hopefully another time.

All of a sudden, Ron, our road manager, came running up to me frantically.

"Quick, quick. We've got to hurry," said Ron.

"Hurry for what," I replied.

"Roger Staubach heard that you had wanted to meet him and he wanted to meet you too. He got up and got dressed. He's in his room waiting for us," he said.

I shot out of there like I was in a cannon. Ron was now following me and I didn't have the slightest clue where I was going. The other Texans in the band were with me. I was like a kid at the park, jumping up and down for joy.

Suddenly, a terrible thought hits me. What if this is like another Mickey Mantle experience? What if he's a real creep? What if he shatters another of my illusions about my heroes? What if, what if, what if? I don't think I can take the pressure. Now, I've got serious misgivings about this meeting.

Well, I really hate to shatter anyone else's illusions. But I have to.

Man, was I wrong. OK. There I said it. Don't expect to hear me admit to that again.

Roger Staubach. What a gentleman. Being termed a "gentleman" in the old South is a great honor. He had actually gotten out of bed and dressed to meet us. But, I figured that Roger, being under the dignified tutelage of Tom Landry, would have that kind of effect on someone. You get it by the process of osmosis. He even promised to call my dad and give him tickets to one of the home games. Wow. Some heroes are the genuine article.

Chapter 20

ACTORS

I'm not sure acting is a thing for a grown man.

Steve McQueen

Actors . . . they like us musicians. Many of them even want to be us when they get rich and famous. But turnaround is fair play because we want to be them too. I know I did.

Have you ever looked into the eyes of Charles Manson? I have. Well . . . at least the man who played Charles Manson. I think that probably is why it didn't scare me much.

As I mentioned earlier, Steve Railsback was another actor that I worked with in a couple of different films. He had actually played Charles Manson in "Helter Skelter" and dozens of other films. Steve had been close friends with a buddy of mine, Alex Rocco. We all knew Alex as "Bo." Alex had worked with Steve on "The Stuntman" and had portrayed "Mo Green" in "The Godfather." Alex was a terrific guy and just had a real great spirit. Alex and I had been in a couple of films together. He had actually been a real live, honest to goodness, bookie/mobster in Boston and ended up in films in California after he figured out he didn't want to die from a gunshot or get turned into little "Goodfella" meatballs in some dark dead-end alley somewhere. He's been in film after film and even won an Emmy for his role of the agent on the TV series "The Fabulous Teddy Z." Alex was a gruff-talking guy, but I knew when I saw him I'd always get a kiss on both cheeks. Those Italians.

So, when Steve and I first met, we were on the set of a film we both had roles in called "Scenes From The Goldmine." I was portraying the drummer in the band, Timothy B. Schmidt (from the Eagles) was playing the bass player, Catherine Mary Stewart (from "The Last Starfighter") was playing the girl singer in the band, while Steve played the brother and agent of the lead singer (Cameron Dye from "Valley Girl") and Joe Pantoliano ("The Sopranos") played the Hollywierd record exec.

When Steve walked onto the set, the two of us just said our formal hellos, glad to meet you's and left it at that. Steve was quite an intense guy. You could see in his eyes alone why he got the role of Manson. Those eyes could bore right through you. We didn't talk much, except to acknowledge each other's entertainment history and that we were both from Texas.

We had been filming for a couple of days and I just couldn't get close to him. Finally, one cool evening, Steve, Timothy and I had a scene together in the parking lot. I was supposed to say, "Way to go Harry" and walk off to my left. We practiced our lines couple of times, got our marks and the director said "let's shoot it." So, when it came time for my line, I changed it and said, "Way to go Harry" then I slapped Steve on his upper arm and grabbed and pinched his cheek between my thumb and fingers and said, "You done splendid." At that point I saw the glaze come off of his eyes. His eyes followed me off the scene. Marc Rocco, the director, yells "cut" and says to me, "Coley, whatever you just did, do it again. That was great." I was forever changing lines, most of the time without asking. They pretty much let me go, because they liked what I would say better than the original lines. I also learned a very valuable lesson. All the lines that I had changed and altered were mine. When the movie came out, the original screenwriters still got the credit for it. Not me. Smart. Very smart. Yeah, change whatever you want to sucker. . . I mean Coley.

The next day, Danny Eisenberg, the producer came to me and said, "I don't know what you did to Steve, but he informed me this morning that if he's got to share a trailer with another actor it's got to be you."

Steve and I got to be good friends. He had been blown away because he once asked me what the largest crowd I'd ever played to had been. I told him "About a hundred thousand or so in Austin, Texas with Fleetwood Mac, Steve Miller, Firefall, Chicago and The Band." We even flew a helicopter into the stage area. He said he'd only played to about a thousand. I could see him doing the math in his head wondering how much money we'd made.

He made me tell that story to Scott Glenn (Urban Cowboy, Silverado) when we all had lunch on Steve's first film as a director, "The Spy Within." Scott said he didn't think he'd ever seen a hundred thousand people at one time. I told him it could be frightening especially if they hadn't taken baths and the wind was blowing in your general direction.

I asked him if he did much riding. He told me "only motorcycles." He hated horses. I found that amusing especially since he'd done so many cowboy pictures. He did have some great stories about being in "Silverado" and "Silence Of The Lambs" though.

I think Steve, Joe Pantoliano and Marc and Danny, the director and producer of "Scenes From The Goldmine" set me up one day. They asked me to do a scene that wasn't in the script. They were always giving me extra lines to say so it wasn't an unusual request. In the new scene I was supposed to be drinking at the bar, turn and see the cocktail waitress and in my most suave Sean Connery pickup voice say, "The name's Bond. Kenny . . . Bond." That was the name of my character in the film.

I thought she wasn't bad looking, but a little big boned. Not my style in women. She obviously worked out and had huge bicep muscles bulging from her sleeveless dress. I just assumed that she was a body builder. So, before we start the rehearsal they introduced me to the waitress and quickly scurried away. I was friendly as usual, and said "Hello." Then in the manliest, lowest and most gravelly voice I'd ever heard on a woman in my life, she said, "Hi, my name's Hope." I could almost see a beard begin to grow on her as I stood there.

With a pinched-up face I looked over at the four of them and they're all looking in my direction and laughing at me. They'd set me up with a guy in drag. I just stood there thinking, "There's going to be blood on the walls before we leave here today."

I turned back to him/her/it and said, "Hi. My name's Naive."

Come to find out, she claimed she really was a woman . . . on steroids or testosterone or something else manly. Who knows. I didn't do any hands on investigating. I just took her word for it. Maybe she actually did used to be a man that got hooked on steroids, but it changed her or him. I guess if you value your manhood, stay away from steroids. But, I'll admit . . . she, he or it certainly did have some big muscles.

****

I also got set up by another actress on the same film, Pamela Springsteen. Yep, you guessed it. The sister of Bruce. She was beginning to act in films and had gotten some acting roles and later went on to producing videos. Now, it's tough to make it on your own in this business, but, it's even more difficult, at best, to follow in the footsteps of a sibling that has made it big time.

She privately told me one day that she had spoken to her brother Bruce about me being in the film with her and he told her how much he liked my music. She even told me how he had told her to give me his number and to call him about opening a couple of shows for him and the "E Street Band."

I was floored, but acting as cool as possible, of course. Bruce Springsteen. Cooler than cool.

Then I said, "Really. He said that?"

"No. I was just acting. Did I get you though? Tell me? Did you really believe me? . . . I've been studying real hard," she enthusiastically said.

I'd been had. Major league had. As long as I have been in the business I couldn't believe I fell for that. But she was so sweet. Looked more innocent than green. You couldn't help but like her.

"Yep. You had me. Your timing was perfect. Those classes are paying off. You're a pretty good little actress all right" I dumbly said.

She's smiling and happy. Her day's been made.

"I've gotta watch out for you, don't I," I mumbled. "But in case you talk to Bruce, here's my number."

She seemed pleased. I'm still waiting for Bruce to call. I'm sure he will. And Bruce, if you've lost my number, I'm in the book.

****

Back to Steve. Steve was a gifted actor and studied the "method acting" style. I recall once I did a short film with him and Doug McClure called "Aces and Eights." Steve and I were in the first part of the film as cowboys in a deadly fateful game of poker. Steve's character was the really cold, mean-spirited, bad guy and my character was in the game because he happened to be the friend of the card player that Steve kills

We filmed in Northern California in an old ranch house and it had to be 30 degrees in there. There was no furnace or heat until the end of the shoot. We filmed all night long and were freezing. I played a former Confederate soldier and was dressed in a hat and Confederate long gray coat. Even the long johns were no help. Steve was dressed only in a thin shirt and vest. We were all trying not to blow smoke when we delivered our lines so as not to show just how doggone cold it was. Steve was chilled to the bone and shaking like a leaf in a cold February blue norther, teeth chattering and rubbing his hands to generate some heat. Then Lee McConnell, the director said "Quiet on the set." The slate board claps out the numbered scene and Lee quietly said "Action." All this time Steve has slowly been calming himself down to the point that by looking at him you would have thought that it was the middle of August, at the beach and Steve was as warm and comfortable as a baby in his mother's laundry basket. He was entirely focused on the task at hand.

He said his lines, completely calm. It's a great take. As soon as the director yells, "Cut", Steve sat there for about five seconds and then all of a sudden began to violently shiver and shake exactly the way he had done before the take. He's freezing. I was laughing myself silly watching him.

I said, "Man, you are one focused guy."

He shot back, "I'm freezing my can off. We should be getting paid for this. I'm only doing this because you asked me to."

So, I told him to shut up and act like a man. Next thing I know he's throwing punches and I'm dodging them, getting in a few good shots of my own. The crew is desperately trying to separate us, my wife is yelling at me to stop, Steve's yelling that I broke his nose and he and his agent both are going to sue me. The makeup people are furious at us because it's cold and they don't want to remake us up, the director's trying to get it all on film, I'm claiming mutual combat and . . . .

No. Wait a minute. My mistake. That was a dream I had about Neil Diamond. I'm mixing up my stories. It's hard to tell which is which anymore, but I do remember that particular dream had a happy ending . . . for me.

Anyway, that's how I learned to be a "method-musician" by watching Steve Railsback. Did you know the swastika on his forehead when he played Manson was the first temporary tattoo? He started a whole cottage industry. I don't think he got credit for it though.

****

One Saturday night my wife, Dana, and I invited Steve and his wife Marcy to a polo match that we'd gotten tickets for. Dana and I were horse people and spent a lot of our time at the Equestrian Center in Burbank. We got to the arena early and lo and behold there happened to be some sponsors for one of the polo teams throwing what looked to us like a come-one, come-all party. It wasn't.

So, the four of us just walked in. Now understand, polo can be a very snooty sport, or at least the people that attend them can be. Horses are just horses, people are not. Refer to the scene in the film "Pretty Woman" where the ascot crowd was so rich and uptight, but had no soul and you could freeze ice on their rear ends. Lovely picture.

When we first got there we ran into an old guy that used to manage Steve, but his claim to fame was that he had discovered Farah Fawcett and kept talking about it like somehow it was important. He kept using his cane to point out things. He even patted my wife Dana on the head when she said something. I guess he had a thing for blondes. I can understand that. It was a nice evening. We were all having a good time. The sun was setting and the air was filled with the smell of horse manure and other stable odors. I was right at home. Then it all came crashing down. Just like high school, another debutante ball I wasn't invited to.

We were eating all their or'horves, hor durves, heck . . . appetizers, that weren't that good, but must have cost the ascot crowd a bundle. The four of us were talking amongst ourselves, watching the people and wondering why would any of them actually pay five hundred dollars for a forty dollar dress or how many "Meals On Wheels" one woman's ridiculous hat could buy. All the time, they pretended to ignore us and continued chatting amongst themselves, nodding to other guests and maybe talking about their various infectious diseases or something closely related. Next thing we knew, this woman in a white polka dot dress and a security guard came up to us. People all over the room were suspiciously glaring at us, talking in hushed tones to each other and questioning how the riffraff got into their up-tight, phoney-boloney, L.A. party.

Needless to say, we were about as welcome as another tax increase. They rudely asked us to leave. I was obnoxiously explaining, "Don't you know who I am?

Wait, here's my American Express card. No, wait, I don't carry American Express, but I have a passport, although the picture doesn't really capture my inner beauty nor does me justice."

With a half-eaten cracker in his mouth, Steve started telling them what a lousy party it is and to remove him from their list and never ever call him again. He handed the woman part of his half-eaten pate and we were abruptly escorted out. At that point, Steve turned around quickly, stuck his head back in the tent and yells out, "And I hope your horses get a polo stick up their wahzoo and you lose."

The four of us were roaring with laughter for a couple of minutes and finally Steve said, "Whoa. That was fun. Let's go crash some other parties."

Our reputations preceded us before we got there.

However, I did learn something that evening that has helped me on many occasions. If you stick your nose up in the air just a little bit, it can actually give you the appearance of being taller. Something like an optical illusion, provided your nose is clean. I don't know why I tell you this. I just had this overwhelming sensation that someone out there might find it useful.

****

Another time, Joe Pantoliano took a bunch of guys out to a female impersonator club to watch the show before Steve got married. Not my idea of a bachelor party. Both Steve and I were very uncomfortable in there and we made a quick pact and both vowed to come to the aid of the other in the event of . . . well, anything that didn't set right with us. Extremely weird waiters . . . or were they waitresses in there? All I know was ours needed a shower. It was cave dark in the club and you didn't want to touch anything or have to go to the bathroom.

Joe was having a great time. He had been with us in "Scenes From The Goldmine" and was in a lot of great films like "The Goonies," "Empire of the Sun," "The Fugitive," and most recently on "The Sopranos." Joe was always a very amusing and spontaneous guy and fun to be with. You're never lacking entertainment with Joe around.

I'd had a big scene with him, Steve and Lee Ving in "Scenes From The Goldmine." In the film the band was supposed to be shooting a music video while some sissy makeup guy is persistant about wanting to cut off my beard. I was supposed to be furious and defending myself against the director, record company exec and everyone else. It was a fun scene to shoot except for one small detail. I had been greatly lied to about this particular scene. It called for me to be without a shirt. The producers had assured me that I would have muscles for the scene. I didn't. I guess props forgot to order them for me. They say that TV or film adds about ten pounds to you. It must have put on an additional twenty or thirty pounds because of the beard. Those things are heavy you know. Did you also hear that being on TV or film can cause your chest to drop down to where your stomach is? Amazing how that works. Watching the scene reminded me of the song, "I Just Don't Look Good Naked Anymore."

So, anyway, back to Sodom and Gomorrah and the bachelor party. The show started and these five fake girls came out doing a dance routine. Steve leaned over and whispered to me, "Are those girls or guys?"

It was hard to tell, but I took a hard look and said, "Those two on the end are girls, I'm certain. The other three are men . . . or some such thing."

Steve was looking real hard. Much to my surprise, they had begun to use a couple of girls as dancers and I had picked them out. Can't fool me for long. Men and women look different. I've seen pictures.

Anyway, the next act up was this man about sixty years old. He had heavy makeup on and a large aquiline nose. What was left of his grey hair was parted just above his left ear and the few strands were swept over the top of his bald head. The most ludicrous thing was the fact that he was dressed in a small spaghetti-strapped, low-cut, white party dress with bony, bony knees and hairy tarantula-like legs. He stood with one hand on the microphone, one leg forward, one leg back, just staring out at the audience. His other hand was positioned oh-so femininely on his hip. Most everyone was laughing at him.

I've been a spectator at many strange, humanly degrading and disgusting things in my 35 or so years, but hands down, this was one of the most pathetic, embarrassing and humiliating sights I had ever witnessed. I think chiefly because he seemed dead serious. I started to feel sorry for the guy. As everyone continued to laugh at him, he bravely stood there staring back until the laughter died down.

All of a sudden, in the deepest, New Jersey longshoreman accent I'd ever heard he said, "Ay . . . let me tell ya 'bout the time I was down in Jwersay woykin' da docks."

I was on the floor laughing myself silly. That I didn't expect. As a matter of fact, that entire evening I didn't expect. It didn't bother me except I was wondering why no women have ever tried to impersonate me? That'd be worth the price of admission.

****

Another time, my wife and I had gone to see Todd Rundgren. Todd had written one of the songs that Dan and I had recorded, "Love Is The Answer." I think he wrote it on a day when he didn't have his hair painted pink and purple. I had been an admirer of his music long before we recorded his song. If you get a chance, check out his "Healing" CD. It's a classic.

"Love Is The Answer" was a song clothed in spiritual ambiguity and of all the "hits" Dan and I were blessed with, this was my personal favorite. However, it came at a very troubling and turbulent point in American history. It was a time of great confusion that caused a tremendous amount of division within our country. The demarcation lines were pretty well defined, still, even to this day. You didn't know who you could trust, what side they were on. I remember during this disorderly period that children were rebelling against their parents and the clothes got really weird. There was fighting in the streets with people spitting on each other and Hollywood began to make really bad and unnecessary movies about the results from it, even now, still affect some people very negatively and you can especially see its impact on our children and their music today. You were either for it, or dead set against it. I was one of those against it. I hated just about everything about it and could see no redeeming qualities about it. I personally suffered some emotional anxiety and psychological trauma during this time period. By now, I'm certain that the majority of you realize that I'm referring to the "Disco Era."

Now, I know that some of you might have really liked it. But then again you should be ashamed of yourselves. It's not that I didn't like it. It's just, that . . . well, I didn't like it. I recently picked my kids up one day from a school bowling outing and heard this music over and over while I bowled a couple of games. As I listened, my only comment was "What in the world could we have been thinking?"

Although, in retrospect, I do concede to the fact that I was a good five inches taller during that time. Those high heel shoes were cool. However, "Love Is The Answer" was the only song in the top ten that year that wasn't disco. If that fact alone doesn't' prove to you that God is alive and well and He obviously loves me very much, then you might be looking a little too hard.

Anyway, Todd's manager, Eric always gave me passes to see Todd whenever he was in town. Although Todd and I had spoken several times on the phone, the very first time I saw him perform live and met him was in San Diego. I had always wanted to record his "Can We Still Be Friends" song. When I saw him that time he was playing solo. On some songs that evening, he'd play with an acoustic guitar, or piano, or with a computer and even would sing a couple of songs acapella. I've played with a bizillion music acts and all I wanted him to do that evening was stop playing. Just stop. Was he really bad? Was he singing off key? No. I'd never been as impressed with an artist as I was with Todd that evening. I was so inspired that all I wanted to do was to go home and play my guitar and piano. He was the most inspiring artist I think I'd ever seen.

The next time Todd came to L.A. I went to see him at the Wiltern Theatre. This time he was using a band and was more of the rock star image.

About half-way through the show, a girl came in and sat in the end seat next to me and my wife, Dana. After the show was over, we all waited in our seats for the after-party. This lady was very pretty and had sort of strawberry-blonde hair. I noticed that she had on a backstage pass like we did. I began to talk with her and asked how she knew Todd. She said her name was Cassandra Peterson and that she was handled by Eric, the same management as Todd. I didn't really catch the name, but I figured she was a singer or something. However, when I asked her if she was a musician, she said no. I then asked what she did. She quietly said she was an actress. So, being an actor myself, I pried a little further and asked which agency represented her. She haltingly told me that she didn't have a film agent and that Eric was handling her. Now, that's not usually a good sign. So I figured she was just starting out. Although she was very polite, I didn't seem to be getting very far with this line of conversation. So I finally asked if she'd been in any films or TV. The beautiful shrinking violet got quiet and a little embarrassed at all the attention. She said she had done some films. "Like what?" I politely asked.

Finally, with a very sheepish voice, she confessed. She looked at us apologetically and almost under her breath said, "I play Elvira. You know. Mistress of the dark."

My wife's eyes got as big as a harvest moon and she immediately leaned forward and said to her, "You've got a great act. Playing that role must be a blast. You're funny."

I jumped in, "I've seen you a lot. Wait. Then weren't you also the biker chick in "Pee Wee's Big Adventure?"

Surprised, she said, "Yeah. You saw that?" At this point, she seemed to relax a little and let her guard down.

So I told her, "We love Pee Wee Herman. He makes me laugh. And whether you like him or not, anyone that would appear on nationwide TV on the MTV awards after being caught in a scandal like he did and have to live with all the snide remarks and crude jokes and then challenge the audience by asking 'Heard any good jokes lately?' has something going for him."

She finally asked how we knew Todd. I told her we didn't know him personally, but I was an agent for the Internal Revenue Service and we were here to confiscate his earnings from the show for back taxes. Then I asked her if she owed Uncle Sam anything while we were here, maybe save us a trip.

Now, she was really curious about who she was talking to. I told her to guess. She said something about me looking like that guy that hung out with Cher. So, before the conversation completely went south I told her who I was. Three times I told her. I remember when it clicked for her who I was, all she said was, "Oh."

I was really let down by her response. About the time I was going to list out a couple of my songs, in characteristic Elvira, she said, "I know your songs. I was just acting."

I guess Elvira showed up. I always liked Elvira but now I liked the person that played her.

I'd always enjoyed watching Elvira's zany behavior on her shows, but I would have never recognized her in a million years sitting next to me. Elvira's bold and brassy and has that big black hair thing going, among other things. Cassandra seemed shy and quiet. I love the contrast. That low cut black dress must just bring out another personality. She was very sweet and told us she had been getting a lot of flak about her character and it had made her a little cautious. We told her to ignore it. It was probably from people who wished they had come up with the concept for Elvira.

We all went to the after-party together. You never know who you might be sitting next to.

Chapter 21

THE ILLUSION OF MOVIES

The older you are, the more slowly you read a contract.

Leonard Lewis Levison

Another film that I was involved in was "Dream A Little Dream." Although I only had a small role in it about three-quarters of the way through, it was one of my most enjoyable films to be in. I got to beat up Cory Feldman, drug Meredith Salenger, kiss Susan Blakely, be an absolute evil creep on screen and although I didn't film at the same time as they did, be able to say I had been in a film with Jason Robards and Harry Dean Stanton.

It was my second film with Marc Rocco and Danny Eisenberg. I was only scheduled for three days worth of work. Thanks to Susan Blakely for pulling me into more scenes with her and the fact that none of the kids in the film knew their lines, I ended up staying for two weeks. I really looked forward to this, because although the part wasn't much, it gave me a chance to do some image changing on screen. I got practice almost from the first instant I landed in Wilmington, North Carolina.

I went straight from the airport to the film set. I got there around midnight and one of the first people I ran into was the make-up girl I had worked with before on a couple of different films. She asked me to stand by her and protect her from some guy on the set who'd been hitting on her. My chivalry kicked in and I said ok. As I got to where the filming was going on I saw Corey Feldman ("Stand By Me," "Goonies," "Lost Boys") and Corey Haim ("Lucas," "Lost Boys," etc). (also referred to as "The Two Coreys") walking down the sidewalk doing their scene. They messed up and started laughing. As Marc Rocco, the director, dropped his head and yelled "cut", people groaned and rushed to reset the scene. The camera people start cussing. In a couple of minutes, they began the scene again. The slateboard slapped and he yelled out, "Take 23!"

Take 23? You've got to be kidding me. Take 23?! I'd have pulled those boys off to the side after "take four" and we'd have had a short, but serious talk where I did all the talking. I thought, "This film's going to go way over budget." It did.

On my first film for these guys, I happened to ask the producer, Danny Eisenberg, how much a roll of film stock cost. He told me approximately $600.00 for a roll of film that lasted about ten minutes. I gasped. After that, I never messed up my lines again. I learned them well.

So, next I was introduced to King Baggot when he came over to flirt with the make-up girl. He was the Director of Photography (DP) and also the man who found the gun Tex Watson used at the Sharon Tate murders. The DP really had the control of the film and lighting. He could make you look good or he could make you look really bad. He looked at me in a distinctly sharp manner. He then headed back to the cluster of film crew and after a second or so they all looked my direction. After that, the make-up girl explains that he's the one that had been hitting on her.

Now, I was really ticked. My sense of chivalry headed South in a heartbeat and I harshly said to her, "You mean the DP is the one that's hitting on you? Why didn't you tell me he was the DP!? Do you realize what kind of lights, if any, I get now? He's going to make me look horrible!" Self-preservation in the film industry is essential and it can take a real bite out of any sense of honor.

I figured I'd had enough for one day, but I was getting into my film character's personality quickly.

I waited around on the set for four days before I even got to get in front of a camera. I had only originally been scheduled for three days of shooting. I was being treated pretty coldly by the crew and especially the camera operators. It seemed to work from the DP all the way down.

Finally, my first scene came up. I was supposed to stop Corey Feldman from coming into the house. I portrayed Ron, a yuppie (so that I really knew I was acting) and Susan Blakely was my girlfriend in the film. Susan didn't feel it was right for me not to be in the scene at the house with her when Corey Feldman came by. So, I landed in a lot of footage I wasn't scripted for. In the first blocking rehearsal, I do admit, I hit Corey a little too hard. Since the very first night and after four days of waiting around and being snubbed, I'd developed a lot of pent-up hostility. It all came out on poor ol' Corey. I almost knocked him backwards down the stairs and off the porch. He complained to the director. I didn't apologize, but smiled at him. That was just the first of several throw downs, wrestling matches, knocking-his-hand-away and pushing-him-away-from-the-door experiences I had. However, he was a good kid with a smart mouth. Fortunately, I liked Corey. Otherwise, I could have hurt him easily.

I got the feeling that I had been quite convincing in my acting abilities. After that rehearsal, no one ignored me anymore. As a matter of fact, it was "Mr. Coley this, Mr. Coley that. Is your trailer good? Do you want a soft drink, cheese whiz, crackers, just don't hit me." And that was just from the camera crew. Even the King was nice to me from then on. I had to tell people to use my first name. Some did, some preferred to still use Mr. Coley.

At the end of two weeks, I was pretty much done. I had roughed up as many people as I could. I had had a good time, but working with kids had shown me that I didn't want my children in the acting profession. When they grow up, the decision is theirs. But there was no parental control. Especially fathers. Even for the ones that had mothers there; the kids ran the show and the parents catered to their every whim. They lived vicariously through their children's experiences and had none of their own. Sad.

Several years later, I happened to drop off some photos to my film agent one day on my way to Disneyland with my family. I took my youngest son in with me. They were all over him like piranha on a bare naked leg with steak sauce on it. "John, get us photos. We can get him parts. He's perfect for it. Look at those big eyes. He's cute; he's blond, ca-ching, ca-ching."

I picked him up and said, "Nope. You stay away from my son. I've seen what happens to kids in the film industry."

They tried to coax me into it all the way to the door. They failed.

At the premiere of "Dream A Little Dream," I received my biggest compliment of my acting career. I had taken my oldest daughter, Ahnjayla to see it at the Mann's Chinese Theatre in Hollywood. It was a big deal. Everyone was there. Alissa Milano, Gary Busey, Roger Rabbit. I even got to see Herb Alpert again who sat a couple of rows in front of me.

In the scene where I gave Meredith Salenger a glass of spiked wine, and then acted like I was her best friend, the lady seated in front of me, blurted out loud through gritted teeth, "What a jerk!"

I looked at my daughter. Her wide-eyed expression was one of, "Daddy, be kind. She obviously doesn't know what she's saying."

I just looked at her, smiled and winked. Great compliment. I did my job.

I tapped the lady on the shoulder and when she turned around I said, "Thank you very much."

Her eyes got big and she slumped down a little in her seat.

I said to my daughter, "Funny thing about it is, she probably doesn't realize I'm acting and possibly even thinks that I'm really like that."

My daughter looked back at me. "You are," she said.

"You mean I wasn't acting?" I said back.

I love the illusion of movies.

****

Sometimes you get caught on the wrong kind of film.

My wife, Dana and I, (is it "I" or "me?" I never get that right, I studied literature not grammar) had gone to Santa Barbara for the film premiere of "The Spy Within" with Scott Glenn and Teresa Russell. We had both written some songs for it and this was Steve Railback's directorial debut after Clint Eastwood (who, by the way, is a mighty fine cowboy actor and after he reads this will hopefully make another "Outlaw Josie Wales") told Steve he would be a perfect director. We were really proud of Steve and wanted to be there for him.

As we got closer to Santa Barbara, the heavens opened and cascaded down a torrential gully washer and most of the town got flooded. Cars were stranded everywhere along with drowning frogs.

We were attempting to get downtown to the theater but the streets were choked off with rain water. It was getting closer and closer to the time of the film's screening. So, I foolishly attempted to go through rising water. The water flooded our car and we got stranded in the middle of the rising river. We were in a fire engine red BMW so you couldn't miss us while the water continued to rise. The water was barely above my door and I had to get out of the car and try to push it out of the water. I'm up to mid-thigh in running water, filled with all sorts of animal feces, muck and smudge. It's cold outside and the water is even colder. My mom and dad almost drowned in a flash flood in New Mexico when I was in my teens, so I'm getting fresh encouragement from their story to get out of this mess and quickly.

About the time I'm getting the car pushed to drier land, two guys jump out and start helping me push. Then all of a sudden, blinding lights flip on and lo and behold there's a local TV film crew filming the unfortunate people stranded in the ice cold flood water for the evening news. The other guys are waving, slipping down and splashing water at each other like they're at Camp Drownyourrumpus or something and obviously have never heard anything about hepatitis. I'm sure the film crew is hoping that someone actually gets drowned and dies, so they catch it all on film and can sell it to "Real TV" and make a bundle of even colder cash or else get to move to a news station in a bigger town where real news happens.

I'm thinking, "I'm not going to a film premiere looking like this."

We ended up on the evening news. I looked like a drowned rat. My blonde wife is waving to them out the red BMW window, telling them to "come on in, the water's fine."

I'm drenched and could probably make a drowned rat look good, but trained to smile for the camera. The car engine won't start. The distributor's wet. I'm cold. I squish when I walk and we're missing the premiere with all-you-eat-free buttered popcorn.

When the car did finally start, the premiere was well over. However, we couldn't get out of town to go back home. All of the roads were shut down because they're flooded. Cars stuck everywhere up to the wheel wells in water. The freeway has had landslides, mud blocking both directions and we're stuck in the outskirts of Santa Barbara. Oh yeah, it's a nice little town when all the seafood places are open and you can walk up and down State Street in a hypnotic Yuppie trance and buy all sorts of kitchy, useless things and "Baby on board" placards and pretend that you're in an outside cafe somewhere in Paris making fun of the people walking by in their plaid, stock-broker shorts and argyle socks with penny-loafers, while you're drinking 873 different blends of exotic coffee and eating pastries that never seem to have enough sugar in them and you're trying to figure out how many run on sentences you can come up with and still say it all in one breath. Neat little side-show. But right now all the hotels were filled up and we couldn't move because the blasted town was under water and Noah's Ark is still stuck on Mt. Arafat somewhere. Scuba diving was an option, but I don't scuba dive.

My wife removed her black spandex leggings from underneath her dress and gave them to me so I'd have dry pants. Now I look like a guy ballerina or whatever they're called. I have no dry socks, we have to spend the night in the car and I'm in women's clothing. Unlike some people I knew in L.A., I wouldn't be caught dead or alive in this stuff at home much less out in the public eye, thank you very much. Thank God I was in California that night instead of Nebraska or something. I'd have some tall explaining to do. All the department stores are closed and Wal Mart doesn't open for another eight hours, so I can't get any sweats or dry clothes. (And I'm re-living this once again, just when I thought I was over all of this trauma-drama with its resident psychological scaring long ago, so obviously the therapy didn't help).

Anyway, very early the next morning we were able to get to a "Denny's" for some breakfast, or whatever it was they were passing off as breakfast. The place was filled to the brim with other stranded travelers. However, according to the way they were dressed, I don't think any of them got wet or spent the night in their car.

I'm walking past people to the booth in my finest ladies skintight spandex leggings and I'm starting to question my mental health now because those things are starting to feel good. I was getting visions of "Tootsie" and I'll be singing Stephen Bishop's songs soon. My shoes are still squishing and it's hard to deny that the footprints of water left on the floor behind me are not mine. My voice drops about three octaves into my most manly man's voice as I go past people. Especially guys. I say to them, "Hey. What's up?" They pretend not to pay any attention, but I know they're thinking I'm some weirdo from one of the even more weirder sections of Hollywood. But, I'm not. I'm really in an, until now, undiscovered version of Hell that's been completely omitted from "Dante's Inferno," and it's located on the outskirts of Santa Barbara, California.

There are times you feel like you're in the middle of "Spinal Tap," which is really a good film. At least the first ten minutes are. Then it starts to hit too close to home.

All I need to make this less than religious experience complete is to hear "Hi, John. Nice . . . pants," turn and see Steve Railsback, the actor-turned-director and Clint Eastwood, chief-instigator-of-turning-actors-into-directors, staring and pointing at me. Image is everything in Hollywood.

But, as I scan the restaurant for anyone I know I should hide from, no one has any clue what's going on in my soggy head.

I'm thinking, "That's the last dang time I go to a film premiere out of town, friends or not and definitely not without a change of men's clothes in the trunk."

And that, Steve, is the reason we didn't show up to the premiere. I mean it.

Chapter 22

MUSICIANS

Good judgment comes from experience. And experience?

Well, that comes from bad judgment.

Anonymous

Welcome to my world. The "normal" everyday life of a musician where all the pieces fit and we all pay our bills on time.

I think one of the biggest thrills I ever had was when I had just moved to L.A. from Dallas. Friends of mine would come out from Texas to either try and get recording deals or just to see a grossly over-populated city, Disneyland, attempt to use their high school Spanish and hope to experience all the charm of an earthquake before they went home.

A couple of the people that used to come to my house and sleep on the couch was B.W. (Buckwheat) Stevenson and Mickey Raphael. Mickey ended up playing harmonica for Willie Nelson from about 1972 on. Mickey was funny. He'd whisper all these funny things to people on stage, but would never say them into the microphone himself. Then, whoever he said it too would relay it to the audience like it was his own original thought, or at least until it wasn't a funny original thought and then they'd blame Mickey.

B.W., Dan and I had played at a folk club called the Rubiyat in Dallas and became great friends. B.W. was a big guy with a soft heart and a hard exterior and almost always wore a black Stetson on his head. He had been a bull-rider and was also a very gifted singer/songwriter, but a complete misfit in the peace and love '60's that drifted into the early '70's. I remember once when we were at the store down the street from my place and this huge anti-longhair type saw B.W., and asked him what he'd do if he took his hat. B.W. looked him dead in the eye and calmly replied, "I'd break your ****** arm." The guy said that he thought all us longhairs were peace and love types. B.W. told him "Well you figured wrong didn't cha." The guy left him alone in a hurry.

One night I took B.W. to the Troubador club when we were opening for Carole King. He even played a song for her in our dressing room. Carole was very gracious in listening to his song, especially since she was getting hit on all the time for people to get her attention. B.W eventually recorded "Shambala" and then he and Three Dog Night went to battle over it on the radio stations. B.W. lost. However, he went on to write "My Maria" and had a huge hit with it. Even Brooks and Dunn had a hit with it a couple of years ago.

B.W. moved back to Texas, even though we tried to get him to stay in L.A. We figured he'd have much more success there. He told me, "I was born in Texas and I'll die in Texas." He proceeded to do just that. What an absolute waste. B.W. died of a heart attack in Dallas. Couldn't have been forty. He had some serious talent cut down way too short.

However, B.W. and Mickey had formed a really close relationship with Ali MacGraw from "Love Story," and Steve McQueen. Both B.W. and Mickey had been around at the set where McQueen and MacGraw were filming "The Getaway" in Texas.

Now, Steve McQueen had been one of my all-time favorite actors since he was first in the TV series "Wanted: Dead or Alive." I think I'd seen just about everything he'd ever filmed, including "Junior Bonner." I still watch "The Great Escape" every chance I can. I even had a large poster of him on his motorcycle from the "The Great Escape" on my dormitory wall my first year of college. If James Dean was cool, Steve McQueen was the epitome of cool on screen.

One morning I was up kind of early and the house was pretty quiet. Everyone was sleeping and I was looking out of my window to see if I could see the mountains. I had lived in my apartment in Glendale for about two weeks before I knew there were mountains surrounding me. The smog was so thick I could never see them. Anyway, all of a sudden the phone rang. I jumped over to pick it up pretty quick so as not to wake anyone up. This real low, gravelly voice that sounded like he'd been drinking all night, hadn't quit yet, didn't plan on it and hadn't slept in a week said, "Is B.W. there?"

I could almost see the weeks' worth of unshaved beard growth on this guy and told him that B.W. had been out pretty late and was still asleep. Who was calling? The man on the phone says,

"Oh . . . well . . . just tell him Steve McQueen called."

Whoa! Steve McQueen is calling my house and I'm talking to him. Life is good. My friends back home are going to be so impressed.

So, having the presence of mind to think sharply that early in the morning, I quickly said, "Well, let me get him up. I'm sure he'll want to talk to you." I tried to sound so nonchalant. I don't think I did a very good job at it. That's when I figured I needed acting lessons.

Anyway, I'm calling all my friends back in Dallas, telling everyone that Steve McQueen keeps calling my house all the time. Yeah, he's got my number. They're impressed. I think I have successfully proved to everyone that I went to high school with that I'm a "somebody" now. Yep. I'm running with the big dogs. They were smart to be friends with me. Just wait for my ten-year reunion. I'll probably win the "Most Successful" trophy.

After that, Steve's inviting me over to his house on the beach all the time. We're watching re-runs of his films, Ali's out in the backyard fixing steaks on the grill and Steve's teaching me how to jump the fence on the motorcycle like he did in 'The Great Escape" while I'm teaching him guitar chords. He's talking about how I can maybe be his stunt double since we look so much alike and he'll get me a good agent and attorney to make the best movie deals. He's grooming me to be a star. We're pals.

The next thing I know, the phone's ringing at the same time the earth is convulsing from another 3.5 earthquake and I wake up. Was it a dream? I don't know. But I do remember it was Steve on the phone. He wanted to talk to B.W. again, who slept through his first earthquake.

****

Sometimes you learn some valuable lessons through your experiences. This happened on the set of "Scenes From The Goldmine."

There was this young girl that really wanted to be in the film. She was quite friendly and tried to talk to me about music and things like that. I was the former rock star turned actor and she was impressed that I had accumulated all these hits and what was it like to have so many hits, travel around the world and make a living doing what you really love, and are the Gold Records really gold, etc, etc. She was songwriter too and even got to have a song in the film. Her song was the very last one in the film and I was in the scene playing piano on it. It was a very good song. She was a good songwriter. She asked me if I wanted to write with her sometime. I should have written something with her.

She was even able to get a couple of speaking lines in the film as the dress shop clerk. I think they might have taken out her line in the final cut though. My entire final scene with Catherine Mary Stewart ended up on the editing room floor. It happens to the best of us. Ask Kevin Costner about "The Big Chill." (He was the dead guy whose face was never shown).

I never did anything musically with this young girl. A couple of years later, she was taking home Grammy Awards. Melissa Ethridge was her name. Forgive me Melissa for not writing with you, but I am available next Tuesday.

****

I traveled to Nashville in the spring of 1999 and had a lunch appointment with Harry Warner at BMI. Harry had managed Jerry Reed and was a great one for stories of the town. As we drove down Music Row, he looked over to his right and said, "I see an old buddy's car. Would you mind if I asked him to have lunch with us?"

I didn't mind. It's always great to meet new people.

We went into an office and I saw the back of this older gentleman sitting in a chair facing the desk talking with the secretary. I didn't pay much attention and walked around to the other side of them. Just then Harry said, "John, I'd like for you to meet Chet Atkins."

My mouth dropped open and my jaw was hanging down to my belly button. In one swift movement, my left hand grabbed the hat off my head in respect while at the same time my other hand shot out to shake hands with him. I don't think my hat has ever come off of my head as quickly as it did that day. He chuckled at my klutzy, twisted up mannerisms and said, "I know your name. You play good music."

Wow. This was musical royalty as far as I was concerned. To meet Chet Atkins was one thing; to get to have lunch with him was an extraordinary unforeseen honor. He told some terrific stories.

I think my favorite was how he had once gone on a cruise ship with his wife. She had made him promise that he wouldn't bring that "infernal" guitar along. This was to be a complete vacation for them both and a guitar would just bring up business and she needed the vacation. Chet reluctantly acquiesced. His wife was in heaven. A real vacation for once. However, about the second day out, he needed his guitar fix. That's a thing that happens to us musicians. If you don't play, you'll never understand it. But, it's very much like an addiction, complete with shakes and everything.

At any rate, Chet was walking alone on the deck and spied a fellow playing a guitar. He said he looked around for his wife. When he didn't see her he then decided to sit down next to the man in hopes of getting his hands on the man's guitar. Chet listened to the man play for a while and then asked him if he would mind if he played his guitar. The man passed it over and Chet began to play. Chet played and played. Finally the man said to him, "You're a pretty good guitar picker. Mind you, you ain't no Chet Atkins or nothing, but you're still pretty good."

Chet said he just thanked the man for the use of his guitar and never told him who he was. All of this occurred without his wife knowing. She later told him how happy and relaxed he looked and that they needed more vacations like this one, without the guitar, naturally. Chet just kept walking the decks. Alone, of course.

****

I'm a real believer in following your intuition, which to me is a language all its own. I never, under any circumstances, mess with it. I listen.

So, to show how that intuition works, listen to this. When I first came to Nashville to record "I'd Really Love To See You Tonight", Kyle Lehning, our producer, and I ran around town a little. Kyle had been an engineer over at the Glaser Brothers studio and needed to pick up some of his equipment. He showed me around the place, where he had worked with Waylon Jennings and others. I was beginning to get fidgety and the hair on the back of my neck was starting to stand up. We went back downstairs and he asked me to wait in the lobby while he packed things up. I stood around in the lobby, looking at photos on the walls, gold records and talking with the secretary. Before I knew it, I found myself anxiously pacing back and forth across the lobby. I had tried to sit down a couple of times, but I'd be right back up pacing all over again. Finally, everything in me said "Get out of here, now." I bolted from the lobby and stood in the parking lot waiting for Kyle. I don't mess with intuition. Something's being said to you . . . listen.

About twenty minutes later, here comes Kyle. He said, "I've been looking all over for you. How long have you been out here?"

I said back, "I decided to wait here in the parking lot for you. There's something really wrong inside that building."

Kyle read me for a second, shook his head and pursed his lips. Then he said, "It took me over two years to figure that out. It only took you ten minutes? Wow."

He collected his stuff and we were gone. I don't know what it was that was there, but, whatever it was, it wasn't friendly and there was this high pitched maniacal, hysterical laughter. Perhaps it was the secluded coven where attorneys had secretly plotted to take over the music industry and come up with contracts 350 pages longer than the Declaration of Independence. The kind where the artists never make any money. Who knows exactly what it was. But it was that same kind of evil.

After we left, Kyle wanted to stop by and see a friend of his, Shel Silverstein, the children's author who wrote such classics as "The Giving Tree" and "Where The Sidewalk Ends" and the song "A Boy Named Sue" for Johnny Cash. Shel was at a studio recording with Bobby Bare. Shel had to be one of the most energetic people I'd ever come in contact with. He bounced from place to place. It was like watching Spider Man or Tigger. I'm trying to keep up by walking, but I'm falling far behind. He bounces us into the studio where Bare is practicing the song he's about to record. I was a fan of Bobby's and this was going to be a real treat to meet him. I can now tell everyone at home I was at a Bobby Bare recording session. Home, meaning Texas. None of my friends in L.A. would have known who he was.

Country wasn't big anymore since CBS mistakenly thought that the Beverly Hillbillies had lowered the IQ of the entire nation and they couldn't talk about banjo music without making a reference to "Deliverance" and squealing pigs. Now remember, this was before Garth, Alan Jackson, Patty Loveless, Trisha Yearwood, The Judds, Vince Gill, Restless Heart and many more really terrific country groups made Country music cool again. Plus many countless talented artists that were my personal favorites, like Rob Crosby or Georgia Middleman, or Matt King that should have made it big time, but for some reason or another got lost in the A&R shuffle.

I'll never forget the instrumentation that Bare had. He was seated at the head of the musicians on a high stool, playing an acoustic guitar, with a high cowboy hat sitting on his head and peering out through dark sunglasses. He had a Fender Rhodes electric piano player, a baby grand piano player, an acoustic guitar player, a classical catgut guitar player, an electric guitar, an electric bass, and a drum kit. Every one of these players was playing the exact same pattern. Boom, chink chink, boom, chink chink, boom, chink chink, boom, chink chink, boom.

I listened with great anticipation for Bobby to sing, because country lyrics are usually really well thought out. No one can write a lyric like a country songwriter. Nobody. Except maybe Joni Mitchell, Dan Fogelberg or Alanis Morissette.

Bobby cleared his throat and started to sing. As I listened I stood there with my mouth wide open, wondering why he needed so many instruments playing the same thing for this. However, one of his biggest hits was about to come out of that golden throat and I was there.

"Dropkick me Jesus through the goal posts of life . . . , End over end, neither left nor to right . . . ," he sang.

I stood there for a couple of seconds; eyes wide open, smiling to myself. I'm really trying not to bust out laughing thinking "That's it. That's what you're recording?"

He came to the end of the first verse, "I've got the time Lord if you've the toe . . . So drop kick me Jesus through the goal posts of life . . . ."

Then in a flash I have visions of tornadoes, hurricanes and earthquakes. The building falling down on me and everyone else, children screeching and this very apocalyptic disaster of Biblical proportions happening right before my very eyes, bodies rising out of the ground over by the Kroger store, record executives pleading for mercy and begging for forgiveness, but the forgiveness ship for them sailed long ago. Taking a lesson from Shel, I didn't hear the remainder of the song because I bounced out of there pretty quickly, just to be safe.

That vision must have just been in my mind though because the song became a hit and a classic. Heck, I was there. Just not for long.

However, to end a less than perfect day, when we drove up to Kyle's house, his wife was giving their 4-year-old son Jason a real serious tongue lashing. She's letting him know just how the cow ate the cabbage, as my momma used to say. (For those of you not from the South, this isn't a good thing). Now I always liked Jason, but I was certain that he was going to have real trouble in school because I don't think I've ever run across a brighter kid in my life. That kid was major league sharp. Sharper than most 30 year olds. Bright children don't usually do well in school. They're too far ahead already.

Jason had been playing in the street with some older children when his mom saw him out the window and was on him like stink on a skunk. She's got him in the front yard, just giving that poor boy the dicken's. She finally said, "You know not to play in the street. What in the world could you have been thinking?"

He looked up at all of us with that deer-in-the-headlights look. In his thick little Southern accent he defended himself by explaining, "Why momma . . . I must'a been temporarily outta my mind."

When kids are in trouble and say something so completely beyond their age and funny to boot, it's hard to stay in that "boy, it's too wet to plow, you're in serious trouble now" mode. What do you say? We're all doing our best not to fall over laughing, but we're turning our heads, coughing, shoving our hands deep in our pockets and clearing our throats. Jason, with his best puppy-dog face is looking dolefully up at everyone in a "Who knew?" kind of bewilderment. Kyle's wife, who is choking back her own laughter, says, "Kyle. What should we do about this?"

Kyle's a man, a problem solver, a quick-decision maker and he knew exactly how to handle this situation. So he quickly said, "I think you're doing a fine job with this on your own honey. There's really nothing more I can add."

So, we went in the backyard and played basketball. Jason is now a successful engineer/producer, just like his dad. Hanging around all those studios, I'll bet he's a good ping-pong player too.

****

I had run across Garth Brooks on several different occasions when he visited the Los Angeles area. I had been introduced to his managers, Pam Lewis and Bob Doyle, by Jennie Frankel, a girl that I had written some songs with. Pam had worked with my former partner, Dan, in Nashville and wanted to hear my side of the breakup story. I told her I didn't tell stories since lying was a Biblical prohibition and that our involvement was ten plus years ago and anyone that lived in the past was condemned to the past. It was the '90's and I had been stuck in the late '70's for years.

My wife had told me once before that I should make the move to the '90's. However, it might be a better idea if I would attempt to move into the '80's first. I'm getting closer day by day. Even though we're almost a decade into the new millennium, I think I'm personally almost up to 1989.

Pam and Bob invited my wife and me to see Garth play at a small movie theater for one of the local radio stations. I hadn't seen a country concert since I had played with Eddie Rabbit and I was prepared to listen to some good music and hear some good yarns. I was not prepared for what I saw. There were some huge country fans in L.A. and that really surprised me. Country music in L.A? Get out of town. Most people in that town didn't know one end of a horse from another or even what a horse was. Then I remembered that many in Nashville had become big country artists, with boots, belt buckle and tall Stetson cowboy hat and didn't know one end of a horse from the other either. I remember sitting in one of the songwriters-in-the-round at the

Bluebird Cafe in Nashville and one of the writers told about a country artist who also had the boots, hat and big belt buckle and on his video he was supposed to ride a horse. He had never seen a horse or saddle before. He was afraid of that big beast and ending up not riding but walking the horse around. They called these kind "all hat, no saddle" country singers.

I was not familiar with Garth Brooks music, but I certainly was after that night. I didn't know if I was at a country concert or a heavy metal concert, but I hadn't been that entertained in years. He was running around like a maniac on stage, jumping, dancing, swooning, crooning, even playing Billy Joel songs and doing them really well. So, I began to change my idea of country music. If this was country, count me in.

I met Garth later that evening and I was refreshed by his humble demeanor. A gentleman. Took off his hat and everything. I had lived in L.A. for so long that I'd forgotten what polite was.

Good talent is easy to spot if you know what to look for. I told him when I saw him a couple of days later that he had some "serious talent." I don't say things like that just because I'm at a loss for words. He told me he was completely surprised by everything that was happening to him and genuinely didn't understand what the appeal was. I told him it didn't matter if he understood it or not. Ride the wave. Figure it out when you're in your sixties. You only get a small window of opportunity to make your mark and fortunately for him he's blessed with the talent to back it up with. He seemed to appreciate it.

I saw him a couple of times after that. Once at a party that Emilio Estavez gave for him I asked him if he'd had any time to do some riding. I really hate to talk business all the time because there's life out there and I refuse to allow business to dominate my every waking moment. He looked at me with suspicion like I wanted something and said he hadn't been able to write because he'd been so busy. I laughed and said "No. Ride, not write. Horses." He seemed to only want to talk business. I thought, "That's what you have managers for. He'll get tired of that pretty quick." By the distant look in his eyes I could tell that the pressure was settling on him already and he didn't know who his friends were anymore or if he really even had any. Been there, done that, to coin a phrase. I recognize it when I see it.

So, I left him alone, and Craig T. Nelson from "Coach" and "Poltergeist" and I talked the entire evening. He was a great guy. One that hadn't let show business go to his head. He told me how those mechanical bulls could really slam you into the ground. He had played the prison guard and tried to ride one when he was on the set of "Stir Crazy" with Gene Wilder and Richard Pryor. Dang. Craig's really tall. I felt like his knees started where my hips began. I hate having to stand on chairs to talk to people.

I have a songwriter friend named Kent Blazy. Kent and I have played several songwriters in the rounds together and gone out metal detecting and collecting for Civil War artifacts. He has written more than quite a few great songs for Garth. I like being around Kent. He's like "iron sharpening iron." Once I had a songwriter-in-the-round planned with Georgia Middleman, Byron Hill (another tremendous Nashville songwriter) and Kent. Kent got a call from Garth to come to Oklahoma and help him write for his next CD. Kent apologized to me and said he had to go. I told him it was ok but because of canceling the show with me he had to tell Garth he would have to put one of my songs on his CD for messing us up.

I called Kent about a week later to do some metal detecting and left a message about how I hope Garth liked the song of mine he was putting on his new CD for canceling Kent out of my show. When I came back home and checked my messages, I had a strange one. The message said "Hi John. This is Garth Brooks. I really appreciate the song you sent for me to record and as great as it is I'm going to pass on it for now. I decided to record another Kent Blazy song instead, but you can call him yourself and talk to him about it." I was falling all over myself. It was Kent's voice and he never even attempted to disguise himself.

Garth has retired more than Michael Jordan and played baseball and several different things. I hope the next time he un-retires that his next adventure is bull riding. I watch bull riding you know.

Chapter 23

KEEPING MY HEAD
AND WATCHING WHAT I BREATHE

All I need

Is the air that I breathe

And to love you

Sung by The Hollies

My mother always told me to watch what I eat. She never warned me about watching what I breathed. There are just some things that I have intentionally stayed away from. Many things, as a matter of fact. Lost friends over it and wasn't invited into certain groups, but I would never change it.

When I was in the Southwest F.O.B. in Texas, all of the band members went to different universities. There, they began to be influenced by yet another less than lovely crowd. Let's see. Our drummer and trumpet player got busted for drugs in Dallas. They spent the night in jail and one of them almost ended up in prison for dealing. You don't want to spend jail time in the South . . . or the North, East, West or Mexico for that matter.

Larry (Ovid), our guitar player loaned his brand new Plymouth Barracuda, that he had received as a high school graduation present, to a guy at school, who immediately got busted for marijuana possession and got Larry's car impounded. I don't think Larry ever got it back and if he did, it certainly didn't look like the car he'd gotten for graduation. Getting busted with drugs in Texas meant only one thing. Jail time. We were nervous for Larry and being the prude type that I was, I didn't do it or understand it.

To let you know why I didn't understand it, I have to go back a little further. When I was about twelve years old, my parents let me stay home one Wednesday evening from church. I happened to see a TV program about a boy in New York City who was hooked on heroin and was trying to get off of it while at the same time trying to keep his younger brother away from it. The convulsions and withdrawal pain that he went through had such a profound impact on me. It scared me to death. To this day, I can still see that boy writhing around on the ground as though it's in indelible ink etched in the lobes my brain somewhere. As a result, I never got involved in any of the drug things that were going on everywhere. Also, when I was younger, I suffered from stomachaches much too often. They said I had a nervous stomach. As a result of that, I'd watch my friends getting drunk and throwing up like crazy. Therefore, I pretty much avoided anything that would make me sick or made me feel like throwing up. I hated getting sick so much that I once went from 1969 to 1985 without ever throwing up. I finally broke that record. But hey, I'm off on another quest. I wouldn't even smoke a cigar until 1995 because I didn't want that nausea feeling. But I must have outgrown it by then. Besides, I'm of the same opinion as Nancy, Lady Astor, "One reason I don't drink is that I want to know when I am having a good time."

Once we were asked to be part of the Mardi Gras in New Orleans. That was a wild time, but completely tame by today's standards or perhaps rather, lack of standards. We rode in the parade with Wolf Man Jack, who I'd met before when we played the "Midnight Special." I had a great evening firing my beads down on people. I mean I was launching them. I was trying to lasso them with bolos and they were yelling for more. A sadist dream.

Anyway, on the way to the parade, Wolf Man, his assistant, Dan and I rode over in the limo. Wolf Man Jack starts to fire up a marijuana joint and offered it to me. I declined and said I didn't mess with it. He looked at me like I was a poor specimen for a rock musician and said, "You can't be a real musician if you don't do drugs. You mean you don't do heroin or nothing?"

I stared straight at him and said "Nope. I don't. And I'm a real musician."

In my mind, I'm thinking "Come on. Get it over with. Tell me what a boring guy I am and let's move on."

Instead, he took me completely by surprise. He said, "Wow. I respect that. Someone who's got their act together."

He continued to smoke the joint.

I said, "What makes you think I've got my act together?"

He said, "I'm not for sure, but I plan to follow your example and change my ways. I'll start first thing tomorrow."

He and his assistant are getting a good laugh out of that. Now, I'm in a confined space. Smoke is filling the air. I'm recalling to mind the night when Dan and I opened for John Hartford and the Ace Trucking Company in San Diego. John and his band were all in the dressing room between shows and the air was extremely heavy with marijuana smoke. I was young and stupid so I just sat there. I didn't know any better. Unlike most musicians and singers I never let cigarette smoke bother me. I'd been playing in smoke filled clubs and bars most of my life and clubs were where people came to drink and smoke. However, this was a different kind of smoke, but I didn't know the difference.

By the time I hit the stage, I couldn't stop laughing. The audience was laughing. I think we had a forty-five minute set, of which I talked for about thirty-eight minutes of it. Dan couldn't shut me up. It must have been non-stop jokes and Dan's fighting just to play a song. I'd start to play a song and start laughing again and tell another joke. That much I recall. But I really remember the "what happened last night, why am I so darn hungry" feeling the next morning and laughing uncontrollably while staring though a haze of smoke. I heard from everyone but Dan that I was really funny.

So, back at Mardi Gras, I rolled down the window in the limo to get in fresh some air. Wolf Man said, "Hey. Good idea."

When we got out of the limo, Wolf Man pulled me off to the side. After he checked over his shoulder he told me, "I was serious about that respect line man."

Now, here's the funny part for me. I used to watch guys in college and other musicians and get all of these great ideas from them when they were stoned. They would never remember what they had said and sometimes what they had said made it into my songs. I used to watch other musicians go out of the studio and come back in and stumble through a piece of music that ten minutes before they could have played with their eyes shut. Do what you want to on your own time, but just don't cost me money.

****

I have a real aversion for anything that would keep me away from reality. Reality is my friend. Call me a reality control freak, but I like being in charge of myself. Besides, I may know how something works in principal, but it doesn't interest me so I don't become involved in it. Ignorance can be bliss at times, but it can also throw you out of touch with pop culture. Case in point.

I was headed out for a road tour and would be gone several weeks. I allowed a really laid-back songwriter friend of mine use of my place to write songs. I had a terrific baby grand piano and he liked to come down to the beach and write. The atmosphere was great. The only thing about living at the beach was that I didn't get much business done. I would be writing or playing music, catch a glimpse of a Frisbee go by, see the people on the beach having a good time and just naturally have to go play in the water. I had a great tan, was physically fit, but checks were about the only thing I was writing. It was like a permanent mental vacation.

My friend mentioned that he wanted to bring another songwriter that had some big hits to write with him and if it was ok for him to be at my place. I knew of this person and he was a major druggie. He knew I didn't want any weird stuff going on at my place. No drugs I told him. That would be all I would need. A drug bust at the Coley house. I lived in a small community.

I came home from the tour, walked into my kitchen and what do I find . . . a large baggie of white powdery substance. I hit the roof. I'm furious. I called the guy up and he answered with this stuffed up, nasal sound. I'm on him like ugly on a stick. I didn't even give him the chance to say anything. I started reading him the riot act, ranting and raving. I must have ripped that boy up one wall and down the other. He just listened and didn't say a word. He's wrong, he knows it, and he knows the rules for working at my house. What defense could he possibly have? There was nothing he can say? There's a big bag of cocaine sitting on my kitchen counter. I wanted to hear him explain that!

Then, with his stuffed up nose, nasal toned, he pedantically says, "Oh. That's my ascorbic acid. I was wondering where I left that."

"What?!!! That's a bag full of crushed up vitamin C? That's what I'm looking at?" I stammered. Boy do I feel dumb now.

"Yeah. I've been sick. You didn't just smell it or taste it?" he said.

"Now that makes perfect sense doesn't it? I'm going to stick my nose in a bag of what I've just thought was cocaine and end up looking just like Al Pacino in "Scarface?"", I blurted out.

Then like nothing ever happened he said, "But I got a couple of good song ideas while you were gone. Wanna hear them?"

I'm still feeling pretty dumb. So I said, "Not now. I'm going to the beach."

****

Being a writer and sometimes living vicariously through others, I will admit that all of my filing away other people's experiences helped me when I played a drug dealer who got murdered in an episode of "America's Most Wanted."

That ended up being one of the toughest things I've ever had to do. From everything the script suggested and from what eyewitnesses explained to me about my character, Vance, he was a less than desirable individual. He'd been involved in every drug known to man and beast. His arrest record showed that he was violent to the point of breaking teeth on girlfriends. No one I talked with seemed to care for him. I did some photo research at the scene of the crime with the detectives on the case and saw all the evidence they had. But the guy the police were actually after was even worse. I was prepared to play the role. I had my character's part down pat.

About midday on the first day of the shoot, all that came tumbling down. One of the detectives came over to me and said, "John, I'm really sorry and no one knew this was going to happen, but Vance's daughter is here and wants to tell you some things about her dad."

Although I was prepared to play the role, I was not prepared for what lay ahead. I thought, "Oh, no. Lord, give me wisdom on this one."

I spoke with this beautiful young twelve-year old girl and her family for about twenty minutes. This very sweet little girl began telling me all the great things about her dad and how he did this for her and did that for her. She was so broken and fragile and thanking me for helping them find the man who murdered her father. All I wanted to do was hug her and tell it was all going to be all right.

I went back to the trailer, locked the door and just stared at the wall. I was so depressed. This role had now become a very heavy cross to have to bear. She didn't realize what I was going to have to do in order to help catch her dad's killer. I now had the task of remaining true to the script, police files and eyewitnesses and at the same time attempt not to destroy the image this young girl had of her father. I don't know if I succeeded.

We backtracked to the actual location of the crime. It was so far back into the mountains, we had to four-wheel drive into most of it. Only way you could get there. I'd never been that far in the sticks before in my life. And I've been in the backwoods often. There in the middle of nowhere, I was lying in the exact location where Vance had been murdered. Right there in the puddle of his dried blood doing the filming. Eerie.

That particular episode ended up being one of "America's Most Wanted" fastest captures. Caught the guy in about two and a half hours. I talked to one of the detectives after I saw clips from our episode the next week. It showed how they had captured him. He said that "Sixty-three minutes after the show aired on the East Coast, they got a call that the murderer was in Chicago. Ninety-minutes later, he was in custody." He was actually in custody almost a full half-hour before I saw the show on the West Coast. Amazing. I felt like I was a part of something that had actually accomplished something meaningful.

At the same time, we did have a fun time on the set. I almost got attacked by the police's German shepherd while I was filming one of my scenes. The dog was getting agitated and about to attack me while his owner (off camera) was giving him the signals to stay down. The dog kept barking and whining and cutting into my lines in the middle of the scene. Without skipping a beat, between one of my lines, I yelled at him, "Shut up dog" and continued the scene. They kept it in the film. Everyone was laughing after the scene. Sure glad that dog didn't attack me though. I've been bit before and it hurts.

While we were shooting on the set, no one there could believe that I'd never done drugs. Even after the episode aired, my own wife, was quizzing me, "Are you sure you never did drugs? You certainly have the mannerisms down."

I almost broke down and confessed I had tried it once. But just once. And that was when I played a gig in Little Rock, Arkansas at a political rally with Bill Clinton. Neither one of us inhaled. That's the honest gospel truth.

Chapter 24

<u>THE TOWER OF BABEL</u>

I don't need bodyguards.

Jimmy Hoffa

The first section of this chapter could also be titled "The Tower of Babel." Well, what do you know? It is. Babel means confusion. When God did this, He knew just what He was doing, like that should really surprise anyone. Traveling around the world, you encounter a lot of strange accents. I just didn't know there were so many in the U.S. So, this is actually about language.

Once we had a gig in Boston. I love Boston. Had my first taste of clam chowder there. Whoever first made that stuff should have a permanent seat in the Third Heaven. I'd read all about Boston in my history classes: the Tea Party, the Revolution, Paul Revere. I enjoy history. Boston's full of it. (I know that didn't sound quite right, but I actually meant well).

But after being in the Northern states, I'm firmly convinced that any war between the North and South was not fought over anything other than the fact that they simply couldn't understand one another's accents. When some dirt poor, backwoods Confederate soldier said that he was "phittin' for hes rats" ("Fighting for his rights" for those of you who don't speak redneck), they probably thought we were all like that, talking funny, eating rodents and crickets and it must be their duty, as the only obviously civilized section of the nation, to teach us to eat and speak properly. The real problem is, we like the way we eat and speak and the war began because it. Of course, they neglect to tell you little truths like this in your high school history classes. States rights, slavery, independence? None of the above. It was over food and dialect. Just listen to me because I've done years of research. And although one could possibly argue the uncovering and bringing to light of such astounding facts, you must admit that they are equally as accurate, or perhaps questionable as the reasons for the war that I've read in any of my or my children's school history books. And the jury's still out.

So although I like visiting the Northern states, I do laugh a lot when I'm there because people eye me with great suspicion, lean in and ask me to speak faster. Heck, I already do speak fast . . . well, for a Texan anyway. I, in return, ask them to speak more slowly. Only, their "slowly" is "lickedy split" for me. I never have to explain to anyone that "I'm not from around these here parts." But I know I do add a little bit more twang to the accent just for fun. Can't seem to help myself. Hey, by the grace of God, I am what I am and rightfully proud of it.

Now, when you're on vacation, this is ok, you've got time to kill and figure out the lingo. When you're touring and on a vicious time schedule, understanding language should never be your primary handicap, especially when you're in your own country. I love foreign languages and have taken classes in several; French, Spanish, Hebrew, even German courses. But heck, I live in the United States and we've only got two things that unite us anyway - language and money. Wait. I'm wrong about that. I forgot that I lived in Southern California for awhile and the borders have been stripped away. Shoot, there's eighty-six languages spoken in Los Angeles County alone. Sorry 'bout that. I guess the pejorative "they" are working overtime to make certain that money is the only thing that unites us.

Anyway, we were looking for the theater we were playing at. We'd already asked for directions. Four different times. You should only have to ask for directions once.

The first time we played in Boston we didn't have this problem. We were opening up for Carole King. She had asked Dan and me to play the Boston gig with her after we had opened the show with her for a week at the Troubador in Los Angeles. This was during her "Tapestry" album and she was the hottest thing in records. I couldn't count all of the people that came in the club that week. I was up on the stage looking down on everyone, playing my heart out when I noticed Judy Carne from "Laugh In" in the front seat, smiling and staring right up at me. Barbara Streisand was over to my right. We're playing for such people I admire like James Taylor, Herb Alpert, Karen Carpenter, Candice Bergen and Joni Mitchell who were taking in our part of the show. The list went on and on. I'll admit, it was hard to play to that crowd. They received us well, but we were virtually unknown because our first A&M Album was just coming out, and they were there for Carole. But I'd never played to so many celebrities in one place before.

Carole was an absolute sweetheart, pregnant and ready to pop any minute. She took all of the attention in stride and never missed a beat. She even took the time to listen to a song by a buddy of mine from Texas, B.W. Stevenson, who was visiting me at the time and sleeping on my couch. She, like so many of the well-known artists we toured and played with, was so generous and kind to us.

But back to the Boston story. Fortunately, there were plenty of local guides and record people to get us to the right venue.

On this trip to Boston, we were the headliners and on our own. We couldn't find the venue we were supposed to play. People we'd ask directions from told us to go down to "Pack Street" and turn left. We did. Over and over. We still couldn't find it after we looked and looked. Finally, we ask someone else. "Ahh, ya missed it. Go back up to "Pack Street" and take a right." We traveled down the same road over and over looking for "Pack Street." There is no "Pack Street." However, plain as day and big as life, there is a "Park Street." We learned that in Boston, they don't "park" their cars. They "pack dher carhs." Fortunately for me, I speak four vernacular of one common language. English, Southern, Texan (my mother tongue), fluent Redneck and body language. Did I say four? I meant five. I'm proficient in all of them. But those are only good south of the Mason-Dixon. None of them work in Boston. Luckily enough for me, clam chowder is pronounced close enough for me to recognize it in Boston as it is from where I come from. Almost, but not quite nearly.

If you ever have trouble with the language, resort to spelling and writing it down. I used this in Montreal, Canada. I spoke Parisian French to them. They spoke something back to me, that was almost nearly, but not for certain, Quebecois French. We ended up writing everything out.

****

In the Northern states, I took spelling to a new level. Once, Dan and I were playing in Bar Harbor, Maine, pronounced "Bah Hahbah." Don't even ask. Nice little town, great lobster.

After Dan and I had finished with the gig, this young girl came up and was asking for an autograph for her album. I politely asked her name. She said, "Dawn."

"Dawn," I repeated.

"No, Daaawwn," she said.

"Daaawwn?" I said again.

When you get the ol' hands on the hips and rolled eyes routine, you're well on your way to an unpleasant autograph session.

"No! Daaawwwnn!" she gritted through her teeth.

I repeated verbatim what she had said to me. Wrong again.

This kind of banter goes on for a couple more seconds and it's, going nowhere quickly. I've still got a line of people behind her with albums to sign. I'm tired. I'm hungry. I want to go eat. But they're fans and you want to treat them nicely. After all, they just paid their hard earned money to come see you. So, you make an effort and be as polite as you can in these head scratching situations, but, it's easy to become irritated.

So, I resorted to spelling. It worked in Montreal and we're not that far from the Canadian border. Why not here.

"D-A-W-N," I spelled out. "Right?"

Now, she's really exasperated with me. I thought for a second she might try to hit me. Where's security when you need them? Oh yeah, it may be all fun and games for them during the show, but afterwards the guards are all eating up the food in your dressing room. There's never any more M&M's when I get back after signing stuff for people. They usually only leave some tea bags and opened and smashed crackers.

Now, this girl starts twisting her lips like I may be a rock star, but I'm a dumb one. "NO! What is wrong with you! It's DAAAWWWNNNNNN!!!! Spelled, D-O-N-N-A," she spit out.

"DONNA," I fired back.

"Uh yeah, finally!" she nastily said.

Now there are times when you just want to smack people upside the head. Hard. But, I just stood there looking at her, wondering how in the world do you get "Donna" out of "Dawn?" Or better yet, the demon out of "Donna," whichever comes first. By now I'm bored with this. So, I signed England Dan's name to her album. I don't think she knew the difference. Now, I'm ready for Denny's. She didn't even say thank you.

****

While Dan and I were traveling with Elton John in England, I was at the hall we were supposed to play in Leichester waiting for a sound check. Out of nowhere, this little old man who couldn't have been more than five feet tall, dressed in an old fuddy, greasy cap, who I took to be a stagehand, ran up to me and urgently said, "Whtaha aoiht ahioao a nanlk. Hone aint'a toina' pyalyylyl."

I think he was speaking in tongues and I needed an interpreter. So, I politely said, "Excuse me sir, but I didn't understand you. Could I ask you to say that again, please?"

He waved his hands all around, like he was flagging down a taxi as he repeated the phrase again.

Now according to Mike Douglas, who Dan and I co-hosted his show with him once, said to his audience, "If there's ever an emergency, I want to you two around. You guys just don't panic."

So, not being one to panic, I must have looked at this stagehand like I did their steak and kidney pie. With great curiosity.

I do well when people get agitated. Then it becomes interesting to me. I like games. However, I didn't understand him any better on the second 'go round', but I figured if I could get him to say it once more, I'd decipher it. It all sounded like some cryptic code to me.

I spoke slowly, "Sir, I'm a little hard of hearing. Could you repeat that one more time?" I'm doing my best to act as grave and concerned as I possibly can.

He put his hands on his hips, slumped his head down and then looked back at me, as close to dead in the eye as he could and said something that makes me think that somehow I've just been cast in the role of the "Spanish Inquisition" in a Monty Python film and John Cleese is hidden off in the wings somewhere, filming the whole thing. I'm looking for cameras and struggling to keep from laughing, because this poor old guy looked and spoke to me like he hadn't been smart enough to stay home when he'd had too much to drink. However, he certainly seemed serious about whatever it was. It was a language I'd never heard before and I can testify that I've not heard it since. Besides, casually looking around, I certainly didn't see anything that resembled any kind of emergency.

He repeated himself once again. Only slower this time. I didn't understand a single word he said.

So I did what I do best. I faked it and said, "Oh, oh? Really? Yes. I understand now. Thank you very much."

Funny thing about it was he understood me every time. He nodded his head with a quick jerk in a kind of salute, straightened his cap, turned in military fashion and walked off. Dan came up to me and asked who the funny man was and what did he want. I just looked at him and said, "I don't know. I don't speak English. But it sounded important." So, we went and ate dinner.

When we came back, the theater was still there. It just doesn't pay to panic.

****

Now, this one was told to my old manager from her ex-husband showing that being on the road is not for the inexperienced.

His group had a manager in training. She was trying to learn the trade because she didn't have a job and thought she would make a fine manager. She could have, given some help. Her mother, who owned the same management company Dan and I were with, agreed, gave her the job, and she was thrown out into the world of radio and road tour hell with no experience to help the group promote their new record. Admit it. Isn't nepotism a cool thing?

They were in one of their first of many radio stations doing live interviews, answering stupid questions and just generally trying to wine and dine the stations into playing their record. When asked where they were performing next, the group asked their novice manager, who was in the control booth with them. She willingly looked at her schedule and replied, "PhilaPenn." Everyone in the booth looked confused. They all said, "PhilaPenn? Where is PhilaPenn?" She didn't know. She's just as confused as they were. When they asked to see the piece of paper she was reading from, it read: Phila, PENN. Live on the radio. The DJ was hysterically laughing, "Philapenn? That's Philadelphia, Pennsylvania."

Bless her heart, she's really embarrassed and I felt bad for her because she was a nice girl. However, the final straw seemed to be when they missed a gig because none of them could figure out where "NY,NY" was.

****

There are times when things come out of your mouth and there is no way in God's green earth you can take them back. Especially when 4000 plus people have heard you. It's like when John Lennon attempted to explain what he meant by his line about "the Beatles being bigger than Jesus Christ," and later in an attempt to undo the damage, trying to tell everyone that what he meant was not "bigger," but "taller." Nice try.

I had several of those happen to me. One such trauma drama happened in Altoona, PA. Hopefully everyone has forgotten about it by now, at least until they re-read it here.

On this date a comedian named Billy Braver was the opening act for us. Billy could be quite funny at times, but on this date, nobody in Altoona thought he was. I was watching his act in the wings. I was laughing and holding my sides in the wings because he's looking helplessly at us after each failed joke. He looked at me often because it seemed that each joke failed. Where Billy was really funny was with girls. He used the most awful, trite, banal lines to get girls. "What's a nice girl like you doing in a place like this?" One is all I can force myself to repeat. What made it funny, is that they'd fall for it. Every time.

Anyway, when Dan and I took the stage, I had the audience laughing at almost everything I said. It's quite baffling to Billy. I could see him in the wings shaking his head. He must have been thinking, "They laugh at that and I get nothing on my stuff? Pigs, idiots!" I think he started stealing my material. I didn't usually plan anything to say. Something would occur to me and out my mouth it would come. It's kind of like divine inspiration. Sometimes though, what I needed was divine intervention.

But they're sure laughing with me and I'm on a roll. Dan's not laughing and is beginning to look like a man that's just had a hernia operation and has to carry in bags of heavy groceries.

Finally, we came to the place in the show where Dan and I would go back to our folk club days. Just two acoustic guitars. I particularly enjoyed this segment. There's nothing like acoustic guitars and vocals. However, Dan had broken a string and was quickly getting it changed. So, to kill time, I fell back into a story that I remembered. It was one I'd used once or twice before and it always got a good response.

I began, "I used to have this dog once. He was a really great dog, not a pure-bred, just a mutt with short hair. He was brown, had white spots, his ears were brown with white spots and even his nose had a white spot on it. I named him Buster. Buster and I did everything together. I really loved Buster. He'd sleep in my room and wake me up in the morning by licking my face. The only thing wrong with Buster was that he didn't have any legs. So, every afternoon, after school, I used to have to come home and take him out for a drag."

The audience was in stitches. Dan's looking at me like, "Funny. Now let's play. Serious, you know."

I've been standing center stage most of the evening except when I'm off playing the piano. Now, center stage again, I happened to look off to my right out into the audience. Somehow, the lights seemed to get a little dimmer and I could actually see people beyond the tenth row. But, what I saw made my blood run cold. Off to the right side of the room were about 20 people, all in wheelchairs. They weren't laughing. They weren't smiling either. I'm sunk.

I abruptly turned my back to the audience, closed my eyes, covered my mouth with my hand and thought, "Oh, Lord, I didn't say that! Give me that one back." I pretended to tune my guitar. My comedy streak came to a screeching halt for that night. Ruined my entire evening, but I turned back around and smiled like nothing had happened. I played the remainder of the night by rote and serious. Now, at least Dan's happy.

After our shows, we would usually meet people and do the autograph thing. However, that night, I had stayed in the dressing room as long as possible to avoid any chance of dealing with the situation. I was thinking that if they're out there they're going try to kill me and although Altoona is a nice town, the last thing I wanted to do was die there.

I finally went out after Dan had been out for there for awhile. Much to my dismay, there were a couple of the people in wheelchairs. I was going over in my mind what I was going to say to them and how much groveling I'm going to have to do. The first one up in a wheelchair says, "That story about the dog . . . ."

I'm getting ready to apologize my guts out.

"One of the funniest things I've ever heard. I've got to tell my friends that one," he continued.

What??? Up to this point, I was having visions of anyone of these people, waiting in their car in the parking lot with a rifle, like the sniper we encountered in Scranton, PA after one of our concerts. He sat in his car, waited for us, pulled the rifle out of the back seat and was swinging it around to aim when I saw him and yelled "He's got a gun!" I was still jumping in the car when our driver spun out of there in a hurry, headed up a one-way street, the wrong way, and we lost him. That was a nerve-wracking experience. I told you I was shot once before and it hurt.

A woman in a wheelchair behind him chimed in and said, "Yeah, you're a funny guy. You should have opened the show with your comedy act instead of the other guy. He wasn't funny."

Comedy act? I just don't have a governor on my mouth, that's all. What I think usually just comes out. I was totally dumbfounded and actually relieved at the same time. I'm not going to get killed in Altoona and will be able to see if the Denny's here has a different menu than all the rest of them. It could happen.

However, I stayed on my best behavior. I said, "Well, I hope I didn't offend you with the joke."

"Offend us? Naw, we tell jokes like that all the time," he said.

I'm still not taking any chances. I don't tell that dog story anymore. I've had to come up with newer and more creative ways to inadvertently offend people. I've come up with dozens.

Chapter 25

ON THE ROAD WITH SEALS AND CROFTS

Sometimes when reading Goethe I have a paralyzing suspicion that he is trying to be funny.

Guy Davenport

I've traveled for years and years and years. I've met some very interesting people and some very eccentric ones. In a lot of cases, you really have to be there because if you heard all the stories you'd probably think we're all just a bunch of liars.

Once, traveling with Seals and Crofts we'd had a very hard road trip. Traveling with these guys was always hard. Not because of them but because of some of the people their management would surround them with.

There are people who can really put their best skills to work in an office environment and direct others quite effectively. However, you don't want them on the road as road managers. Above all, a really good sense of humor is an essential quality you must have. Much to the dismay of many former road managers that have held this coveted position, being in charge on the road with a bunch of musicians is closer to being a counselor at a Boy Scout camp minus the smores. It's in our musician's DNA. We just don't think normal and always have our own ideas about how to do everything. The phrase "herding cats" comes to mind.

First of all, it's dang near impossible to do much with musicians who usually don't get enough sleep and have problems with dictatorial authority to begin with.

Unfortunately for us all, as well as Seals and Crofts new road manager, their management company had picked a pre-menopausal, two or three time divorced, both overtly hostile and covertly hostile feminist, (depending on which day you talked to her) for a road manager. She also appeared not to like little impish boys or men in general for that matter. Oops. Bad judgment on their part. Now I don't have any witnesses and I can't prove it, but would have bet you she carried photos of her idol, Frau Blucher, in her wallet. She had no road or musician experience, was a control freak, had absolutely no sense of humor and was mostly always angry about anything said, done or even thought about. I was surprised that she didn't have us make up our beds in the hotels in the morning before we checked out. We could have felt bad for her, but since she wouldn't let up, nobody wanted to.

We gave her an extra amount of grief just because. Like the food fight in the New Orleans airport. Totally spur of the moment, frustration-releasing fun. I think she was digging banana out of her ear for weeks. We had to pay for the cleanup, but it certainly eased some tensions. I mean, it wasn't like we threw forks that stuck in the wall or anything like that. We'd give her wake-up calls two hours ahead of the one she left or put glue on her doorknob. We'd look for fun wherever it presented itself. Most of us knew more about open-heart surgery than she did about being in our non-politically correct jungle.

Jimmy Seals was truly a gifted, might I say, dyed-in-the-wool musical genius. And having that kind of gift really leaves you open to a tremendous amount of difficulties and at best you can't have that kind of talent without having the same number of demons associated with it. I really admired Jimmy's talent, but he was difficult mainly because the management knew he was their bread and butter and acquiesced to everything he might want to do.

When you are starting out and don't have any hit records to your name, you can have a bad night playing, go to your hotel room and tell everyone you're so angry you're going to throw the TV out the window. You'll have the people around you saying, "Sit down, shut up, what's the matter with you. Who do you think you are?" After a few hit records, you can have a bad night and announce you're going to throw the TV out the window and those same people are now unplugging the TV, opening the window and saying, "Yeah, go ahead. We're with you." It's easy to lose perspective.

Jimmy, bless his heart, was cursed with a hearing problem. He never heard the true note, but all the wavering vibrations that surrounded it. It drove him crazy. He was forever tuning and tuning, and then, he kept turning his head away from the microphone when he sang because of his insecurities about hearing the right pitch. What the audience mostly heard out front was Dash Crofts' wonderful harmonies. At one point, the sound people had about three different microphones surrounding Jimmy so that no matter which direction he turned he'd be in front of a mic. But, being the crafty rascal that he was, Jimmy found a way to avoid those mics' as well. Ironically, on their worst performance they sounded far better than most other bands. Jimmy just never believed it though. All of this drove almost everyone to the brink of wrist slitting insanity.

I simply stayed away most of the time because it wasn't my battle and not being incestuously related excluded me from most of the decisions by committee anyway. Just about everyone that worked for them was married to some member of their organization. I wasn't.

One night, in the middle of a performance, Jimmy was throwing a hissy fit because he couldn't hear the monitors. He was good at it. He'd had lots of practice and it's Hell when you can't hear yourself sing. Dash was trying to calm him down and continue the show. The road manager was screaming at the monitor guys who were desperately trying to fix something that probably didn't need to be fixed anyway. It was absolute chaos. Just another normal, average day.

At this point, the drummer, Jeff Pocaro, who went on to become the drummer of "Toto," had had enough. He stood up, threw his drums sticks in the air and screamed out at the top of his lungs, "I'm only doing it for the MONEYYYYYYY!"

Jeff stormed off the stage. Everyone was in shock and it was graveyard quiet in the audience. The crowd who came to hear some beautiful harmonies filled with a peaceful, loving message, sat stunned.

All of a sudden, the light truss on stage right began to teeter.

Everyone scattered.

The light truss fell right through Jeff's drum kit and demolishes it.

Gasps from the audience could be heard and then, a deafening hush.

Jeff would have been killed.

He quit right after that. They had to get another drummer.

Or was it that Jeff was playing with his snare drum tied around his neck and was out front with the band on the encore. Then the light truss fell through his drum kit and would have killed him? No, I like the other story better.

Either way, it was just another day in Paradise.

****

Despite all of this, Dash was always fun to be around. He was such an easy going, fun loving guy. I liked spending time with Dash. If you couldn't get along with Dash, you couldn't get along with anyone.

Jimmy had been a great help to Dan and me in getting to know people in the business when we first got to Hollywood. I really appreciated his help and greatly admired his talent. He was a tremendous songwriter but he was just a little bit too intense for me. But, he taught me how to juggle and he also taught me how to play golf. You know, hit a ball, break a club. Hit a ball, break another club. I gave up golf. I couldn't afford that sport. I learned something from everyone I ever worked with.

When Dash and I first met in L.A. in 1969, he was this barefoot hippie guy running around. We were in his car once going to the Sunset Grill (long before Don Henley made a hit song of it) to get a chili cheese on a Kaiser hamburger. Very unexpectedly this guy swerved his huge Buick out in front of us and took over our lane. I was ticked and ready to pull the man out of the car and give him a good talking to about manners and courtesy and such.

Dash was entirely unfazed. He just blinked his eyes and without an ounce of malice in his voice said, "Hey mister . . . if it means that much to you, you can have it. I don't mind."

I learned something from that exchange. I can't really think of what it was at the moment, but I'm sure it was something and one day it will be useful.

Once, in Kansas City, Dash and I were sitting backstage atop the anvil cases having this nice conversation about what the main ingredient in "Jack's Secret Sauce" was and the possible effect of "Global Warming" on the peanut crop and important life altering stuff like that. We'd been on the road for about 6 weeks and everyone was already past the point of slap-happy and moving quickly toward "cranky." Looking up to the stage, I happened to notice that one of the lights on the truss was pointed out toward the audience. I laughed and told Dash. We made jokes about someone in the audience being under the spotlight that night and hoped they weren't there with someone else's wife. Dash said that we'd tell somebody later and they could take care of it. In other words, it was minor.

Bam!!! Just like a bolt of lightning streaking through a clear, blue sky, up runs Jimmy. He's pointing, waving his arms and screaming about the light. He had overheard our conversation and what was minor to us, was a major league issue to him. He runs up on the stage, castigating the light men, pointing to the light, directing them to fix it and fix it now. They assured him they would.

Jimmy stormed past Dash and me, shaking his head and mumbling to himself about the light. Unfazed, Dash and I just sat there. I cynically smiled to myself and scratched my head. I told Dash, "I certainly hope he's never around when there's a real emergency."

Dash did too. We continued our conversation, but failed to solve the dilemma of "Global Warming." However, I think the answer to the question of "Jack's Secret Sauce" is Thousand Island Dressing.

****

Since we're on Seals and Crofts stories, let's continue.

They had their own airplane, called Thunderfoot. It was formerly the President of Mexico's personal airplane. It was a big twin engine prop and all the band and crew rode in it. They had their own personal pilot, Pete, who disappeared in the jungles of South America, along with the plane in the late '70's. I always thought that it might be Pete in the scene of the downed drug plane in "Romancing the Stone." Then again, maybe not.

Anyway, we were playing in New Jersey one evening and were leaving for Cape Cod, Massachusetts after the show to play there the following evening. We were socked in with heavy fog that reached all the way to Maine. All the airports were closed. There was no way, shape or form that our plane was going to take off, and if it did take off there was no place to land.

Seals and Crofts manager insisted that we were going. Pete, our pilot, was futilely attempting to explain to her how desperate the situation really was. She's arguing with him, not listening to any wisdom or experience he's had and was doing her famous "Go ahead . . . try and reason with me!" act. She would not budge.

However, since we were still at the hall, I was listening and I could see what was happening outside. My intuition was kicking in big time. Everything in my being was screaming at me not to fly. I really do my best not to mess with my intuition. When I do, I generally regret it. I was seeing death, destruction and above all, I didn't want to die in New Jersey either. So, I said that I wasn't flying. She told me I was, too. I told her I was not and that I would be riding in the equipment big rig with the driver and his wife.

With hands on her hips she starts telling me that if I know what's good for me that I'll be flying into the fog with everybody else. Now it became a test of wills. I told her that this was insane and that I had no intentions of flying in weather like this, especially without a place to land.

I realize that I can be very difficult at times and quite the smark-aleck. It's a gift. So here we were just having a nice friendly little disagreement when she attempted to bring out the guns and knives into our little card game. When she said something about "O ye of little faith" I told her that was Luke 12:28 and it was also in Matthew. Then I asked her if she'd ever actually read it in the Bible or had someone just told her about it. That made her even madder. I proceeded to ask if she had ever read Deuteronomy 6:16 about "You should not tempt the Lord, your God" and something else to the effect that as much as I was enjoying the Bible lesson if we stayed here quoting Scripture out of context long enough maybe eventually the fog would lift. She huffed off.

After the show, everyone else was hustled into the plane. I refused to go and drove in the big rig all night with the truck driver and his wife.

The truck got to Cape Cod the next morning. I was so tired and my eyes looked like road maps because who can possibly sleep in a big rig. Do you know how many toll booths there are between New Jersey and Cape Cod? There's got to be a bijillion of them. If I'd ever entertained the notion of being a truck driver, that trip pretty much sealed the answer to that question. The answer is NOOOOOOOOOOOO! That's really rough on your rear end. While I'll admit that it was fun to be able to see over all the traffic, I had begun to think I'd really made a mistake and my intuition had mislead me the night before.

I finally checked into the hotel and asked what room Dan was in. The hotel clerk told me that they hadn't checked in yet.

What!? They should have been in by midnight. At this point, I was a little worried. Should I begin to check with the hospitals? What if they crashed in the fog? I began to watch the news to see if anything had happened to them. While I was surfing the tube I ran across the tennis match at Wimbledon between Jimmy Connors and Bjorn Borg. I had been looking forward to that tennis match. I loved to watch Jimmy Connors. I mean, of course, I was concerned about the safety of everyone in the plane, but hey, this was Wimbledon. I chose to watch the match. Connors won. That's who I was pulling for.

The troupe didn't show up until well after noon. Or let's say they "dragged in" well after noon. They were tired and they were not a happy bunch. Several said I'd made the smart move and next time they would too.

Dan later told me that Pete, the pilot, kept calling the tower to get clearance for take-off. The tower kept telling him he was crazy and there was no place to land in Cape Cod. It was completely socked in with fog. The manager kept telling him to take off. He continued to vacillate. The control tower continued to try and talk him out of this brainless maneuver. The manager prodded again and then made the mistake of saying something to Pete about "being a man."

That did it. Pete told her he wasn't flying in this weather and if she was so darn determined to fly out tonight, she could sit in the pilot seat and fly it herself, without him. They had to get hotel rooms in New Jersey for everyone. Surprisingly, Pete kept his job.

I had made the smart move again. I always seemed to make the wise move when I refused to follow her lead.

She didn't talk to me the entire time we were in Cape Cod and two days after. Dang near broke my heart.

****

You got time for one more ex-manager story? Ok.

I've had several managers over the course of my career. You have an occasional disagreement but it's business and you get back on track pretty quickly. However, this management situation was different and difficult for me all the time.

Now, this woman and I had already settled our relationship a couple of months after I first came into her management company. She and Dan lived in the same community and would discuss what was going to happen in our career. No one ever discussed anything with me. Dan would just come and tell me what the two of them had decided. I resented this and often objected. Like for example the time when they decided that I was going to be gay for publicity. Now, that would be fun to explain to my parents. "Not really mom. It's just a publicity gimmick." Yeah, right. I shot that idea in the foot quickly. They were mad at me.

So, another time, Dan came and told me what they had decided we were going to do. I objected and Dan hit the roof. He told me to go take it up with her. I said I would.

What made all of this so exasperating was that I was raised to honor women. I didn't object to fighting with men, but fighting with women wasn't considered a gentlemanly thing to do and besides that, women don't know how to fight. They really try to hurt you. So, I learned that it wasn't only considered not a thing men, it was downright dangerous. Yeah, I slipped up with her every now and then, but it always bothered me. Working with these people I'd have to be nasty on purpose just to keep from being run over. It was just plain twisted and I was in over my head.

I already knew that I didn't fit in their organizational grouping almost from the first instant I spent time with any of them. To make the point, I once asked one of the many people hanging around what he did for a living. He glared at me and replied "A Ranger." So, I asked him if he worked for the Forest Department and took the job for the peace and quiet of the outdoors. The tone in his sneer said, "you ignorant backwoods hayseed ignoramus" and he snarled back at me "Not a Ranger . . . Arranger . . . like in music. You have those where you come from?" You could see where I might have been easily confused.

I really liked L.A. at first. It was nothing like Texas. Until I figured it out though, living in L.A. was confusing and being around some of our management's people was pseudo-enlightening. The real down side was that I had moved there around the time of the Civil Rights Movement. I was taking endless flak for my Southern/Texas accent and for calling a "Laundromat" a "Washateria" and an "apple turnover" a "fried pie." I mean, not speaking Californian, it seemed like an easy enough mistake to make. The hard part was that I tried to fit in. I just didn't do a very good job of it.

But they patiently took me aside and lovingly explained to me that wasn't I aware that all Southerners were the reason for the Civil Rights movement and the universal deterioration of mankind in general, the assassination of JFK, the KKK, the War in Viet Nam, the Bubonic Plaque, The Stock Market Crash of '29, Hee Haw, banjos, Dairy Queens, moon pies, hula hoops, Orange Julius, uneducated barefoot girls getting married at 11 to their equally uneducated barefoot cousins, Bible thumping snake handlers, Edsels, and the phrase "fixin to," what does that mean? Do you always have to put "Sir" and "Ma'm" in front of "yes" and "no", tah yadda, tah yadda. Makes you kind of dizzy doesn't it? I'm swooning just reliving it.

In an equally loving and patient manner, they explained how this list didn't include Elvis . . . or Dan, of course, "because he's like Jimmy's brother and although like Jimmy and Dash were like from Texas, they had like escaped many, many years like before and had like lost their accents and like everything and like therefore Dan's Texas association like didn't count," like, etc, like, etc. At first I thought they just liked to get me mad, but I got to where I enjoyed playing the dumb hillbilly. Asking where I could get grits, watermelons and fried okra and openly laughing at their reactions. I'm easily amused and it became my defense. But, well that's my side of the story and I can't help but think theirs might differ a little.

So back to planet earth and the manager story.

After talking with Dan I called our manager, set up a meeting and went into her office in Hollywood. I was there simply because Dan believed in her after she had become a millionaire. I'm not impressed by people with money, especially new money. They can lose it by having the same bad business managers the rest of us musicians have had. Besides, I was almost a thousandaire myself.

Now, being a Southerner, I was trained in the fine art of knowing how to meander in a conversation and finally get to the point in a most polite and non-offensive manner. I had also lived in L.A. long enough and as a matter of survival had adopted some of their mannerisms of dropping a nine-pound hammer in your lap by being very direct because "time is money," a "basic lack of training in courtesy" and just in general an "I'm here to win the argument and the heck with the truth" kind of attitude. Both very useful and quite fun, depending on the situation and the people being dealt with. For this particular meeting, I opted for the L.A. approach.

Dealing from the bottom of the deck I went in, sat down and despite the two guns ready to be drawn and blaze away, I actually began a pleasant conversation with her. She then asked what I wanted to talk with her about. Now to be fair to her, I admit I can be contentious at times. What happened next, at least to the best of my recollection, went a little something like this: "Well, just so we can get our relationship in right order, know that I don't like you a nickel's worth and don't trust you as far as I can throw a baby grand piano. I think that about covers it."

Cold? Yes. Blunt? Yes, I guess so. Very ungentlemanly? Yes, yes, yes. I'm guilty. But I was in their world now and not in my own any longer. Felt like Dorothy not being in Kansas anymore. At the same time, I concluded that I had been quite unambiguous, concise, direct, and made my point more than convincingly and didn't waste anyone's time, because again "time is money." We now had our relationship set up on the proper foundation in just two simple sentences. She then proceeded to tell me how I had an attitude problem. I agreed with her that I had an attitude, but that I personally had never considered it a problem.

She retaliated by saying that "she didn't much care for me either." I told her "I would have never guessed it. I thought everyone liked me because I was so lovable." She later attempted to come between Dan and me and break up our partnership. She almost did it. The relationship between she and I continued in this manner until Dan and I went to new management. Free, free at last.

Dan was anxious to know how the meeting went.

I said, "Great. We understand one another now." That was all that needed to be said. He seemed relieved and happy it went so well.

Meanwhile, back to the camp of the Philistines.

****

Seals and Crofts themselves always treated us good and I really did enjoy being around them despite the craziness. I suppose we rather mirrored each other. But, in opposite directions. I think even though Dan and Jimmy were brothers, Dan resembled Dash more and I resembled Jimmy, not in looks but temperament. Dash and Dan were both laid back while Jimmy and I were pretty hot-tempered and prone to more violent unpredictability. I've mellowed much since then. But I suppose that's why we didn't hang around each other a lot because we were so much alike. Jimmy's intensity would dwarf my intensity and I know when I'm upstaged. He was my mentor. So, he was fun to watch from a distance and learn from. I used to say, "If I could only get that crazy when I go off. That'd be so cool!" What a misguided ambition.

For sake of illustration. We had traveled to play a gig in Cleveland, Ohio and were flying out after the job and heading to Miami and then, on to the Bahamas for a few days rest. We left everything on the plane. When I came back after the show, I noticed that my camera bag was missing. I was livid. I'm a camera nut. Lenses are expensive and mine were gone. Jimmy was trying to calm me down and I didn't want to be calmed down. Then Dan noticed that some of his things were missing too. He was furious. Jimmy attempted to calm him down and told him everything was going to be ok as well. Dan calms down. I was still pitching a fit. Other members of the band started finding things missing. Jimmy's new mission in life became the soother of frayed emotions in a volcano of spewing lava and flaring hostilities. Forget any notion you might have that musicians are all about 'peace and love.' Jimmy began to resemble a talk show host running up and down the stairs to get the next person's comment. He was doing a lot of calming everyone down. He was a busy man.

Then, Jimmy noticed that some of his things were missing. Whoa. Now we have a whole new person emerge. Mr. Peacemaker was now screaming, yelling, throwing stuff and fit pitching like it's going out of style tomorrow. His fits make my fits look like I'm calmly sitting in a Lazy Boy reading Dickens, drinking an R-o-C coke-cola and eating a moon pie. We all just sat down and watched Jimmy. I practiced my juggling that Jimmy had taught me and finally got it. He stormed around and carried on for some until the police came. No one made any attempt to stop him. He was fun to watch and Lord knows we needed the entertainment.

The detectives came, figured they knew who did it and we got all of our things back several days later. But just watching Jimmy go off was worth the couple of days without my camera gear. Everyone agreed.

Chapter 26

<u>INTERVIEWS AND CRITICS</u>

Rock journalism is for people who can't write

Interviewing people who can't talk

For people who can't read.

Frank Zappa

If you've never been interviewed by a reporter, you've missed one of life's greatest phenomena. There are some really wonderful and intelligent journalists out there who really dig a little deeper and bring out hidden gems in you, provided you have any to begin with. But, in many of the interviews, I can almost guarantee you of a certainty that whatever you did say will be misquoted, perverted, changed, hacked up or altered in such a way that you will be left wondering if you happened to be at the same interview at all.

Also, I found great delight in using the phrase "off the record." At that point the journalist had better put the pen down. That means you get to say all sorts of things and if it gets printed, they're in trouble. Law suit kind of trouble. But never in my wildest dreams could I ever imagine that they'd ever print anything that wasn't true.

So, rule number one for anyone giving a newspaper interview, "Always double check." Rule number one for readers is "Don't believe half of what's written in print." It's probably wrong, (except for my little antidotes, of course, which can be considered as gospel).

I personally am of the same theory as Elton John when he said that if he reads something about himself in the papers, he just says that it's a lie and didn't happen or at least not in that manner. However, when he reads an interview about someone else, he's the first to say, "You're kidding! Really!" The same thing happens to me.

While performing in Miami I once read an article in one of the Miami papers that talked about a big party that had happened the night before. It mentioned how I was there and according to them, was pretty much the life of the party. I was dancing with all the beautiful ladies, laughing and having a regular evening of wine, women and song.

When I read it, I remember that my only comment was, "Sounds like I had a really good time. Sure wish I'd have been there."

****

In Oregon, I was slated for a phone interview for an upcoming engagement. I spoke with the interviewer for about 20 minutes. He was quite good at asking questions. We had a very friendly conversation and when I got off the phone I felt as if I'd been talking with an old friend. However, I felt there was a Benedict Arnold masquerading as my interested friend when I read the article he wrote. The opening line read "John Ford Coley, the last of the Hostess Twinkie Cowboys . . . ." The rest of the article went downhill from there. The people I was playing with were beside themselves in literal rage. They wanted to call the guy up and personally describe the levels of Hell he would be facing in the world to come. They were new to this business so I remember calming them down by saying, "Oh look at that. He spelled my name right." They were baffled at my lack of not being outraged by it. Like I said, they were new to the business.

****

In Anchorage, Alaska I was scheduled for an interview with the local paper. It was a pleasant talk and as usual everything seemed to be going fine. The journalist asked a question, I answered. She asked. I answered. She took notes. I spoke slowly. No room for mistakes. She asked. I clarified. Even gave her a bio. How can you go wrong? I also happened to have a friend sitting with me at the time of the interview.

The next day, I got the local paper and found the interview. We sat in the airport reading it. Virtually nothing was as I remembered our intimate chat. As we read the article out loud, I found myself shaking my head saying, "Didn't say that. I didn't say that either. I also didn't say that. Oops, she messed up because I do remember saying that." My friend sat with me saying, "No. I don't think you said that either." But it sounded familiar, so I think I must have said it, unless perhaps I'd heard it from someone else and adopted it as my own. Sometimes it's difficult to recall all of what I did say. But I usually remember quite clearly what I didn't say, unless of course they make me sound terribly intelligent at what I didn't say and at that point who in their right mind would want to argue with the press?

Sometimes you just have to laugh, otherwise the stress of having people try to "one up you" will make you very defensive and skeptical all the time.

Once in upstate New York, the TV station sent out a crew to catch us as we got off the plane and before we got to the gig. The camera man hadn't shown up yet, so we stood around in the baggage claim area talking with the interviewer. It was a pleasant time. I think we must have talked about everything from music to literature to how to clean cow manure off your boots with a Popsicle stick. I was thinking that this was going to be a good interview for the local TV station. When the camera man finally rolls in the only question that the interviewer had to ask us "on air" was, "Does it bother you that no fans showed up to greet you?" What do you do? You're on the air and can't make a nasty comment back because then you look bad. So, I told him that "yes it did because usually they bring us cookies and stuff and I'm kind of hungry." That question rates right up there with "Are you somebody?" He was such a nice guy. I hope he learned to ask better questions.

****

The worst case scenario is having to do back-to-back radio or newspaper interviews. Everything seems to run together and you find yourself toward the middle of the third interview wondering, "Did I say that already?" and foolishly repeating yourself or if you actually said it two interviews ago and can't remember. You quickly envision yourself spiraling down into the ever deepening abyss of "interview Hell" trying to remember and not give way to the fact that you really have no earthly idea what you're talking about in the first place. That's where the lack of sleep, boredom, and being asked the same questions over and over and over again creates the vacuum that sucks all the remaining intelligence out of you, causing your left eye to twitch while the brain does the old Texas two-step. And it all occurs waiting for the next question.

****

One of my all-time favorite interviews was held at the University in Ada, Oklahoma. I remember it so well because I almost died that day.

Ada was the hometown of the healing evangelist Oral Roberts. Now if you want to read some good uplifting spiritual material, grab one of his books.

On a different note, it was also the town that had lynched Jim Miller and some of his men after they had murdered a local rancher in the early 1900's. Jim Miller was the man that had killed Pat Garrett, the sheriff famous for shooting Billy the Kid. The townspeople obviously didn't like attorneys either and so they cheated them out of some work. Isn't history interesting?

Anyway, in Ada, Oklahoma, the chief journalist of the University paper missed the interview session the day before. He had sent his subordinate and didn't like what they had delivered. He called and asked if he could meet us before we left for our next date. I don't know why, but we agreed to meet with him. The gig was already over and there was no need for the interview. Besides, it was an early flight. Here I was in my natural "next to exhausted" state and I'll admit I wasn't in the mood to be sliced, diced, blended and dissected all over again definitely not that early in the morning.

He was really late. We had already waited about fifteen minutes for him to show up and I'm prepared to get the heck out of Dodge. He finally arrived with an assistant who was carrying his tape recorder. It was a huge two-track and looked like a real hernia maker. Without apologizing for his tardiness, he sat down and pretended to get organized. By now, neither Dan nor I are the slightest bit amused.

I'll never forget the very first question out of his mouth. It went exactly like this:

"Now that you've played Ada, tell me . . . What are the psychological advantages and or disadvantages of playing in a geodesic dome as opposed to playing in a regular rectangled-house roofed gymnasium?"

What????? We've got our patience limits, but this interview just received the kiss of death. For a brief second, Dan and I looked at each other in complete disbelief. Then I proceeded to blow through that guy like a hailstorm through a cheap teepee and said, "Plaid! My favorite color is plaid! Turn that tape recorder off!"

We chewed him out, knocked him down and stood him up straight. He probably never rode with both feet in the stirrups again. Through clenched teeth with smiling faces, we informed him that we were not going to be used as guinea pigs to complete any thesis for his Masters that he may or may not be working on. We showed up for the first interview, which incidentally he had already missed. That and being late, which obviously showed a habitual lack of excellence on his part (probably a closet bowler and couldn't help himself), meant simple questions were the order of the morning for interviewers, especially when they didn't have the common courtesy to bring any stinking donuts.

Needless to say, we rode that boy hard and put him away wet. Both Dan and I were laughing and patting each other on the back as we left. Now, that's a mighty fine start to a very early day. However, I wouldn't venture to guess that he wrote about how wonderful and peaceful we were in his school newspaper article.

****

I remember a radio interview we had in Hong Kong once. It was quite unusual. We waited forever for the interviewer to come in. We waited and we waited and then waited some more and were just about to leave. They only had magazines in Chinese, or Korean or maybe it was Japanese. To the unskilled eye it all looks alike, but the photos were pretty. I love Asia and Asians, so I always try to think the best when I'm there.

Finally, she shows up. By now though, we're feeling a little contrary and me in particular. In all fairness though, I think I woke up on the redneck side of myself to begin with, so that might have colored my mood a little. Besides, I was struggling with the Chinese accent and for the life of me just couldn't get right. I'd say "thank you" in Chinese and with my accent and pronunciation it would come out "Life like bowl fish lips." Our interpreter constantly corrected me. So that ticked me off.

Anyway, she was dressed in a Mao uniform, complete with cap and red scarf and looked just like the little Chinese soldiers out of National Geographic magazine. She was one pushy un-feminine girl or soldier or whatever she was trying to be, and honestly had about all the personality and charm of a plastic fork.

In a short choppy sentence and all in one breath mind you, she quickly demanded of the assistant, "Get me tea, make it English and black, no bread" and the assistant quickly shuffles off with head hanging and shoulders slumped. Then turning her focus to us, again in one breath she pedantically says, "I will ask you what you are doing in Hong Kong, you will answer, I will ask you how many days you will be here, you will answer, I will ask a little about your music, then you will answer, understood? Let's go. Turn on the recorder."

Now the only problem was, neither Dan nor I do well being bossed around. We were generally easy going, but we can throw off your timing in a heartbeat if we feel like it. We've had practice on some of the best in the world.

Most of the time, interviews I find fun and interesting, maybe not for the interviewer, but for me at least. Interrogations are neither fun nor interesting, unless you're the one doing the interrogating of course. It's a bit like torture. As long as you're not on the receiving end it's actually kind of fun. And if you've got a good imagination you probably don't get bored with your work. I just realized how sick that sounds.

Anyway, she rapidly fired off her first question, again in her characteristic one long breath.

"I'm talking with England Dan and John Ford Coley, what exactly you doing in Hong Kong and when you leaving?"

I glanced at Dan. He nodded back to me. Slowly, with the most pleasant smile I could muster, I politely answered. "That's a really nice uniform you're wearing. Is that like a Mao Tse-tung style? That's a nice little hat too. Olive green really highlights your skin complexion. Looks very good on you."

Dan's playing along. He didn't like her style much either.

She's thrown. Her eyes got big, her chin shot out and her head arched back. This is not what she asked. Answer the question, NOW capitalist pig! She's accustomed to being in charge and it's obvious that compliments don't work on her. What she wants she gets or maybe somebody comes up missing. She didn't understand my attempts at the Chinese language either. I never did get the darn accent right. Or those slippery plastic chopsticks either. Needless to say, it went downhill all the way.

When the brief interview was over I remember we all stood up at the same time without shaking hands or even bowing and just said "Goodbye." I think that "Goodbye" about covered it.

I had fun in Hong Kong. Especially that radio interview.

****

My other favorite review was at a film festival in Houston. The producers of "Scenes From The Gold Mine" had flown several of us down to be part of the festival and represent our film. Granted, the film was no "Ghandi" or "Gone With The Wind," but it wasn't any "Revenge of the Papparazzi" where they run around beating up movie stars either. It was about a rock band doing whatever it takes to make it. Although it made the headline article of all the papers in town, the critics had an absolute field day of trashing the film. One was even so bold as to state that this was not the way that the music or rock and roll industry worked in general. That's funny. In those articles, I just about had nearly all of my musical industry experiences nullified by someone that's never done it or been involved in it. I was willing to give them the benefit of the doubt. I mean, it's possible they knew something I didn't.

So, again in the words of one of my favorite writers, Mark Twain, "The only reason why God created man was because he was so darned disappointed with the outcome of the monkey." I'm not for certain, but in some odd way I think that quote applies here. I really do love reading reviews though.

****

On our very first trip to Japan in 1972, the press corps surprised us with full-blown press conferences. Can you believe it? Press conferences. That's only for Presidents and football coaches and people that have serious apologies to make. I felt like I was apologizing all over Japan.

On one occasion in Tokyo, we had a beautiful Japanese interpreter that would start to translate immediately after we began to answer the questions put to us. She was a very serious lady who was intent on performing her skills with excellence. So, she was translating while we were talking. If you made a hand or face gesture while you spoke she made the same gesture to make certain the full meaning was translated. She was really very good.

It was annoying at first and I couldn't get a clear thought in my head. So, the real John came out I decided to trick her. I think the question went something like this: "This your first trip Japan, how you find you think our country of and they liking your music thank you very much your polite answer?"

I answered. "I think I'm having a wonderful time tripping up and down and over the garden hoses on the sidewalk in Tokyo and the only music I've heard is the Mr. Donut song in every donut shop over and over, makes me think how much I miss yogurt trees growing in the alleys and let me see . . . ."

Now, I was watching the interpreter's facial expression the entire time. She was diligently attempting to quote verbatim what I was saying. Dan and our manager have that frozen smile, teeth showing "oh no, not again look." I began to laugh and laugh. Those that spoke English in the press are confused but smiling or laughing too. I apologized profusely between my laughing so the interpreter wouldn't lose face.

Then told her I was only playing a dirty American trick and answered the question properly. However, she continued to eye me with great suspicion just in case the "Tricky American" decided to come to life again. I haven't done press conferences since, although I do have a tremendous amount of things to apologize for.

****

One of the most interesting interviews that I remember was for Radio Luxembourg. It was recorded in London when Dan and I were there traveling with Elton John.

We arrived at the studio, guitars in hand; all prepared to maybe play a few songs live and answer every possible question put to us. One problem. There was no interviewer. Now, I'm from the old school. You know. Someone asks a question. I answer. They ask another question. I answer. It's a simple process. I know how to do this.

However, what they had in mind was for us to interview each other and they would piece our answers together and send it to Radio Luxembourg. The interviewer at Radio Luxembourg would then formulate his questions based on our answers and put them on the tape. Somehow, through the miracle of modern technology, it would sound as if we were all sitting around the campfire together drinking tea and Dr. Peppers, smoking cigars, punching one another on the arm and swapping lies like we were friends or something.

Now I know how to be interviewed, but I do not know how to interview. Even to this day, having been interviewed so much, I don't generally think to ask questions back when someone is talking to me. They'll say, "How are you?"

I'll say, "Great."

Then it dawns on me that I'm not being interviewed. It's supposed to be a conversation and it becomes my turn to ask them how they are too, not just wait for the next question.

So, Dan and I muddle through this so-called "interview," asking stupid questions and telling really long, slow, drawn out stories of epic proportions. Things like, "So Dan, you're a fisherman. How long does it take to scale a catfish?"

After a moment of reflective thought, Dan replied, "Well, John, you don't actually scale a catfish, you skin one. You see, your regular fish, like bass or trout, have scales that have to be scrapped off before you eat it, but a catfish . . . ."

It's a guy thing, ladies.

However, when our version of what we considered an "interview" finally made its way to Radio Luxembourg, it turned out to be the shortest interview in history. However, I felt blessed to be able to add another useless experience to my already long line of other useless experiences. It might come in handy someday. Like college algebra.

****

Now some of the least favorable reviews from critics have come from my own State. In Houston, Texas no less. The first review was when Dan and I played at the Celebrity Circle Theater. It was one of those theaters-in-the-round, or more commonly referred to as the "rotisserie." After about an hour and a half of turning round and round in circles and never going anywhere, under those hot lights, you can stick a fork in us and we'll be fully cooked.

I could tell that the reviewer was really working at being nice, in a very underhanded manner of course. Provided you were able to get through the entire review, the last line of the article was the killer. It read, ". . . from the best vantage point and see the bald spot on the back of Dan Seals' head peer back at you like a peculiar third eye while he sang." That's brutally and unnecessarily cold.

Now, I have to tell you I'm not quite for certain what he was attempting to get at, but since that review I've come to believe that the artists should be allowed to write their own reviews of their shows. Had I written it and reviewed our show it might have come out something like this.

"It was a hot night in Houston, both with the humidity and music played by ED&JFC. We came on stage (a theatre in-the-round) to the deafening roar of applause from an enthusiastic audience. We started off a little slow as we seemed like we had to get our sea-legs with the stage first turning left, then suddenly stopping and starting to spin to the right. Once, in the middle of "Westward Wind" the drummer slid off his seat, falling to the floor and knocked over his cymbal as the stage unexpectedly jerked to the right. He said he wasn't hurt and it was the first time he'd fallen off the stool sober. After that, everyone seemed to settle down as we played all of our hits including several new songs from our newest album. The live versions seem to have more life to them and there's more time for long instrumentals. The audience sang along on almost every song and the newer songs were met with wild cheers. Dan seemed a little wobbly at times and remarked about not knowing they had been booked for a cruise-ship. John told the light operator that he felt sufficiently cooked by now and would he mind turning off the french-fry lights that he had bought from McDonalds. Both comments drew a big laugh. The musical versatility became quite apparent as Dan would trade out between guitar and saxophone and John would be at the piano one minute and playing guitar the next. The audience loved the Texas humor and laughed, cried and danced all through the concert. At one point, John tried to jump into the audience mosh pit only to fall on some seats when no one caught him. That's when he discovered he was about ten years ahead of his time. The only difficult thing was the bright light reflection coming from somewhere that none of us could figure out its actual location, but at times had a disco ball effect. It might well have been the lights bouncing off John's freshly polished guitar. But a great time was had by all and we can't wait to come back to Houston."

Now that's a review. Simple, to the point and no one gets unmercifully or unjustly destroyed because they sent a heavy metal lover to review a soft-rock show. Also, no one has to be reminded that the role of a reviewer is to critique, not criticize or just try to make a name for themselves by ripping apart others work that they obviously cannot, could not or ever possibly do. Look for the good things. Believe it or not, we work hard and have fun for the money. Well, most of the time.

However, back to the cold, cruel real world of critics where hard working people slave to purchase books about celebrities. Just remember, I do appreciate you spelling my name correctly or in the words of fellow musician Stephen Bishop, "Bitter, Bitter. Party of one. Your table is ready. Bitter. Mr. Bitter." There's some sort of perverted justice in there somewhere.

Chapter 27

<u>HOW DO YOU KNOW WHEN YOUR TIME IS UP?</u>

Don't Fear The Reaper

Blue Oyster Cult

The statement earlier about almost dying might have piqued your curiosity. I guess even the Grim Reaper has a bad day and misses his chance every now and then. I'm thankful to God for guardian angels. Some brief stories.

Dan and I had a private turbo-prop plane that we had leased for a tour that included Ada, Oklahoma. We were looking forward to avoiding some of the commercial airline nightmares that we had been experiencing. As we were speeding down the runway, suddenly the right engine caught on fire. The co-pilot, Jack Brunner, happened to look back while all the band members were screaming that the "engine's on fire" and without authority, shot all the foam from both engines on it and put out the fire before we were able to get off the ground. The pilot stopped the plane and when the doors flew opened everyone except Dan, Nancy and I shot off of the plane and ran half way to the next county before they stopped. The three of us just sat there. The fire's out. Problem solved.

At that point, the pilot, Robert Fowler, came back to get off the plane and assess the damage. He was a former Viet Nam jet pilot and had flown many missions. However, this time he was sweating bullets and his clothes were drenched. He saw us sitting there and told us how close we came to dying.

"If the plane had gotten off the ground we'd have crashed and we'd all be dead now, just like Jim Croce and Buddy Holly," he said.

That kind of thing sobers you up in a hurry.

I flashed back to a time when I was playing my guitar in my hotel room in Chicago, enjoying the peaceful view of Lake Michigan from my window. I just happened to watch a single engine plane take off from a local airport on the Lake, climb, hit a flock of birds and nose dive into the water. It was over that quick. I called down to the operator and they called the police. Later I heard on the local news that it killed a doctor and his family.

The only time I thought I had really died on the road was when the seat of my stage pants ripped out once in front of about 8000 people in Colorado Springs and I didn't have any other pants to put on. People were laughing and pointing. It was "tuck and run." Talk about a serious near death experience. Wheeeeeeee.

Wow. One story just leads to another. But back to the plane mishap. I remembered what our road manager had told me once, "Close only counts in horseshoes and atom bombs."

I thought, "Well, either you die or you don't. And we didn't crash and we aren't dead. Besides, I didn't get on this plane to die. I've got someplace to go."

I was truly amazed at how detached from it I was. Dan and Nancy seemed to feel the same way. I felt that same sense of detachment when I was almost shot by policemen in my own house. Someone called the police when they saw me climb in through a window when I forgot my keys and the front door was locked. Death was just a heartbeat away. But once again, either you die or you don't.

So, we got another plane and went to the next date. End of story.

Except when I got back home and told the story to a record exec he dropped his head, looked back up at me and sadly told me, "Man, if you'd have crashed and died, just think what that would have done for record sales. You'd have sold millions."

I could see how disappointed he was as he did the mental math. So I told him I'd take that into consideration the next time.

****

Also, there was the time when LeBlanc and Carr, another Big Tree recording act used to open up for us. We'd known Lenny for awhile. He used to come and watch us record in Nashville. They had a big hit with a song called "Falling." We met up with them on the road and here was Lenny LeBlanc and the band, but no Pete Carr. I asked Lenny where Pete was and he told me that "he couldn't take the pressure and had quit."

I said, "What pressure?"

Lenny explained how they had been on tour with Lynard Skynard and they were asked to fly on the plane with them. Lenny and Pete felt that it wouldn't be right for them to fly when the rest of their band had to drive, so they declined the offer. That day the plane with Lynard Skynard crashed and killed a lot of the guys on it. When Pete heard about the crash the next morning, he quit and went back home to Muscle Shoals. Lenny finished the tour on his own and later went on to write many hits for Christian radio.

****

Some things are only the kiss of death. Here's another story about how death almost kissed me on the road.

We had just arrived in Denver and were standing outside the hotel. While the bell-man was getting our luggage out of the van, I decided to take a walk to stretch out my legs. There was man in a business suit walking toward me. For no apparent reason, I turned to started walking back toward the hotel lobby. Poof. Out of the blue, someone or something broke a plate glass window on the 10th floor. Shards and splinters of sharp glass came raining down near us. I wasn't hit, but the man in the business suit wasn't so fortunate. He survived, but he was sliced up from head to toe. Definitely not a good way to start your morning. We never did find out how that window broke.

****

Odd and funny things seem to happen all the time on the road and for the most unexplained reasons, which leaves all of us wondering how we've lived so long.

One good example:

Burleigh Drummond and Christopher North from the band Ambrosia got a little jolt when I was with them on our most recent trip to New Orleans. They were walking in the French Quarter looking to buy some pralines or something and happened upon a voodoo joint or shop or whatever they're called. Maybe they were secretly hoping to find some Love Potion #9. They watched with great curiosity as a man explained his so-called religion to a couple of people there. He had his back to Burleigh and Chris and the other people that had come in. The man never looked at them, but he began to grow increasingly more and more agitated and excitable. After a couple of minutes, quick as a cat he spun around toward Burleigh and Chris and shrieked in a high pitched voice, with bulging eyes, foaming mouth, waving and pointing his finger at them screeching like a wild banshee, "YOU!!!!! GET OUT OF MY MIND!!!!!" Talk about demons.

Burleigh, Chris and everyone else cleared out of that place in a three-alarm-fire hurry. They tried to act cool about it and laugh it off. However, after they explained the story I understood why Burleigh played the kick drum on 2 and 4 and the snare on 1 and 3 that night, instead of the other way around, and Chris's hand would lose control, keep flying up in the air and playing air organ. At least it wasn't a strong back beat on 5 and 7 like Turkish music. Some areas of curiosity are better left undiscovered.

****

Once while we were in Hong Kong, Ovid, our guitar player had a rather eye-opening, not-soon-to-be-forgotten, if-I-didn't-drink-or-pray-before-I'm-starting-now experience during our second day there. We went to see the sights of Hong Kong. As he walked along the street he saw an old Chinese man squatted down making some kind of craft. When the old man saw Ovid taking a picture of him, he began waving his arms, talking excitedly in a language that Ovid clearly didn't understand, but he knew it wasn't any dialect of English he knew. Then, the old man flung a meat cleaver across the ground at Ovid almost hitting him. Ovid jumped as it skidded under his feet, ran away and lived to tell about it. Although he had an interesting story to tell, I really don't think he enjoyed Hong Kong as much as I did.

The fact that Ovid lived to play another day was not only good for him, but it meant I didn't have to find another guitar player or have to explain to his momma how he was almost dispatched, and on my watch mind you, to the world beyond where he would receive either a harp or an accordion for his earthly deeds for all eternity. We discussed this scenario a couple of times and Ovid was quite certain he would have received a harp, provided, of course, God didn't bring up that unfortunate little incident in Salt Lake City. Also, hopefully the small occurrence in Charlotte would go unnoticed as well. But, then again . . . there was that nasty little thing in Chicago. . . .

****

Sometimes life and even death comes at you a little faster than you might have expected it. Case in point:

On Valentine's Day, February 14, 2005 I was in Manila (Makati) in the Philippines. I had played there several times before for Valentine's Day. I had been invited again and was sharing the stage with Gordon Waller (of Peter and Gordon fame) and Chris Montez. Chris had the unique history of having a huge hit in England in the very early 1960's and who opened the show for him? Believe it or not, it was the Beatles. Quite a legacy there. Also, Paul McCartney had even written hit songs for Gordon's group. I was sharing the stage with living legends. Although I had never played with or been around the Beatles, I had stayed at a Holiday Inn at some point. I guess I could do one of those commercials.

Valentine's Day is a very special day in the Philippines. The Filipinos really admire love songs and tonight was the final show of our tour there. We had already had a pretty eventful day having been taken to the Presidential Palace for a tour and meeting with the Presidential Spokesman for the President. Coming back, traffic was horrendous as it always is on Valentine's Day.

I sat in the hotel restaurant eating dinner with Gordon and my friend Vanessa that used to work at the record company there. We were having a pleasant conversation when BLAAAAAAM. It was the loudest and only explosion I'd ever heard in my life. The building shook a little as did the table and glasses. We all looked at each other with a "what in the world was that" expression." I told them, "That's far too loud to be a car backfire." My first instinct was "bomb." I knew that there were Muslim insurgents in the south of the Philippines that were ticked off over one thing or another. However, we were almost a thousand miles from any of that. No one in the restaurant seemed overly concerned, so we continued eating, but still wondering what it had been.

As I came down from my room to be taken to the show, one of the doormen told me of the bomb that had exploded on a bus at the Ayala Station. It had killed three or four people and had wounded seventy plus others. The Ayala Station was only about 100 yards away from our hotel. When he related the story to me, I don't recall being frightened or anxious in any way, but I do remember how livid I got. I really love the Filipino people. We had just passed by the station about forty minutes before the bomb exploded. Cowards really make me angry and that was about the most cowardly act I'd ever been that close to. There are so many wonderful things about the Philippines and I prefer to dwell on those. I'm not much impressed by the works of the demonic.

Ironically, the year before as I toured the Manila and Cebu area of the Philippines, I'd had been asked by a television reporter if I was afraid of the terrorists. I replied that "Cowards don't scare me much. I'm in God's Hands and He knows my comings and goings."

However, would I ever go back to Philippines given the circumstances that occurred on Valentine's Day? In a New York minute.

Now to further complicate the story. I was back in Manila in October of 2007. As I was taking a walk around the Philippines Cultural Center, I heard a very loud explosion. I thought, "Oh no. Not again." I ran down the street to where people were pointing and a long cable was dragging the street. Seems that a power transformer blew up. I was so relieved it wasn't a bomb and no one was injured.

However, within a week, another explosion occurred in Makati, close to where the bomb had blown up in 2005. Again, many people died. We continued to think it was another bomb, but it turned out to not be a terrorist event, but an underground LPG that had exploded. Danee Samonte, my friend the promoter and Howard Medina were jokingly accusing me of being a jinx and the bombings only happen when I come there. I told them that it wasn't my fault this time. Josh Groban was in town too. Let him take the blame on this one. They thought that was funny. We laugh a lot when I'm over there.

I was there again in May of 2008 and no bombings occurred on this visit. However, I did eat "sisgue" and that did cause a nice little explosion in my stomach.

Chapter 28

OK, IT'S TUESDAY, WHO WANTS TO BE ME?

My one regret in life is
that I'm not somebody else.

Woody Allen

One day, in 1997, I received a call from my publishing administrator in Nashville. They strangely began the conversation with a series of unexpected questions, almost as if they didn't know me. They wanted to know if I'd been to New York recently. Had I played there? Had I done any interviews? Had I spoken with this disk jockey? I told them "No." They then informed me that I had a problem. There was a man claiming to be me, booking gigs in clubs, doing local radio and cable TV interviews on Long Island. I remember my first lighthearted comment was, "Really? Well, if he wants to be me so much, tell him I've got about 60 bales of hay to unload. Get over here and help me feed these horses." I didn't really give it much thought at the time, but it turned out to be something that dramatically affected by life.

They told me I needed to call the radio disk jockey, Tom Pantaleo at WRIV in Long Island. When I finally called, I was greeted with great suspicion. I had never gotten so many personal questions about my life and career before. I was actually having to prove that I was me. He asked. I answered. He asked. I answered. He asked. I answered. But because, more than anyone else, I just so happen to know a lot about myself, it was amusing. Getting a little tired of it all, coupled with the fact that I had to call him long distance to tell him I didn't particularly think my life was all that interesting, I finally said, "Look, does this guy live on Long Island and have a northern accent?"

He said, "Yes he does."

So, in exasperation, I said, "All of my bios say I'm from Texas. Now tell me, do I sound like I have the accent of someone from anywhere above the Mason Dixon line?"

At that point, he believed me. That and the fact that I was familiar with the most intimate details of my life and could answer things about me that the impostor couldn't.

But my question was, "Who in the world would want to be me? How did they choose me, again?"

Over the last several years I had been keeping a very low profile and was actually rather difficult to locate. I loved music and film but I had finally had enough of the music and film industry. Not the music or film, but an industry where I felt I knew more about nuclear physics than most of the people in those industries knew about music or film. Talk about nepotism. I affectionately referred to it as "The Attorney Business." For those of you in this industry, this might sound familiar.

For the most part, I was raising horses and working for the courts in L.A. in child abuse. Talk about depressing. Not the horses. That's fun. But try working with dead and abused children day in and day out and keeping a sense of humor. Working for the courts negatively affected my life, but this impostor business transformed my life dramatically.

I'd had this impostor thing happen to me before. In the late 70's, some man in Indiana, claiming to be me, had gone into a music store and tried to purchase all kinds of musical equipment on credit and billed it to somewhere in L.A. It was a pretty hefty dollar amount. The store manager got suspicious and did some checking around and found out he wasn't me after all. The impostor ran out of the store without any equipment and without getting caught.

But this impostor was different. He was, in a very public manner, attempting to be someone and something he wasn't. I told the disk jockey that anyone can claim to be anybody they want to and there's not much you can do about it. But as it progressed, it became even more and more bizarre.

It appears that this wanna-be had hooked up with a doctor at the VA hospital on Long Island, who just happened to play in a band, and convinced him that he was one-half of the duo, England Dan and John Ford Coley. He was able to get several paying gigs. He progressed on to finding a booking agent, Beth, whom he wooed into trying to find him playing gigs. She had spoken with Tom Pantaleo at the radio station and the whole scam began to crash.

When I spoke with Beth, I had never been treated with such caution in my life. I guess this guy scared them. Finally, as she quizzed me on the easy things, she suddenly asked me if she could ask a very personal question. I thought, "Oh no. Just how personal?"

So I teased her by saying, "Well, if you're referring to that little jacuzzi incident down in Jamaica, it's a lie. I was never there. I don't care what the Enquirer said."

She stumbled around and said, "Oh no, not that. But how are your wife and your sister?"

I thought, "What kind of fool question is that?

I told her, "My wife is fine and I never had a sister. Why?"

She then proceeded to inform me that the impostor had told her that his wife and sister had been killed in a car crash. He had been so traumatized by it that he hadn't been able to play the piano since, which was quite convenient.

I said, "You mean to tell me that I had a sister and then lost a sister all in one phone conversation? That's terrible. But I still play the piano and I can do all of my songs to prove it."

Now it's my turn to ask questions. I wanted to know, "Since it's rather obvious that this guy doesn't have both oars in the water, do I possibly need to get a Federal gun permit?"

She seemed to think that might not be a bad idea.

Cool. Good answer. Perhaps a little 380 for my ankle and a Glock in a shoulder holster and maybe a 40 S&W for my back. All legal of course, cause I've got a friend in the FBI. I could be the next Ted Nugent. Fire up the grill Ted. I'm coming over. Let's kill something.

She then told me that she had gone out one evening to see the impostor perform and thought, "John Ford Coley has really lost it."

Now, I'm really ticked. I'm definitely getting the gun permit. The words "lost it" with my name in the same sentence are coming up far too often in this conversation for my liking. If I'm not going to actually play, at least make me sound good. You can't imagine how angry I get when I walk off the stage not feeling like I did well. I would wager my impostor didn't feel the same amount of remorse as I do.

Then, she put the capper on it. It appears that he had been writing rubber checks signing my name to them. Now, I'm furious. So, besides bouncing checks in my name, all I need is for this idiot to get some girl and/or girls pregnant and they come looking for me with paternity suits.

I put a stop to it. With the help of my attorney friend, Blake Rummel, (now look what a hypocrite I've turned into. But Blake's special because it isn't often that I use the word attorney and friend in the same sentence) we sent out cease and desist orders to the club on Long Island he was playing in. I called the District Attorney's office in the area where he lived, filed a complaint and the party got rolling.

Before long, I was receiving tapes from the police of cable TV shows he had been performing on as John Ford Coley. The first time I saw him on those tapes I was floored. He had a long face with a salt and pepper beard. He wore this 'old salty dog' sailing cap and had hands about the size of the state of Oklahoma. His east-coast accent was so thick any seventh year law student who hadn't passed the bar by their fourth attempt could have told you he wasn't from Texas or anywhere close to the South.

Then, I heard him sing. Now I understood what the booking agent had been talking about. He actually sounded pretty good, in a 1960's Las Vegas kind of way. Not my style though. I began to actually have compassion and feel sorry for the guy.

The law enforcement teams gathered their information and made their arrest in August for "petty larceny, criminal impersonation and a scheme to defraud." Those were all misdemeanors. They dropped the most serious "1960's Las Vegas style of singing" charge, which should be a Federal offense and it's just bad taste.

It appears that the impostor had been at a karaoke bar one night and got up and sang a couple of songs. Some people asked him his name and for some unknown, never to be explained reason, my name popped into his mind. Why my name? I'll never know. All the police were able to get from him was that after he told everyone that he was me, the free drinks kept coming.

Yeah, I guess life's all fun and games until you end up on the karaoke playlist somewhere. Next thing you know, you hear your music when you step on the elevators and you can kiss your career goodbye.

Before I knew it, I was being very easily found. My days of low profile were behind me. This event appeared in the news everywhere. I must have hit on a slow news day. No war, earthquakes, stock market plunges or aging movie stars slapping policemen. I was asked to go down to the ABC TV station in L.A. and they did one of the link-up interviews for New York. I'd never done one of those before. I never knew I had actually been doing the interview and that it was over until they said "Thank you." I just thought I was talking with some guy I couldn't see that was prepping me for the interview. It's on the evening news all over the country. My cousin Kay even called me from New York. Not bad for someone who's hard to find.

The late night news L.A. anchor even mispronounced my last name. I laughed at that one because like I said, I've lived with that problem all my life. I had watched her as an anchor on several occasions and thought she faked sincerity pretty well. That little tear in her eye on the abandoned puppy story was killer or the little sniffle at the four gang bangers who had been gunned down while robbing a convenience store. She was one of those very young, pretty girls, who obviously wasn't even born when my music was playing. In other words, she was no Connie Chung or Diane Sawyer, but certainly beautiful without their experience.

Now, here's where it gets fun. I was listening to Mark and Brian at KLOS in L.A. the next morning and lo and behold, they've got the story on the impostor. I'm surprised. My ego's getting huge. It was a big deal to me, but it certainly wasn't of the proportion it was made to be. I had called the cops, they arrested the impostor, he got time in jail and nobody got pregnant. Pretty simple really.

They made their customary zany jokes about it and were quite funny as usual. I had played for Brian's birthday party a couple of years before and you could sort of say I knew them. I mean, we didn't go bowling together or anything like that, but they were good guys. They told me they used to take a boat out on the ocean and play my music really loud, so no one would hear them singing my stuff when they only played hard rock on the station. My music played really loud. That's funny in itself.

So, I decided to call and talk a little bit with them about it. However, their assistant on the line hesitated like she was stumped. Finally she said, "Well, how do I know it's really you? You could be an impostor yourself." No matter how hard I tried, she would not let me through to talk to them. For the life of me I couldn't convince that girl that I was me for love, money, chocolate or marbles.

I began to see my immediate future written in un-erasable ink on the bathroom walls. "John Ford Coley is an impostor," or "John Ford Coley sings karaoke." Talk about the kiss of death. Ugly.

Quite literally, from that point on, I had to produce a photo ID and two other forms of identification anytime I called a radio or TV station. With every radio interview, I had to give the contact name of the person who set the interview up, answer personal questions and reassure them to the best of ability that I was genuinely myself. One radio station even hung up on me, and another put me on hold, called the person that set up the interview to verify that I was actually calling. Talk about a darn nuisance. I almost gave up interviews. If I'd have known this impostor thing was going to cause me so much trouble, I'd have asked the DA to double his jail sentence or just shoot him in the foot or something. Of course, a couple of my true friends assured me that the impostor couldn't possibly be half the jerk that I was. I agreed and thanked them for their encouragement.

Shortly after the story broke, my son was at the gym and happened to see the "Daily Show with John Stewart" on "Comedy Central." To his surprise, they had done an entire piece on the impostor story. I love comedy and wanted to see it. I called and finally got to the producer of the show. He seemed a little relieved that I hadn't seen it. I suspect that he thought if I was really me that I had called to chew him out. I told him I'd like to see it and requested a copy of it. He began to profusely apologize. He told me that they hadn't been very kind to me on the show and had taken a few potshots at me. So I told him, it wasn't comedy if you didn't take potshots. He sent me out the tape.

When I saw it, I laughed and laughed. They had placed a photo of the impostor along with me in one of my least favorable photos from one of our album covers. They told how the impostor had wanted to be me. But next they placed a photo of England Dan next to my photo and told how I had really wanted to be Dan. That was funny. I wonder who Dan wanted to be.

Tom Pantaleo, the disk jockey who broke the story to me, called the next morning. He was so depressed. It seems that he was taking a lot of flak for busting the impostor from the New York ABC radio affiliate's morning disk jockeys. They had apparently been on the impostor's side, thought it was all in fun and what was the harm in it. However, he told me that the only one that had stood up for him was Howard Stern. Way to go Howard.

Before you know it, I'm on Real TV and other shows. They're showing me video footage of the impostor playing at backyard birthday parties in New Jersey, claiming to have written songs I'd written and making me prove who I am. I didn't mind doing that show. I got paid for it.

I spoke with my former partner, Dan, shortly after this and his comment was, "What's the deal with you and impostors? That's the fourth time."

I corrected him and told him it was only the third time.

He corrected me back and said, "Did you forget about the guy in Texas when you were in college?"

I had forgotten about him. Heck. I've got to be the most impersonated guy I know. But why, I don't know.

I tried out for the gymnastic team in my first year of college at North Texas (University of North Texas - see my forward about the degree they're giving me after they read my book/thesis). I happened to be talking to the only other guy there with long hair. He told me that he played organ in a band. I asked him which band he played with. He told me, "The Southwest F.O.B." I just stood there and looked at him, stunned. That was my job.

The next thing I knew, the coach yelled at me to hurry up, that it was my turn. I told him we'd talk after I came back. I ran down the mat, did an improper triple back flip, bounced off the chin bar, swung up on the ceiling grid and came down into an agonizing stick position on the mat. However, I seriously sprained my ankle when I landed. Dang near broke the sucker. I don't think I really did all that flip stuff, but the memory begins to play tricks on you after two or three identity thefts. Anyway, I do remember spending the night in the college hospital. I never did see my first impostor again. But, it was thoughtful of Dan to remind me of it.

On the tail of the New York impostor, I got word that another person had begun impersonating me in Miami, Florida. Probably had me singing karaoke in Spanish. But I didn't pursue this one. By now I'm bored with it.

When I moved to Nashville from the L.A. area, I got a call that my Long Island impostor was loose and back at his old tricks again. Real TV flew me to New York and this time I was going to personally confront this guy. There were questions I wanted answers to. However, so many calls had come into the club about me playing; my impostor must have gotten wind of it and disappeared. Too bad. I would have liked to have met myself. Maybe I could have gotten an autograph of myself. I wonder what I would have gotten for it on EBay.

So, if you're reading this book and are as of yet undecided about your path and purpose in this world or what you would consider a life-long career and are possibly tossing back and forth the idea of choosing the role of being an impostor or not, a word to the wise. Although I'm flattered at being chosen so many times for such a prestigious, albeit rather dubious honor, please, pick someone else. I know for certain that there are plenty of lonely celebrities out there that probably need the publicity. I don't. Truthfully, I'm impostored out.

Well, I've still got many stories left to tell, but I think I'll save the rest for my next thesis when I apply for my Ph.D. Besides, I've been writing all day and right about now I'm pretty worn out so I'm going to sleep. I covet sleep you know.

Now, on a final note, a word to all you that are choosing the life of a traveling and recording musician. Remember my experiences. It's not the destination, it's the journey. Look out the window and enjoy the ride. You'll probably start out with nothing; but don't worry, because at the end of your career you'll probably still have most of what you started out with. And in the words of the visionary Steven Wright: To steal ideas from one person is plagiarism; to steal from many, is research.

EPILOGUE

On a serious note, I couldn't let this book end without mentioning some of the ones that have already left this life. Most of them were my friends and I had worked and spent time with them. A couple of others were ones that I have greatly admired for their skill, music and their gift to the world, but never had the opportunity to sit down and talk with. I regret that I should have spent more time with them or gone out of my way to get to know them better. Probably like you, I miss them all.

"England" Dan Seals – my partner for 15 years. I loved the music we made.

Karen Carpenter – what a sweetheart. I miss that voice.

James Griffin - (guitar) - Bread

Mike Botts - (drums) - Bread

Terry Kath - (guitar) - Chicago Transit Authority

Harry Chapin

Jim Croce

Paul Davis

Dan Fogelberg

Joe Schermie - (bass) - Three Dog Night

Dee Murray - (bass) - Elton John's Band

Eddie Rabbit

Dennis Wilson - (drummer) - Beach Boys

Carl Wilson - (guitar) - Beach Boys

Jennie Frankel - (songwriter)

Nicolette Larson

Dewey Martin - (drummer) - Buffalo Springfield

Jeff Pocaro - (drummer) - Toto

Dennis Yost - Classics IV

Mike Bloomfield - (guitar) - Paul Butterfield Blues Band

Gene Page - (Arranger)

Larry Londin - (drummer)

Kenny Buttrey - (drummer)

SOUTHWEST F.O.B.

PERSONAL MANAGEMENT
Theze Few Productions

exclusively
with

Picture above: Promotional picture for the band from Texas. Pictured left to right are: DocWoolbright, Randy Bates, Dan Seals, JFC, Zeke Durell, Ovid Stevens.

Picture below: England Dan and John Ford Coley performing at University of North Texas in 1970.

DE MONTFORT HALL, LEICESTER
Wednesday, 24th November, at 7.30

TICKETS: £1.00, 90p, 80, 60p, 50p, from B.O. Charles Street   Tel. 27632

ELTON JOHN
with Dee Murray & Nigel Olsson
also England Dan and John Ford Coley

Pictured above: Playbill for Elton John when we toured England with him in 1971.

Pictured below: Backstage. Elton John, John Ford Coley, Dee Murray.
Elton's sticking his tongue out.

Pictured above: my red vest so it must be 1977. Pictured below: my first gold record for Nights Are Forever, 1976.

Pictured above: New York Atlantic Records party. Left to right: England Dan, John Ford Coley, Roberta Flack, and Blues Brothers: Dan Aykroyd, and John Belushi.

Pictured bottom: John and David Soul (from the original Starsky & Hutch), 1977. Pictured below: Garth Brooks and John, 1992.

Pictured top: Corey Feldman, Susan Blakely and John Ford Coley in the feature film, "Dream A Little Dream."

Above: John Ford Coley, Cameron Dye, Joe Pantoliano, Steve Railsback, Timothy B. Schmidt (Eagles) in the film "Scenes From The Goldmine."

Pictured above: The 'real' Pirates of the Caribbean, Englishman Joey Molland from Badfinger and John Ford Coley in St. Croix, U.S. Virgin Islands, 2006.

Pictured below: My good friends. John Ford Coley, Jimmy Griffin (Bread), and Englishman Terry Sylvester (formerly of the Hollies) 1999.

Above: Front Row: John Cafferty, Michael "Tunes" Antunes, Joe Lynn Turner (Deep Purple), Governor and first lady of Tennessee, John Ford Coley. Back Row: Larry Hoppen (Orleans), Jimi Jamison (Survivor) 2009.